REDEMPTIVE HOPE

FORDHAM UNIVERSITY PRESS   NEW YORK 2015

COMMONALITIES
Timothy C. Campbell, series editor

REDEMPTIVE HOPE

From the Age of Enlightenment

to the Age of Obama

AKIBA J. LERNER

Copyright © 2015 Fordham University Press

All rights reserved. No part of this publication may be reproduced, stored in a retrieval system, or transmitted in any form or by any means—electronic, mechanical, photocopy, recording, or any other—except for brief quotations in printed reviews, without the prior permission of the publisher.

Fordham University Press has no responsibility for the persistence or accuracy of URLs for external or third-party Internet websites referred to in this publication and does not guarantee that any content on such websites is, or will remain, accurate or appropriate.

Fordham University Press also publishes its books in a variety of electronic formats. Some content that appears in print may not be available in electronic books.

Visit us online at www.fordhampress.com.

Library of Congress Cataloging-in-Publication Data available online at catalog.loc.gov.

Printed in the United States of America

17 16 15   5 4 3 2 1

First edition

*To my wife and kids for being the source
from which all my hopes spring*

CONTENTS

	Acknowledgments	ix
	Introduction	1
1	Redemptive Hope and the Cunning of History	21
2	Revival of Messianic Hope	40
3	The God of Exodus and the School of Hope	65
4	Richard Rorty's Social Hope and Postmetaphysical Redemption	90
	Conclusion: Between Pragmatic and Messianic Hopes	113
	Notes	127
	Bibliography	173
	Index	193

ACKNOWLEDGMENTS

The gratitude I have for all those who have assisted me in exploring and developing the ideas in this book cannot be fully contained within these pages. These acknowledgments are but grains of sand in the vast beach of my true feelings of gratitude for all those who have contributed, directly and indirectly, to the creation of this manuscript.

The seeds of this book took root early in my academic life when, as an undergraduate at the University of California at Santa Cruz and later Berkeley, I gained a greater appreciation for the competing redemptive narratives that have culminated in this book. As a history major, I was inspired by the writings on hope of first-century Jews, struggling with the culture of Hellenism and political subjugation under the Roman Empire. Then, in my graduate work at Stanford University, my interest in narratives of redemptive hope was further piqued as I struggled through the process of my own disenchantment and re-enchantment with religious thought. I must begin by expressing my profound gratitude to my principal adviser, Arnold Eisen, for encouraging me to think boldly and to not lose touch with the vocational spark that should be the driving force within all academic pursuits. I remain truly grateful that Eisen's demand for rigorous critical thinking and writing was coupled with a willingness to break from the boundaries of the traditional Jewish Studies canon, encouraging me to continue a conversation I had begun with Richard Rorty over the nature of religion, pragmatism, and the enduring importance of hope for twenty-first-century intellectual life. In addition, I thank Tom Sheehan and Amir Eshel for the roles they played in shepherding my early scholarship. I am particularly grateful to Amir Eshel for his ongoing feedback as I further developed this manuscript.

Eisen sagely advised that one should have both living and dead conversation partners. This book is a direct outgrowth of my conversations with Richard Rorty during the last years of his life, conversations that fundamentally altered my worldview. Rorty's passing at the end of my graduate career was a tremendous loss, but I am eternally grateful for the conversations we had, as well as the comments and support he gave my scholarship. Since his death, I also feel fortunate to continue those conversations, albeit in a different medium. Although Rorty was not a big fan of metaphysics, this book in many ways serves as a metaphysical tribute to the ongoing debates his ideas continue to inspire in me since his passing.

From my earlier years at Berkeley, and then later as a graduate student, I feel especially grateful to Martin Jay for his teachings and mentorship. Daniel Boyarin, Eric Gruen, Jonathan Beecher, Bruce Thompson, and David Biale were early teachers who set me on an intellectual path I continue to travel to this day. From my studies at Hebrew University, I thank Paul Mendes-Flohr for his advice and encouragement to keep the "secular" messianic Jewish voices of Bloch and Benjamin within my work.

I also thank the generosity and support of Stanford University's program in Jewish Studies and particularly Steven Zipperstein for his leadership, as well as the efforts of Charlotta Fromrober and Vered Shemtov for their contributions to supporting Jewish Studies graduate work. I also thank Joshua Landy for his very thorough readings of my early scholarship and for modeling how to cut through metaphysical underbrush. As a friend, Josh has a wit and a shared love of working in San Francisco cafés that has carried me through many years of toiling within academia. Jean-Pierre Dupey brought me into the exciting world of French intellectual history and introduced me to the challenges of Girardian thought. I must also thank Mark Brilliant, not only for his generosity in providing close readings of my work but also for our discussions while riding through the hills of northern California on our mountain bikes. Rob Reich also provided valuable mentorship and feedback on my work. From my time at Stanford, I also thank Van Harvey, Lee Yearly, Hester Gelber, Brent Sockness, and Carl Bielefeldt. Significantly, Greg Kaplan's ability to combine scholarly insight with practical advice on navigating the world of academia continues to be a welcome source of support.

During my postdoctoral period at Stanford, I was fortunate to teach in the IHUM (Introduction to the Humanities) Program and in the Religious Studies Department. In particular, I am thankful to Hester Gelber for providing the opportunity to teach a course developed with Mark Gonnerman entitled Hope and Prophetic Politics. Mark's combination of Zen master–like humor and flashes of deep insight is coupled with genuine intellectual solidarity. The comradeship forged with Mark during this period remains a true gift.

After Stanford, I was extraordinarily privileged to join the ranks of Santa Clara's Religious Studies Department as an assistant professor. The welcome I have received at SCU has given me the feeling of arriving at a true academic home. My experience at Santa Clara has reinforced my appreciation for being in a department with people who are committed to modeling ethical relations, modeling intellectual inquiry, and supporting scholarship that places social justice concerns at the center of what it means to be a scholar-teacher. I want to thank my chair, Gary Macy, for his support and for allowing me to cluster classes so that I could carve out more time for finishing this book. I also thank Peter Minowitz for his insightful feedback and mentorship and David Pinault for his mentorship. Additionally, I am grateful to my department and the Dean's Office, which graciously provided funding to help offset some of the costs involved with the publication of this book.

Through the evolution of writing this book, I was fortunate to have the opportunity to develop some of my ideas through publishing related scholarship. I thank Peter Orchs for inviting me to publish an article entitled "The Dialectical Self: Between Liberal Autonomy and Religious Identity" in *The Journal of Textual Reasoning*. I am thankful for Ken Koltun-Fromm's informal mentorship over the years and for his organizing a symposium at Haverford University in 2011 on Jewish Thought and then editing my chapter titled "Otherness and the Future of Democratic Solidarity: Buber, Kaplan, Levinas and Rorty's Social Hope" in a volume entitled *Thinking Jewish Culture in America*. I also thank Zachery Braiterman, Martin Kavka, and Ben Lazier for their feedback on early versions of my book proposal.

I particularly want to thank the staff at Fordham University Press for all their assistance in bringing my manuscript to print, especially when faced with the tragic and untimely loss of my initial editor, Helen Tartar. Helen was gracious and patient, and her willingness to support young scholars and encourage innovative paths within scholarship is a legacy that I hope this book lives up to. I also owe a huge debt of gratitude to Thomas Lay for honoring Helen's legacy by committing himself to shepherding my book through the delicate period right after her death. I also thank Eric Newman for his careful and thoughtful editorial work and Michael Koch for his very thorough and expeditious copy editing. Additionally, I am deeply grateful to the anonymous readers for the Press for their insightful comments and support. Their thorough readings and demanding questions contributed to the sharpening of each chapter. I also thank Erin Hyman for her early editorial work on my manuscript. Her untimely passing is a terrible loss, but her editorial insights are preserved in the pages of this book.

This book also reflects the love and support of a remarkable circle of family and friends who have helped provide the fortitude required to make it up the academic mountain. Although I cannot include the names of my entire Bay Area–based tribe, I must mention Nathaniel Deutsch for being a true friend in times of need, for his tough-love readings of my work, and for conversations that have shaped my thinking over the years. My debt to his editorial insights and friendship is everlasting. I must also mention Elliot Neaman for being like an older brother to me, for years of mentorship, for bike rides at Mt. Tam, and for invaluable readings of my work. Starting from our early years together at Berkeley in the '90s, Elliot has been an amazing friend at every step along my scholarly journey; Ari Kelman for his loyal friendship and late night intellectual conversations since childhood; and my friends Aaron Tapper, Ben Hurlbut, and Marc Gidal for years of solidarity, great discussions, and laughter.

I thank my father, Michael Lerner, for a lifetime of Sabbath dinners over which we've challenged each other's worldviews and wrestled over life's big questions. I owe much of my understanding of Judaism to his teachings. I also thank him for his editorial insights on earlier iterations of my manuscript. To my mother, Theirrie Cook, and her partner Jerry Horovitz, I owe a debt of gratitude for their loving support, countless hours of babysitting, and early editorial suggestions. I have also been blessed with extraordinary in-laws, Jean and George Rosenfeld, whose boundless love and support of me, my wife, and our children have been essential for making it through the long haul of becoming a professor. I also thank my uncle (in-law) David Aaronson for his sage advice in navigating both life and academia.

I thank my children, Ellie and Jeremiah, for allowing me to experience what unconditional love is all about and for allowing me to become the dad I've always wanted to be. In one form or another I have been working toward completing this book their entire lives, and they know only too well the sacrifices that were required. They are the light of my life and my hope on the horizon. I especially want to thank the love of my life, my wife, Sunny Lerner, who is the greatest companion I could ever imagine, for teaching me that all redemptive hope begins in those quiet, intimate moments when the armor of the ego dissolves. Her unyielding love and support of me have not only allowed me to face life's challenges but have taught me that in the darkest of moments the love a life-partner provides is the best form of hope we can experience in this life. My gratitude to her is never-ending.

REDEMPTIVE HOPE

INTRODUCTION

> Blessed are those . . . whose hope is in the LORD their God.
> —PSALM 146:5

This is a book about our need for redemptive narratives to ward off despair and the dangers these same narratives create by raising expectations that are seldom fulfilled. The story of the rise of secular redemptive hope narratives from the age of Enlightenment to the early part of the twenty-first century has been a story of the struggle between heightened expectations and postutopian despair.[1] The quasi-messianic expectations produced by the election of President Obama in 2008—followed by the diminution of these expectations—was a stark reminder that redemptive hope is seldom satisfactorily fulfilled. Although what led to the dashing of these expectations is still in dispute, Naomi Klein used the term *hopeover* to describe the cynicism that many progressives felt because of Obama's reluctance to implement his vision of hope and change.[2] The ironic suggestion that this cynicism is similar to a hangover is incisive since it alludes to the intoxication that accompanies any historical moment when individuals collectively embrace redemptive hopes. This despair provoked a great deal of theorizing about whether the United States can regain a sense of direction while adjusting to the uncertainties of environmental and geopolitical challenges.[3]

The reelection of President Obama in 2012 was arguably a reaffirmation for his support of the redemptive potential unleashed by citizens facing the challenges of the future together. Nevertheless, something had profoundly changed in how Americans related to phrases like "the audacity of hope."

Although the debate over the significance of Obama's legacy is still on-going, the redemptive narratives surrounding his elections are a reminder that we are still wrestling with what the neopragmatist philosopher Richard Rorty considered to be one of the central intellectual challenges of our postmodern age: Can solidarity with other people serve as a sufficient foundation for our social hopes, or do we need a transcendental force—like God—in order to maintain a grander vision of redemptive hope?

In the decade before Obama's election Rorty made what many of his peers considered to be a controversial proposal—that solidarity is enough of a basis for maintaining social hope. In doing so, Rorty challenged his fellow intellectuals to move away from the metaphysical grounding in transcendental powers that has defined all Western redemptive hope narratives since the story of the ancient Israelites' exodus from slavery in Egypt. To view social hope as a substitute for metaphysical grounding, according to Rorty, is to base the future of hope for liberal democracy "on our loyalty to other human beings clinging together against the dark, not our hope of getting things right."[4] Solidarity based on liberal democratic dialogue can provide an alternative foundation for our hopes to create a better future.

However, can we ground a sense of redemptive hope purely on our solidarity with other people or do we still need a sense of transcendence in order to maintain such hopes?[5] Are other people enough, as Rorty proposes, or are we always destined to "gaze into the starry skies above," as Immanuel Kant put it, in search of a transcendent foundation for our hopes? In this book I engage this dilemma by bringing together Rorty's neopragmatic version of social hope with the work of modern Jewish intellectuals, particularly that of the existentialist philosopher Martin Buber.[6]

Part of what made Rorty's proposal so controversial is that historically most religious and philosophical thinkers have shared the conviction that linking one's hope to a transcendental source—God or the eternal realm of ideas—was necessary. In the Christian social philosopher Gabriel Marcel's words: "The only genuine hope is one directed toward something that does not depend on us."[7] From this more conventional perspective, a sense of transcendence—that is, the sense that the possible can overcome the given—is necessary in order to guard against debilitating depression and even nihilism if one's hopes are dashed. According to Martin Luther King Jr., confronting one's shattered dreams and transforming the "fatigue of despair into the buoyancy of hope" always depends on one's ability to affirm a sense of "cosmic companionship."[8] Finding the strength to hew out a "stone of hope" from a "mountain of despair" almost always requires reliance on some transcendental foundations. Only God can provide the support necessary for overcoming despair and taking what Kierkegaard suggested is the leap of faith toward the possible.

Rorty countered that Western civilization has matured to the point where we no longer need to rely on the transcendental hopes of our ancestors. Instead, we are mature enough to embrace a "criterionless hope" that looks merely to the foundations we create through our solidarity with others.[9] Rather than concern ourselves with the epistemological quest for establishing what counts as real knowledge, Rorty maintains: "What matters is your ability to talk to other people about what seems to you true, not what is in fact true. If we take care of freedom, truth can take care of itself."[10] If we could only give up our pretensions to truth and certainty, he argued, we could gain a stronger sense of public solidarity, coupled with the freedom to create what we want to become rather than discover some timeless essence of what we are supposed to be.

Rorty's appeal to solidarity as an alternative grounding for social hope was particularly intended to challenge traditional hope narratives that either relied on transcendental appeals to God (as in religion) or an idealized notion of subjectivity (as with the Enlightenment and romanticism). Yet, Rorty's turn to solidarity as an alternative foundation for his neopragmatic social hope, I propose, contains its own redemptive narrative, sharing important links with earlier mid–twentieth-century religious thinkers similarly interested in reinvigorating hope narratives without relying on the same metaphysical foundations. In this book I explore these connections, for example, by bringing together thinkers like Buber and his existential philosophy of I-Thou relations for the first time in scholarship with Rorty on the question of solidarity as an alternative grounding for redemptive hope.

The comparisons and conversations between religious and liberal redemptive hope narratives I weave throughout this book, however, avoid a facile reconciliation of religion's emphasis on grounding individual hopes in a transcendental source that dissolves individual boundaries and liberalism's emphasis on maintaining the boundaries of civil rights. For example, Buber's interest in the transcendental illumination of a person's "whole being" may not be reconcilable with Rorty's postmetaphysical vision for social hope, yet both provide compelling narratives for imagining solidarity within a vibrant liberal democratic society. More important than the moments of convergence, Rorty and the modern Jewish thinkers covered here provide a new approach for appreciating the kinds of conversations redemptive narratives inspire.

REDEMPTIVE HOPE

This is a book about hope narratives that offer a form of redemption. This is also a book about despair and disenchantment, especially with regard to the failure and potential danger of redemptive narratives. As Hegel taught, the force of desire often defines our hopes, and we despair because desire is rarely fully satisfied. One of the greatest strategies we have developed for overcoming despair has been to create narratives of redemptive hope that promise an eventual triumph over alienation and the attainment of harmony. Redemptive hope springs from the desire for a holistic transformation of the world so as to reconcile creation with the divine, or in accordance with a greater good. As individuals, we may hope for a variety of personal goals. However, when we start to link these hopes to a broader universal vision for how society or the world might someday come to reflect the divine in theological terms, or the supreme good (*summum bonum*), then individual hopes become part of a larger redemptive narrative. The specifics of these ideals have changed throughout the history of the West, yet the constant is that redemptive hope has been transmitted through narratives that inspire individuals to believe in the possible transcendence of what *is* for a higher vision of how things *ought* to be. This is perhaps what Emmanuel Levinas meant when he stated that the "true object of hope is the Messiah, or salvation."[11] When we embrace redemptive narratives, we are hoping for the possibility of achieving a higher good.

In order to reach this ultimate good, most redemptive hope narratives have depended upon a grand teleological model promising that all the struggles within history will be brought to a conclusion at the end of days when, in the words of the prophet Isaiah, "the whole earth is at rest" (Is 14:7). Isaiah's vision of the wolf dwelling with the lamb (Is 11:6) suggests a fundamental overcoming of power relations toward new possibilities of a new order based on love. The promise for an end to history "when the earth is full of knowledge of the Lord" (Is 11:9) is related to the hope that either harmony between nature and providence will be restored (as it was in days of old in the Garden of Eden), or a new creation will come into existence (when God's future kingdom is established here on earth).[12] The origins of time (*Urzeit*) provides the foundations for peace and hope for the eventual overcoming of alienation at the end of time (*Endzeit*). In Hegel's more modern philosophical terminology, a day will come when all the tensions and struggles that fuel the dialectical process will culminate in a new political order based on social harmony and solidarity. Drawing on the vision of universal solidarity developed first among the Hebrew prophets, Rabbi Mordechai Kaplan later summed up that the purpose of all religious redemptive traditions is to provide a sense of existential meaning by linking the individual to grander hopes for one day achieving universal solidarity with all peoples.[13]

Various definitions of hope are interwoven into each chapter of this book. I focus mainly on *redemptive* hope because I am interested in the political and religious narratives that inspire individuals to link their personal hopes to a larger vision of universal redemption. Redemptive hopes, according to my definition, involve the relationship between the individual and what Peter Berger referred to as the broader "cosmic order" within which individuals are located.[14] Redemptive hopes are never exclusively personal, nor purely communal, but always entail a convergence of both realms. For example, one of the greatest redemptive hopes offered by most religions is the ideal that it is possible to love the stranger as a neighbor, or even as a sister or brother.

Hope, as a phenomenon for intellectual reflection, is an extremely amorphous concept—hard to define without either indulging in gross generalizations or lapsing into fragmented minutiae. A famous rabbinic *midrash* states that six hundred thousand Israelites at the base of Mount Sinai each understood revelation in six hundred thousand different ways.[15] This *midrashic* insight into the variety of ways for experiencing and interpreting revelation may also apply to how each individual experiences hope.

Hope is comprised of both affective and cognitive dimensions: the mental image of what we hope for is often accompanied by a sense of anticipation or even an experience of elation.[16] Consequently, hope is always contextually related to particular experiences of hopefulness, that is, a *phenomenology of hope*.[17] Defining the nature of hope and experience, however, raises epistemological challenges. In reflecting on these challenges, Martin Jay in

Songs of Experience suggested that the nature of experience is best captured through the particular "songs" that bring experiences about, not through stripping away its subjective context in order to lay bare a single, transhistorical core meaning.[18] Following Jay's nuanced approach to the topic of experience, I present various "songs" that intellectuals have written about hope, allowing a greater appreciation for the complexity and historical variety of redemptive narratives that have given voice to hope throughout the ages.

Seen through the lens of analytical philosophy, hope always involves a tension between the *realism* of what we consider to be currently probable versus our *idealism* of what we think ought to be possible. Hope thus implies calculations between future possibilities and probability. The "desiderative constituent" of hope (i.e., A hopes that $P = A$ wishes that P), is always relational to what J. P. Day referred to as the "estimative constituent" (i.e., P has some degree of probability).[19] In the words of Adrienne Martin, "hoping for an outcome involves standing ready to offer a certain kind of justificatory rationale for engaging in certain kinds of thought, feeling, and planning."[20] Our "justificatory rationale" for embracing certain hopes necessitates a complicated balance between evaluations of what is *actual* in relation to the probability of fulfilling particular desires. According to Martin, when we hope we engage in an "incorporation analysis" in which we are prepared to offer "a certain justificatory rational for certain activities related to the outcome."[21] Hope is a mode for "exercising one's rational agency" by increasing feelings of excitement and expectation for the actualization of an object of attraction, thus increasing our motivation to work toward its fulfillment.

In order to explicate the redemptive component of hope narratives, I additionally draw on Joseph Godfrey's important distinction between "proximate hopes" and "ultimate hopes": proximate hopes refer to wishes or quotidian desires for particular things within a particular timeframe, and entail a high level of probability.[22] In contrast, ultimate hopes are "superordinate to all other hopes" in that they are higher, deeper, and involve a broader historical trajectory toward the future by pushing the boundaries of probabilities and the "limits of evidence." Most comprehensive doctrines reflect ultimate hopes. Proximate hopes are more confined by a realistic assessment of present probabilities, whereas ultimate hopes are closer to our idealistic wishes for what ought to be.[23] Ultimate hopes entail final vocabularies that give one's life a broader sense of significance and meaning whereas proximate hopes are more easily satisfied and therefore less determinative of a person's view of themselves or overall worldview. For example, my proximate hope for a good meal at night is different than my ultimate hope that all peoples should be able to enjoy a good meal at night.

Rabbi David Hartman proposed that this relationship between hope and future possibilities necessarily challenges the boundaries of empirical verification. As he put it, "hope is a category of transcendence, by means of which a man does not permit what he senses and experiences to be the sole criterion of what is possible."[24] Hope, therefore, always creates a tension between what we know as factual and our desires for the possible, especially with regard to morality.

My use of the term *redemptive hope* draws on these analytical distinctions while focusing on the intersection between personal hopes, solidarity, and narratives that imagine universal transformation for the entire world.[25] Godfrey's analytical distinction between proximate and ultimate hopes is also useful for understanding the history of Western religious and philosophical traditions that have provided foundational narratives for both personal and collective hopes. Drawing on Godfrey's definition of ultimate hope as superordinate to all other hopes, I view the history of messianic, utopian, and social hope narratives as all-containing qualities of redemptive hope through the inspirational narratives they provide.

The biblical story of Exodus and prophetic proclamations—for example Isaiah's vision that the temple in Jerusalem will one day become a "house of prayer for all peoples" (Is 56:7)—gave voice to some of the first redemptive narratives within the Western tradition. For the prophets, working for the establishment of a world based on the reconciliation of justice with mercy represented the greatest hope for both the Jewish people and the entire world by merging particular and universal redemptive ideals. Biblically inspired redemptive hope narratives, starting with the prophets, linked the future welfare of a particular people (Israel) with a broader hope of universal redemption for all peoples when, at the end of days (*acharit ha-yamim*) or in the world to come (*olam ha-ba*), divine judgment will come from on high, resurrect the dead (*tehiyyat ha-metim*), and sweep away the forces of iniquity.[26]

The vertical biblical images of creating a *New Jerusalem* by channeling the transcendent here on earth shifted during the modern period toward a horizontal ideal of secular utopianism that looked, instead, to the bonds of human solidarity as an alternative source for redemption.[27] The greater the despair with human nature (as reflected in theologies that highlighted human sin) the greater the need for transcendental narratives that reinforce human dependence on God's mercy and omnipotence for saving the world. By contrast, the Enlightenment fundamentally shifted the ground of hope toward a new optimism based on unleashing humanity's potential.[28] With the development of Enlightenment skepticism by thinkers like Spinoza— and later with the development of a hermeneutics of suspicion (Marx and Nietzsche, for example)—transcendental hopes for reward in an afterlife gave way to secular forms of utopianism and emancipation predicated on changing this world through the power of science and humanistic values. In contrast to the faith once located in a transcendent God, these new secular utopian narratives were based on the ideals of emancipation, freedom, and revolutionary change whose goal was to bring about greater individual authenticity and social harmony. Instead of the unity of providence and nature in some other realm, the Enlightenment promised self-actualization in this world for those willing to seize the means for their own liberation.

Redemptive hope narratives powerfully express a range of desires that may be difficult to actualize in practice, yet remain a potent source of inspiration. With this history in mind, part of my interest in bringing together Rorty's neopragmatism and modern religious thought is to explore why redemptive hope narratives are also so problematic for liberal democratic societies. Although we need redemptive hope narratives, these very same narratives pose a special kind of danger: Just as redemptive hope narratives raise our expectations and motivation to strive for creating new possibilities, so too they can generate greater levels of despair by reminding us of the disconnect between our expectations and reality. In the words of Reinhold Niebuhr: "An optimism which depends upon the hope of the complete realization of our highest ideals in history is bound to suffer ultimate disillusionment."[29] Following Niebuhr, Cornel West warns us that "despair and hope are inseparable."[30] Similarly, Muysken reminds us that "since what we hope for must remain uncertain, despair remains a constant and strong temptation."[31] Although we need to experience ourselves engaged in larger projects that provide a sense of meaning, ultimate purpose, and transcendence, these larger aspirations can also lead to radical forms of utopianism and idealism that heighten unreasonable expectations.

Despair created in the wake of the dashing of these hopes can also lead to the search for alternative sources of hope, thus resetting the dialectical progression that occurs each time despair gives way to new narratives of hope. With each moment of hope the possibility of despair rises. Yet the fires of despair can also provide the source from which the phoenix of new hopes may arise. It is within the depths of despair that we can discover, according to Jonathan Lear, a "radical hope" that inspires images for new ways of existing in the face of extreme adversity.[32] New descriptions and images generated through moments of hope provide what Adrienne Martin describes as a "meta-confidence" that has the potential to turn the unimaginable into the possible.[33]

Some see God as providing the inspiration that allows the move from despair to hope, while others credit personal will or social solidarity. For philosophers, however, it is impossible to ignore questions about the legitimacy of certain hopes. An added danger of redemptive narratives is that they often encourage an emotional state of hopefulness as a replacement for concrete evidence. Consequently, philosophers from Spinoza down to Richard Dawkins have argued that, although redemptive narratives often function pragmatically as a source of collective psychological comfort, they also rely on emotions that cloud the individual's ability to appraise evidence rationally and face up to the truth of their circumstances. Additionally, from a political perspective, the emotionalism stimulated by hope narratives opens individuals to the dangers of manipulation by either religious authorities or politicians who often depend on emotional bonds, rather than reason, to maintain their positions of power.

THE AGE OF OBAMA AND THE DIALECTICS OF ENLIGHTENMENT

Redemptive narratives—in the form of both left-wing messianism and right-wing apocalypticism—have shaped Obama's presidency. For many progressives, the ideals attached to Obama's rhetoric of hope and change quickly gave way to the realism of Washington power-based politics.[34] In the words of Cornel West, President Obama "was able to mobilize based on a democratic rhetoric and ended up with technocratic policies."[35] West goes further to argue that Obama's spirit of accomodationism has tragically contributed to the evisceration of "Black prophetic fire" needed for the revitalization of our democratic culture.³⁶ This type of soul searching has left many who were originally hopeful about Obama's presidency to ask what happened and why.

Leading up to the presidential election of 2008, the driving slogans of Obama's campaign revolved around the idea that, after nearly a decade of cynicism and despair, America would have the opportunity to pursue its highest hopes for real change rather than settle for a sober and pragmatic accommodation to existing political realities. Although Senator Obama was often positioned as the candidate of idealism (in contrast to Hillary Clinton's cynical realism), his 2006 bestseller, *The Audacity of Hope*, reflected a deeper tension between utopian aspirations and sober pragmatism. Obama encouraged Americans and the world to look to each other for hope, but also to look to the transcendental power of spirit as a guiding source for ultimate salvation.

> The audacity of hope. That was the best of the American spirit, I thought—having the audacity to believe despite all the evidence to the contrary that we could restore a sense of community to a nation torn by conflict; the gall to believe that despite personal setbacks, the loss of a job or an illness in the family or a childhood mired in poverty, we have some control—and therefore responsibility—over our own fate.³⁷

Given the subsequent despair over the weak economy and the increasing divisiveness in national and global politics, Obama's use of hope rhetoric after the election seemed to many naïve at best, and cynically manipulative at worst. A growing fatigue and concern for the despair generated by the overuse of redemptive hope narratives may account for why these slogans were greatly diminished in President Obama's reelection campaign. The one striking exception was his reelection speech given on November 7, 2012. In this speech Obama began as follows:

> Tonight, more than two hundred years after a small group of colonies won the right to determine their own destiny, the task of perfecting our union moves forward. It moves forward because you reaffirmed the spirit that has triumphed over war and depression, the spirit that has lifted this country from the depths of despair to the great heights of hope, the belief that while each of us will pursue our own individual dreams, we are an American family, and we rise or fall together as one nation and as one people.³⁸

President Obama went on in this speech to affirm the importance of solidarity in sharing "certain hopes for America's future." Yet toward the end of this speech, he balanced the transcendentalism implied in his earlier 2006 reflections on hope with a pragmatic critique of the very idealism invoked during his first campaign.

> I am hopeful tonight because I have seen this spirit at work in America. . . . I have never been more hopeful about America. And I ask you to sustain that hope. I'm not talking about *blind optimism*, the kind of hope that just ignores the enormity of the tasks ahead or the roadblocks that stand in our path. I'm not talking about the *wishful idealism* that allows us to just sit on the sidelines or shirk from a fight. I have always believed that hope is that stubborn thing inside us that insists, *despite all the evidence* to the contrary, that something better awaits us so long as we have the courage to keep reaching, to keep working, to keep fighting.[39]

This speech is particularly noteworthy because it not only signaled a return to some of the redemptive hope narratives of his first presidential campaign (messages that were glaringly absent throughout most of his first term as president) but also because it pointed to the crystallization of a more sober postutopian pragmatism and concern with maximalist positions that has become the hallmark of his presidency.

The challenges created by narratives of redemptive hope are crucial for understanding the conflicting pulls toward realism versus idealism that have not only defined Obama's presidency but have also defined the history of America's own redemptive narratives of exceptionalism. The soaring rhetoric often employed by President Obama drew on the horizontal solidarity of "we the people" coupled with the transcendence of a nation "under God" with "inalienable rights." Drawing from the well of religious and secular Enlightenment redemptive narratives, one of the major themes in America's founding mythology is the idea that mere immigrants and refugees are capable of forging a beacon of hope for the world, dedicated to safeguarding freedom and liberty, while providing shelter for the downtrodden.

Obama's desire to include both pragmatic and transcendental elements within the "audacity of hope" also has broader resonances with the historical evolution of Western redemptive hope narratives. Inspiring a nation to embrace their highest ideals is often an essential part of being a good politician. President Obama's earlier affirmation of hope as that force that encourages individuals to strive "despite all the evidence" links his writings on hope with the premodern political philosophy of Plato's *Republic* where the politician is tasked with providing rhetoric that binds a polis together, even at the expense of all evidence.

In more analytical terms, Musyken proposed that reasonable propositions for action based on hopes for the future are never completely removed from pragmatic considerations of probabilities based on what currently counts as fact.[40] Nevertheless, as a defender of religious hopes, Musyken went on to propose that the central difference between hope and belief statements is that belief statements need to be possible in order to cohere, but hope statements are not limited by the same degree of certainty required for belief statements. In other words, legitimate hopes are constrained by probabilities, but if moral, can still be rationally desirable despite high degrees of uncertainty. According to this conception, it may be unreasonable to believe certain propositions without solid evidence, but it may be reasonable to hope without the same standard of evidence.[41]

The transcendence provided by hope helps maintain an analytical openness to possibilities and propositions for discovering new standards of truth that may have remained unknown if we had stayed within the comfortable confines of following the maxim to avoid error.[42] For example, in particular historical moments it may be more reasonable to embrace the audacity of hope as a force for social change than to wait for convincing evidence or simply capitulate to despair over the prospects for genuine change. Thus, President Obama's earlier definition of hope as a call to action "despite the evidence" may violate certain standards of epistemological certainty. Nevertheless, Obama's proposal may still be analytically and pragmatically justified when viewed as a spur to action that induces a psychological openness to striving toward new horizons. The stimulation of individual resilience and agency may in fact be proof for the rational content within any given redemptive hope narrative.

There is, however, a problematic side to Obama's appeal to the audacity and emotionalism of hope as a way to justify beliefs and actions "despite all the evidence." Redemptive narratives that focus our hopes on transcendence rather than on factual probabilities in relation to hard evidence constitute a particular danger in the public arena.[43] For scientists and philosophers inspired by the Enlightenment's commitment to liberating humanity from superstition and blind obedience, truth derived through evidence should always trump transcendental hopes. If, as Joseph Godfrey states, "Hope in X implies the reality of X," then for any particular hope object to count as legitimate, there must be evidence verifying the reality of X.[44] Martin follows a similar line of argument when she states, "it is irrational to form or maintain a hope based on the belief that the hoped-for outcome is either more or less probable than one's evidence indicates."[45] What counts as "reality" is both epistemologically and politically relevant for justifying hope.

The twentieth-century German-Jewish political philosopher Leo Strauss offered a provocative interpretation for evaluating these broader social tensions in relation to redemptive hope narratives. He argued that there is an inherent conflict between the philosopher's quest to arrive at the ultimate reality of truth by penetrating the veil of appearances and social conventions, versus the obligation of political leaders charged with the pragmatic responsibility of maintaining social stability through enforcing collective harmony. Politicians and religious leaders understandably employ rhetoric that promises collective salvation through individual sacrifice because it is their designated role to inspire social harmony even at the expense of truth based on evidence. Going back to the model of Plato's *Republic* and his infamous "noble lie," Strauss points out that the security of the polis depends on social cohesion, so maintaining solidarity among a citizenry is subordinate to the philosopher's concern for establishing the conditions for defining truth.[46] Consequently, the need to affirm social cohesion often leads politicians to use grandiose rhetoric to manipulate our greatest hopes and fears "despite the evidence" for the sake of mobilizing commitment, conformity, and sacrifice for the general good. Strauss's juxtaposition between the philosopher's quest for truth and pragmatic goals of maintaining civic cohesion highlights the challenge of reconciling political concerns for the collective good with philosophical concerns for the ontological foundations behind any claim.

This tension goes to the heart of two competing social goods within political philosophy. The first is the *civic good* of social harmony and motivation that encourages individuals to make sacrifices for a better future. This good is implied in Obama's appeal to the "audacity of hope" as providing a form of spiritual resilience to restore a sense of agency and praxis. The second is the *individual good* based on an Enlightenment ideal of autonomy and freedom from the heteronomy of false beliefs. Echoes of this second good are also found in Obama's warnings in his later speech against "blind optimism" and "wishful idealism." The contrasts between the *soulcraft* of President Obama's use of lofty rhetoric designed to inspire a nation's spirit and the sober pragmatism that has defined his *statecraft,* are directly related to broader intellectual debates over the use of religious narratives that focus on transcendence within liberal democratic cultures. For example, what do we do with redemptive narratives that may be effective at inspiring bold actions that favor the common good yet lack rational grounding in evidence? Do we jettison concerns for truth for the sake of solidarity and protection against despair? Is it more important to utilize redemptive narratives in order to inspire citizens with a sense of personal agency, or is autonomy only genuine if individuals are liberated from false consciousness?

Connected to the challenge of balancing the tension between realism and despair are broader questions regarding the role of redemptive narratives within liberal democratic societies, namely: How do we go about harnessing religious and philosophical narratives of redemptive hope in order to sustain and grow healthy liberal democratic communities? How do we balance legitimate hopes for what people might be capable of with the pragmatism of recognizing human limitations? The tension between needing broader redemptive hope narratives and needing to guard against unreasonable expectations is inescapable.

The early twenty-first century is an important time for reflecting on both the history and future of redemptive hope narratives in the West. We need new strategies for thinking about and managing redemptive rhetoric in the public arena. This requires bringing liberal political philosophy and religious thought together in new and unexpected ways. In the post–World War II period, both religious and secular intellectuals wrestled with reviving narratives of redemptive hope in the face of postutopian despair. The mechanized devastation wreaked by two world wars created a lasting crisis of confidence among Western intellectuals. Jürgen Habermas summed up this sentiment when he stated that there are "reasons to doubt whether the Enlightenment traditions can still generate sufficient motivations and social movements for preserving the normative contents of modernity out of its own resources."[47] What if the hopes placed in science and humanism were no longer sufficient for inspiring civic virtues of courage and self-sacrifice for a greater good?

Some of these concerns stemmed from older discussions, going back to the European wars of religion and the emergence of the Enlightenment, over whether there are discourses within religion that can be rationally rehabilitated for the purpose of metaphysically grounding liberal democratic culture. With the increase in awareness of the political threats posed by religious fanaticism since 9/11, one of the greatest contemporary concerns with allowing religion a greater role in the public sphere is the question of whether religious discourses and traditions will promote openness to liberal values or will only further fuel sectarian differences.[48] How do we allow the best of our private hopes to become part of our aspirations for the public sphere while avoiding the abuses generated by nationalist chauvinism or religious fundamentalism?

USES AND ABUSES OF REDEMPTIVE HOPE

This book raises more questions than it provides answers for reconciling religious and liberal hope narratives. Nevertheless, I propose that our best way forward is to engage liberal and religious theorists who wrestle with the mutual limits and strengths of applying redemptive hope narratives to the civic realm. I am particularly interested in the Jewish contributions (most notably by Martin Buber, Ernst Bloch, Emil Fackenheim, and Eric Fromm) to these debates on redemptive hope narratives, specifically in relation to Rorty's proposal that social hope springs from solidarity born from dialogue. Jewish intellectual writings on messianism in the modern era are part of an on-going two-thousand-year-old discussion over the tension between the idealism of establishing a "new earth" (Isaiah 65:17) and the realism of worldly empires. The Jewish thinkers covered in this book looked to the Jewish messianic tradition in order to ground their redemptive visions in the regenerative powers of community and solidarity as an alternative to both Western metaphysics and the alienation of modern capitalism. The long history of Jewish intellectuals positioning themselves and Judaism in relation to the legacy of Athens provides the pretext for engaging Rorty's postmetaphysical philosophy. Neither fully inside nor outside the Western philosophical tradition, the Jewish thinkers I bring into this discussion share with pragmatism an interest in discarding what they similarly identified as a problematic (Greek) metaphysical tradition based on what John Dewey identified as the "quest for certainty." Additionally, the interplay and tensions between reason and revelation within these religious writers encourage a rethinking of the dichotomy between the secular and religious within the modern era.[49]

I begin by contextualizing my investigation into Jewish thought and Rorty's neopragmatism within a broader history of what I propose are four stages in the evolution of Western redemptive hope narratives. The first stage of redemptive hope narratives emerged from biblical ideals of theological transcendence and providence. This initial stage is defined by the central idea that our ultimate hopes are only justified if linked to the divine. This first stage combines both Jewish and Christian scriptures, as well as philosophers like Saint Augustine, Thomas Aquinas, and Immanuel Kant. The second stage, starting with the Enlightenment, is defined by the emergence of new redemptive narratives based on the materialism of science and secular ideals of humanistic self-fulfillment as an alternative to biblically inspired otherworldly hopes. During this period a hermeneutics of suspicion and a broader sense of disenchantment began to erode religious foundations of hope. Chapter 1 provides an overview of the dialectical interplay between these first two stages leading to the emergence of a third stage toward the end of the nineteenth century.

In response to the crisis of reason created by the technological devastation unleashed during World War I, theologians and secular theorists generated new redemptive narratives in which they combined secular utopianism with premodern messianic narratives.[50] The focus of Chapter 2 is on the recovery of messianic hope narratives by Jewish thinkers—particularly Martin Buber—who in the early part of the twentieth century perceived the failure of Marxist utopianism and secular humanism to address modern alienation adequately.[51] In this chapter I also present my rereading of Buber's work on I-Thou relations as a phenomenology of hope. Buber's great contribution to centuries-old Jewish discussions on the nature and meaning of messianism was marked by his shift in emphasis toward the hallowing of everyday encounters as the springboard for redemptive aspirations. According to Buber, "it is only by way of true intercourse with things and beings that man achieves true life, but also it is by this way only that he can take an active part in the redemption of the world."[52] The recognition individuals receive through dialogue creates the foundation from which broader messianic hopes become plausible. I-Thou encounters function as sites for the performance of messianic hope by "hallowing" daily interactions that provide the foundations for a redemptive horizon. Without these moments of genuine encounter and reciprocal recognition, it is almost impossible to imagine why we would accept the idea that other people can serve as a source of redemptive hope. The phenomenology of hope I perceive in Buber's work complements Rorty's postmetaphysical ideal of solidarity by providing an account for reimagining intersubjective encounters as an alternative foundation for solidarity and social hope.

Most readers of Rorty locate him within the intellectual trajectory stemming from American pragmatism.[53] I take a different path by connecting the thought of Christian and Jewish theologians engaged in a recovery of redemptive narratives after Auschwitz with Rorty's postmetaphysical social hope. In Chapter 3 I explore the work of Ernst Bloch, Jürgen Moltmann, Walter Capps, Paul Ricoeur, Eric Fromm, and Emil Fackenheim—all of whom contributed to the project of reviving redemptive hope narratives as an answer to the failure of both religious and philosophical traditions to adequately address the modern breakdown of humanistic values and the catastrophes of mass extermination.[54] Writing in the shadows of the *Shoah* (total catastrophe, also referred to as the Holocaust) and the threat of nuclear devastation, they were joined together in what they termed the "school of hope," dedicated to creating a new synthesis between premodern and postmodern discourses out of the resources of both religious and secular Marxist utopian redemptive narratives.[55] The "school of hope" took their inspiration from Bloch's conflation of Marxism with eschatology. For Bloch the history of hope narratives had been defined by a tension between our impulses for foundational certainty versus what he identified as our Promethean desire to break from social norms and create something not yet experienced. Bloch's dialectical theology of tradition and transgressions provides an interesting bridge toward Rorty's writings on social hope as a balancing act between Enlightenment ideals of solidarity and postmodern appreciation for the force of contingency and irony.

In Chapter 3 I also turn to the work of Emil Fackenheim, particularly his essay "The Commandment to Hope" in which he presents what I propose is the beginnings of a new redemptive narrative based on what he termed the "dialectics of work and wait."[56] After the *Shoah* the liberatory narratives provided by the Enlightenment's appeal to secular ideals of materialist progress, Marxist hopes for revolutionary struggle, and traditional Jewish faith in waiting for the Messiah as an act of devotion have all become defunct. Therefore, according to Fackenheim, we must *work* for redemption while retaining a sense of discipline and humility embodied by the ideal of *waiting* for the Messiah. After the *Shoah* we still need the transcendental grounding for our redemptive aspirations and, precisely because of the *Shoah*, Fackenheim suggests we can no longer simply wait for a supernatural intervention to save the world.

During this same period—in his 1966 work on radical theology, *You Shall Be as Gods*, and in his 1968 work, *The Revolution of Hope: Toward a Humanized Technology*—the social theorist Eric Fromm also worked to develop a dialectical synthesis of secular utopian and biblically based redemptive hope narratives. According to Fromm, the "paradox of hope" lies in the opposite dangers of "radical adventurism" (usually inspired by premature messianic expectations) in contrast to passive waiting. For Fromm a middle course is found in affirming both the transcendental qualities of hope that allow us to avoid what he referred to as the "resigned optimism" of our consumerist culture, while also affirming the immanence of hope in the form of erotic social connections.

The Jewish and Christian thinkers in Chapter 3 provide an interesting historical antecedent and contrast to Rorty's late twentieth-century proposal for a postmetaphysical form of social hope. Rorty's critique of metaphysics shares with the theologians of the "school of hope" the project of moving beyond the redemptive models provided by the transcendentalism of Platonism and the historical materialism of Marxism toward a new, "postideological" understanding of solidarity.

Chapter 4 is devoted to the fourth and final stage in this evolutionary narrative, namely, Rorty's neopragmatic proposal to ground social hopes in human solidarity. Rorty's writings on social hope reveal a tension between a more pragmatic approach that allows for a recovery of religious narratives as a source of hope, and his secular utopian ideological position that sought to jettison all appeals to what Heidegger termed ontotheological discourses. Rorty's utopian proposal for overcoming metaphysics by replacing religion and philosophy with literature and dialogue, I propose, constituted a new secular redemptive narrative that encourages a new thinking of how religious and secular narratives of redemptive hope might interact within the twenty-first century.

Rorty forged a new path toward fulfilling the emancipatory legacy of the Enlightenment by proposing provocative redescriptions for interpreting the traditional meanings of both hope and redemption. As part of his broader interest in achieving a postmetaphysical discourse, Rorty charged that the concept of redemption has been defined by a vertical hierarchy that reinforces the inferiority of everything within the phenomenological realm of becoming.[57] The time has come for the ontotheological quest for a "redemptive truth" that can provide correspondence to the eternally "real" within both the histories of religion and philosophy to give way to a new utopian ideal based on "the redemptive power of works of the imagination."[58] As part of his lifelong goal to provide alternative models for redemptive hope, Rorty offered a contrasting "redemption from egotism" based on retaining a literary "openness" to "redescriptions" of what we might become.[59] To be redeemed from "egoism" also allows us to give up the search for the timeless essence of what we should already be and instead focus on creating new meanings that can better contribute to human flourishing. The hope and strength that comes from imagining a transcendence of the wickedness and finitude of this world might be replaced with an alternative redemptive hope discovered through the unleashing of our imaginations and creating new bonds of solidarity.

Missing from this alternative mode of redemption, however, is a thick description of how the unleashing of the imagination combined with intimacy of solidarity serves as an alternative for the consolation of foundationalism provided by both religious and philosophical metaphysical traditions. My reading of modern Jewish thinkers throughout this book fills in some of the gaps in Rorty's thin appeal to liberal bourgeois solidarity. For postmetaphysical democratic hopes to flourish, a robust narrative for how individuals should go about establishing social bonds and intersubjective relationships is necessary. For example, Buber's own struggle to provide an ideal of subjectivity that draws on both the transcendental and the intimacy of self-other encounters provides a compelling comparative model. Buber's account of intersubjective encounters as an alternative foundation for redemptive hope helps to answer the challenge of how to imagine redemptive hope emerging from within the reciprocity of I-Thou encounters. I conclude the book by turning back to religious thinkers for this thicker description of solidarity. In particular, Buber's exploration of the libidinal, spiritual, and existential dimensions that bind intersubjective encounters with the messianic ultimately complements Rorty's concept of social hope.

For most readers of Rorty's neopragmatism there is little that would initially suggest compatibility with modern interests in reviving Jewish messianism. It may be impossible to fully reconcile both liberal concerns for social boundaries and religious concerns for addressing a person's whole being. Nevertheless, a mutual emphasis on ethics, education, and the importance of solidarity as a basis for hope creates new opportunities for investigating the tensions and correlations between Jewish thought and Rorty's neopragmatism. Additionally, the critique of Western metaphysics within both traditions provides new avenues for bringing together religious messianic hopes (as refracted through modern Jewish thought) with contemporary secular liberal hopes (as refracted through Rorty's American neopragmatism). Part of what I found appealing as a graduate student working with Rorty during his last days at Stanford was the family resemblances between his neopragmatic approach to social hope and modern Jewish thinkers who similarly looked to postmodern interests in expanding social justice through the power of dialogue as an alternative to standard metaphysics.[60]

The redemptive narratives explored in this book are not only engaging for the possible solutions they offer but also because they force us to ask hard questions regarding the nature of hope and solidarity in an increasingly fractured postmodern world. This book affirms that the best response to these challenges is the maintenance of dialogue. A possible new redemptive narrative for the twenty-first century is one that can draw on the best within religious and liberal thought while also appreciating how their points of tension are a necessary cost for maintaining a vibrant democratic culture. As Rorty stated at the end of *Philosophy and the Mirror of Nature*, once we have abandoned the "systematic" quest to accurately "mirror reality," we can follow "edifying philosophers"—such as Buber—who "want to keep space open for the sense of wonder" by "keeping the conversation going" over what we hope to become.[61] "Keeping the conversation going" may also hold its own redemptive promise against postutopian despair. Redemptive hopes may be impossible to actualize, but sometimes we are made better by the inspirational narratives they provide. The hope behind this book is to add to this conversation.

1

REDEMPTIVE HOPE AND THE CUNNING OF HISTORY

> And I will wait upon the Lord, that hides his face from the house of Jacob, and I will hope for him.
> —ISAIAH 8:17

TRANSCENDENTAL HOPES

The notion that the entire world is capable of total transformation begins with the various redemptive narratives introduced by the biblical tradition. Although the explicit expression of these transcendental hopes changed in each period, the common denominator during this first stage is the assumption that transformation is possible. This first stage includes the Hebrew prophets, Christian intellectuals like Saint Augustine and Thomas Aquinas, and the Enlightenment thinker Immanuel Kant. These theocentric groundings of hope all share the claim that individual hopes for happiness are ultimately linked to a transcendental source, for example, God. For all traditional theologians interested in reconciling Greek metaphysics with the Bible, God became the causal vertical force from which all tributaries of divine grace, mercy, and justice flow.

For most modern commentators on the historical origins of redemptive hope, a biblical ideal of hope for redemption (*geulah* in Hebrew) represented a stark alternative to Hellenistic ideas of fate and determinism. Although later scholars have come to problematize this simple polarity between messianic hope and Hellenistic fatalism, for many nineteenth- and early twentieth-century Jewish intellectuals the Athens versus Jerusalem divide was a useful foil for explaining the tensions between universalism and particularism within Jewish thought. Additionally, nineteenth-century German-Jewish scholars such a Heinrich Graetz and Herman Cohen could counter the anti-Semites of their day who charged that Judaism merely reflected a premodern misanthropic identity by claiming that the legacy of Athens may have a better purchase on the immutable laws that govern the physical world, but the legacy of Jerusalem reveals the laws of human freedom, responsibility, and universal redemptive hope for all peoples.[1] For these nineteenth-century thinkers the biblical tradition also provided the foundations for the notion that history has an ultimate purpose and meaning: to move humanity closer to the eventual reconciliation of individual inclinations to a larger divine will. Hope for this moment of peace in which finitude is reconciled with the infinite also gives meaning to human freedom, since through the embrace of personal responsibility individuals overcome the fatalistic laws that rule nature. Hope for eventual unity with the divine, therefore, was an essential affirmation of individual freedom as expressed through faith in our ability to overcoming the deterministic laws that define the natural realm.

Although Western redemptive hope narratives begin with biblical accounts, in the philosophical tradition Augustine (354–430) and Aquinas (1225–1274) provided the foundational narratives of hope as a theological virtue. In his seminal work, *The City of God*, Augustine elaborated on the crucial link between personal hopes and the redemptive promise of immortal happiness in a future life.

> The hope of the future world—Paul: "For we are saved by hope: now hope which is seen is not hope; for what a man seeth, why doth he yet hope for? But if we hope for that which we see not, we are made happy by hope" (Romans 8:24). As, therefore, we are saved so we are made happy by hope. And as we do not as yet possess a present, but look for a future salvation, so is it with our happiness.... Salvation, such as shall be in the world to come, shall itself be our final happiness. And this happiness these philosophers refuse to believe in, because they do not see it, and attempt to fabricate for themselves a happiness in this life, based upon a virtue which is as deceitful as it is proud.[2]

Deeply inspired by a Gnostic/Manichean worldview that human life is "encompassed with evils," Augustine argued that those philosophers who look to ground their hopes in this world are simply irrational. Human quests for ultimate happiness are only justified if linked with faith in the salvation of a "future world." Only God's perfection and promise of perpetual peace in a future life can guarantee our hopes in this life. Thus, God is what the theologian Karl Barth was to later refer to as humanity's "anchor of hope."[3] Only God's perfection and promise of perpetual peace in a future life can guarantee our hopes in this life. Augustine states:

> The supreme good of the city of God is perfect and eternal peace . . . the peace of freedom from all evil. . . . But the *actual possession of the happiness of this life, without the hope of what is beyond, is but a false happiness and profound misery.* For the true blessings of the soul are not now enjoyed; for that is no true wisdom which does not direct all its prudent observations . . . to that end in which *God shall be all and all* in secure eternity and perfect peace.[4]

Because of original sin, those who look to root their hopes in what they can verify through their experiences (Epicurean philosophers constituting the most classical example for this materialist orientation) are doomed to despair.

Augustine gave hope a central role within early Christian theology, but it was Aquinas who provided a more systematic reading of hope within the constellation of essential theological virtues. For Aquinas, hope has the ability to transform base wishes into something transcendent through the grace of revelation. In his *Summa Theologiae* (1265–1274) hope is defined as an *imperfect virtue* that directs us toward the *perfect virtues* of *love* and *charity*, leading to the happiness of the ultimate union with God.[5] Aquinas states: "The virtue of hope has as its ultimate goal eternal happiness, and the primary agency on which it relies is God's help." When harnessed to God's providence, hope becomes more than just a bundle of individual passions for the fulfillment of desires and longings. One must have faith in God as the ultimate force that makes redemption possible before one can hope to overcome sin and achieve eternal happiness.

According to Aquinas, a disposition of hopefulness straddles the divide between pure fantasy and our imaginative ability to construct new possibilities out of what we already claim to know about the world. What is possible depends on the complex interconnection between God and creation. As humans, we start from a basic desire for the satiation of our appetites. In

Aquinas's words: "Hope is a movement of appetite aroused by the perception of what is agreeable, future, arduous, and possible of attainment." Because "hope, like every movement of desire, springs from some form of love of the thing desired," faith in God provides the eternal spring for keeping hope alive.[6] Without access to this eternal spring—maintained through a combination of intellectual reflection and devotion—our ultimate hopes would wither in the face of corporeal corruption and finitude. "Since hoping for God to reward one inspires one to love him and keep his commandments," Aquinas continues, hope for "eternal happiness" as the reward for achieving "eternal life" is the motivating force that propels us closer to the divine.[7]

As a theologian, Aquinas followed Augustine in grounding ultimate hopes in God, but as a philosopher, Aquinas was equally concerned with the challenge of determining the rational justification for redemptive hopes with reference to actual possibilities. Hopes are distinct from wishes or fantasies because, according to Aquinas, they are grounded and circumscribed by epistemic considerations.[8] Unlike beliefs and wishes, our hopes have to be disciplined by our present knowledge.[9] In the classical terms developed by Aristotle, future possibility (*dynamei on*) is connected to what is possible in the present moment (*kata to dynaton*). According to Aquinas, hope is necessarily oriented toward targets and goals that are attainable, although not inevitable. Aquinas's model for circumscribing legitimate hopes within epistemic considerations based on the factual assessment of probabilities continues to define the analytical standard for determining which hopes are justifiable.[10]

During the Middle Ages, Jewish philosophers like Moses Maimonides (1135–1204), Nachmanides (1194–1270), and Joseph Albo (1380–1444) also contributed to discussions over the necessity of grounding individual hopes for salvation in God's divine justice and mercy.[11] Most premodern religious redemptive hope narratives revolved around the tension over the role of humans in the redemptive process and the extent to which redemption represented a complete transformation of the physical world or merely an improvement on the physical and social laws that already exist. For example, the medieval Jewish thinker Nachmanides saw redemption as more of an apocalyptic rupture with the natural order, whereas Maimonides looked to Talmudic sources as suggesting that immutable divine laws that govern the natural world would continue in the messianic age with only slight adjustments within the political order, most notably regarding the oppression of Jews.[12] Through our reason we can work toward actualizing God's infinite perfection here on earth without relying on supernatural intervention in the form of an apocalyptic transformation of the entire natural order. For Maimonides, redemption involves attaining a deeper knowledge of God, but attaining this knowledge is something that intellectual elites already have the power to access through their intellects and interpretive prowess.[13]

The challenge for both Jewish and Christian thinkers throughout this period was to develop alternative religious strategies for maintaining messianic speculations over how the world might change in the future, while also ensuring that these redemptive hopes did little to stir up messianic agitation that might threaten the status quo. After the failure of the great revolts against Rome, the rabbis had already begun the processes of dampening the potential hazards of messianic enthusiasm by suggesting that the "birth pangs" of the messianic age would entail the disastrous breakdown of the social order and prohibited calculating when the end of time might occur.[14] Although there were slight differences of opinion over whether or not redemption represented a continuation of human nature or a miraculous transformation thereof, religious thinkers continued the process started in the first century of spiritualizing redemptive narratives from scripture into daily devotional acts that could provide a sense of agency while restraining messianic fervor.[15]

A promise for an end to the alienation created by the gap between the divine and the human, both within the realm of politics and the natural world, was also a central redemptive hope. Accordingly, redemption entailed the overcoming of religious laws based on distinctions between the sacred and profane. Gershom Scholem later pointed out that the key to the messianic idea is helping individuals maintain hope, and thus overcome their sense of powerlessness, while also deferring the promise for actualization into an unknown future so as to avoid releasing anarchic forces within society.[16] If redemption means an overcoming of all distinctions and dualism, the challenge for religious authorities (who depended on maintaining a privileged knowledge for how and why these distinctions must be maintained) was to encourage narratives of redemptive hope while insisting that these antinomian impulses should not be acted upon. For Scholem, narratives of

Redemptive Hope and the Cunning of History 25

redemptive hope are less about speculations about the future, and more reflective of an underlying desire to either challenge or reinforce current social structures.

FROM VERTICAL TO HORIZONTAL HOPE

Although an anti-apocalyptic (perhaps even antitheocentric) view of messianism championed by Maimonides has always been a part of the debates over the meaning of redemption, it wasn't until the rise of secular Enlightenment ideals within the early modern period that a real undermining of the emphasis on God as an active redeeming force within history emerged.[17] The combination of religious wars and the ascendency of materialism and science in the early modern period gradually undermined this link between redemptive hope and theological foundations. The established equilibrium between individual soteriological desires and biblical promises for a redeemed world additionally saw new challenges with the renewal of interest in the sciences, arts, and philosophy of the classical period starting in the Renaissance period. The Reformation and the Scientific Revolution both undermined the feudal social order and contributed to the rise of new secular redemptive narratives centered on autonomous individuals. During the age of Enlightenment secular ideals of optimism and progress began to eclipse theological ideals of hope.[18] The foundations for grounding epistemology gradually changed from vertical appeals to God toward a post-Copernican horizontal veneration of human beings as the measure of all things. Subjective grounding in human experience—not divine revelation—provided alternative secular utopian hopes. If humans were capable of unlocking the secrets of the universe, perhaps redemptive hopes for achieving happiness were better placed on developing the human potential for reason and the imagination than on union with the eternal.[19]

The renegade Dutch-Jewish philosopher Spinoza (1632–1677) was the first of the Enlightenment philosophers to employ a critique of hope as a launching point for his broader critique of religion. Leo Strauss points out that Spinoza, as a descendent of Marrano Jews who himself had undergone excommunication (*Herem*) at the hands of his own people's religious tribunal, was primarily concerned with making the modern world safe for truth-seekers like himself.[20] For Spinoza the best way to unleash the powers of philosophy and science was to eliminate the political role of religion and the state in determining matters of conscience.²¹ Redemptive narratives based on scripture had a pragmatic role to play in reinforcing civil and moral commitments among the masses, but should have no direct role in guiding civil administration.

Given his historical position as one of the founders of modern liberal political philosophy, Spinoza's thought is particularly noteworthy because his argument for liberalism commences with a direct challenge to the use of redemptive hope as a form of social control among ecclesiastical authorities. Spinoza starts from the position that hope and fear represent dangerous emotions that can distract from rational reflection on individual strivings for happiness and perseverance (*conatus*). Following in the Stoic ideal of *ataraxia*, the emotions stirred up by our hopes will always threaten to make us passive by weakening our true resolve for self-preservation. Spinoza's critique of hope and fear (*Nec Spe, Nec Metu*) is rooted in his overall view that most desires result from ignorance, and from ignorance we attribute superstitious causes to occurrences without any rational foundation.²²

In his *Ethics* (1677) Spinoza proposed that being a true philosopher means rising above secondary desires toward the higher rational realm of authentic self-sufficiency.

> The emotions of hope and fear cannot be good in themselves. Proof: The emotions of hope and fear cannot be without pain . . . there cannot be hope without fear . . . these emotions indicate a lack of knowledge and a weakness of mind . . . confidence, despair, joy and disappointment are also indications of our weakness. . . . Therefore the more we endeavor to live by the guidance of reason, the more we endeavor to be independent of hope, to free ourselves from fear . . . and to direct our actions by the sure counsel of reason.²³

The emotionalism of hope has dangerous potential to lead us astray from the real forces of causality toward a sensual reliance on stories—such as tales about divine providence and miracles—as compensation for our ignorance and fears of powers beyond our control. The less we know the more we compensate for our ignorance by relying on the blind optimism generated by our hopes.

In his earlier work, *The Theological-Political Treatise* (1670) Spinoza placed his challenge to the abuses of hopes and fears by ecclesiastical authorities at the forefront of his argument for liberal democracy and the sequestering of religion to the private realm. Spinoza begins the preface to his *Treatise* with the following indictment of hope and fear:

> Men would never be superstitious, if they could govern all their circumstances by set rules, or if they were always favored by fortune: but being frequently driven into straits where rules are useless, and being often kept fluctuating pitiably between *hope* and *fear* by the uncertainty of fortune's greedily coveted favors, they are consequently for the most part, very prone to credulity. The human mind is readily swayed this way or that in times of doubt, especially when hope and fear are struggling for the mastery, though usually it is boastful, over confident, and vain.[24]

For Spinoza, during moments of doubt and ignorance religion is able to eclipse sober scientific reflection by giving expression to our hopes and fears. Accordingly, religion relies on narratives that speak to an inner psychological need to experience ourselves in contact with a cosmological order that will both guarantee just rewards and respond to our individual wishes.[25] The raising and then dashing of hopes increases the desire to maintain a state of hopefulness. Similar to an addiction, in order to maintain the emotions of elation and comfort that come from an overcoming of fear through hope, individuals are tempted to disregard countervailing evidence that might lead to a rational reassessment of their expectations.

Conversely, for Spinoza, philosophy conceptualized the divine as a self-sufficient unified power that governs the universe. This power follows the laws of logical determinism, not the pathos that cripples feeble minds yearning for a personal caretaker or confirmation for their uniqueness. The liberatory promise of philosophy correlates to the progress we make through scientific advancements within the natural world. The more we know, the more we emulate God's self-sufficiency. Similarly, the more we know, the less dependent we become on emotions like hope and fear. The philosopher's hope of emulating the self-sufficiency of the divine depends on overcoming our childlike dependency on God as a providential father figure who has chosen us to somehow be exempted from the vicissitudes of his own natural order. Only philosophy, according to Spinoza, can liberate humanity from the stormy seas of emotions that plague the psyche.[26] Paradoxically, Spinoza was the first to give us a hope to end all hopes—for example, a hope that rational reflection will help to eliminate the emotionalism that defines states of hopefulness.

Later generations of Enlightenment-oriented Jewish intellectuals (*maskilim*), such as Moses Mendelsohn, were inspired to follow Spinoza's critique of messianic hope by arguing that faith should be placed in the powers of rational persuasion as a replacement for the revelatory and inspirational sanctification of social norms through religious institutions.[27] For Mendelssohn the messianic ideal was premised on a collapse of the public and private spheres into a single redemptive ideal. Such a collapse, Mendelssohn's claimed, was antithetical to the true meaning of religion exemplified by Judaism. The essence of Judaism was expressed through a civic ideal that celebrates pluralism and diversity within creation. Mendelssohn went so far as to argue that Judaism provided a model for how a multitude of different orientations—religious, aesthetic, and so on—could simultaneously exist within the public sphere. In *Jerusalem* (1783) Mendelssohn presented a vision for a new universal Jerusalem in which religious identities could exist both as expressions of private identities while serving a greater civic good.[28] According to Mendelssohn we should learn to "render unto Caesar that which is Caesar's and unto God what is God's . . . [b]ear both burdens . . . serve two masters."[29] Privately, every citizen should be allowed to embrace whatever redemptive narrative they wish as long as they abide by civil norms of harmony and public peace.[30] The task embraced by Mendelssohn of trying to reconcile Enlightenment ideals to the needs of religious communities reflected the emergence of a new narrative of redemptive hope among intellectuals in the modern period. In the Enlightenment period, intellectuals like Mendelssohn and Emmanuel Kant were unwilling to give up on the hope of reconciling transcendental and communal ideals found within religion with the ideal of individual autonomy.

COSMOPOLITAN HOPE AND THE KINGDOM OF ENDS

As critiques of religion by Spinoza and other fellow travelers gained greater traction, redemptive expectations for otherworldly salvation gradually gave way to imagining secular forms of salvation here on earth that were once thought possible only in the world to come. Yet, the shift toward the corporeal world as an alternative source for redemption was not without its own ethical questions. Enlightenment empiricists had trouble grounding any ethical or aesthetic judgments in empirical proof. While science provided a powerful critique of theological speculation, it had a difficult time explaining why its worldview should be considered a more solid foundation for knowledge, other than to postulate that it had a better predictive understanding of causal forces.

Within these intellectual debates over how to reconcile idealist concerns for an absolute good with empiricists concerns for standards of judgment, Kant (1724–1804) introduced his own redemptive narrative based on hopes for achieving a moral world (*moralische Welt*). With the gradual decline of ecclesiastical power, Kant's thought was particularly noteworthy for modernizing the theological emphasis on hope as a virtue, thereby transforming it into what Rorty argued was a more pragmatic philosophy revolving around a concern for civil rights and ethical relations.[31] By mixing religion's emphasis on transcendence with philosophy's emphasis on autonomy, Kant created a new mixture of rationality and morality that greatly appealed to Western Enlightenment audiences eager to retain the essence of biblical morality without the emotionalism of superstitious beliefs.

The unity created in a moral world, according to Kant, results from the peace derived through the social good of mutual affirmation and individual autonomy. Hope is justified because history is moving toward a cosmopolitan goal of greater unity based upon recognizing the universal ethical imperatives of distinguishing between *is* and *ought*.[32] The great challenge we face, however, is the difficulty of reconciling our nominal ideals of autonomy and infinite freedom with our synthetic observations. Thus, we can only hope that someday nature and virtuous ideals will be reconciled, even as we pragmatically accept that these ideals remain necessary transcendental constructs for the purpose of assuring civic harmony. The essences of things are beyond the realm of synthetic observations, but a priori knowledge of a supreme good provides the rational justification to strive after moral perfection.

Kant's writings on hope in his *Critique of Pure Reason* (1781) stemmed partly from a desire to correct the hubris of natural philosophers, who used the standards of empiricism to argue that it was now possible to achieve a moral rational social order without appeal to any transcendental signifiers.[33] Kant's response to such brazen empiricist reductionism was perhaps best embodied in his famous retort, "I have therefore found it necessary to deny knowledge in order to make room for faith." Synthetic knowledge derived through observation gives us greater predictive understanding, but such knowledge cannot convey the meaning or value of what we observe, much less the whole of existence.[34]

Additionally, humans are driven to metaphysical concerns for foundational answers to what we can know, what we should do, and what constitutes legitimate hope.[35] Kant's answer to his famous question "What may I hope?" is not perfect knowledge, but rather the profound happiness that comes through a more sublime union with our highest ethical principles, both in this life and the next.[36] Through synthetic knowledge we may not be able have a true understanding of things-in-themselves but we can have hope in our ability to harness our reason to arrive at ideals that reflect the supreme good (*summum bonum*).

The ideal of hope, according to Kant, is central to the ethical foundations of any liberal society. All rational individuals hope to become happy, and therefore, all rational persons hope to also live in a moral society based on assuring the mutual right to happiness for all. According to Kant, "all hoping is directed to happiness" because "happiness is the satisfaction of all our desires."[37] Unlike Spinoza, who saw the phenomenon of hope as undermining a rational ethical order, Kant sees striving to become worthy of our happiness as providing the "rational" foundations for a broader redemptive hope that one day will establish a moral society.[38]

The challenge, however, is to explain why anyone who desires to be virtuous is rationally justified in thinking that through the pursuit of moral perfection one will also obtain happiness.[39] Tragically, experience often teaches that the pursuit of moral perfection comes at a price to personal felicitude, thus raising the question if there is a tension between morality and the rational pursuit of autonomy.

From reason we learn that ultimate happiness is not found through mere eudemonistic pursuits (as the ancient Greeks erroneously thought according to Kant), but rather through striving to become *worthy* of our happiness. Reason teaches us how to become virtuous autonomous individuals by adopting the categorical imperative of "common objective laws" that are both universal and within the "realm of ends." And by striving to become virtuous individuals, we are granted the ultimate hope of becoming worthy of achieving a harmonious union between individual happiness and the highest good. This union with the good in turn gives an ethical grounding for happiness.[40]

Kant designated the concepts of *God*, *freedom*, and *hope* in a just order (as expressed through the faith in the immortality of the soul) as *postulates of pure practical reason*. Although God, freedom, and hope are of the noumenal realm (i.e., beyond the realm of synthetic observation), these *postulates* are essential for maintaining a *rational* adherence to moral law among autonomous individuals within an ethical commonwealth.[41] Without hope in a just providential order it is *irrational* for the individual to adhere to the moral law, since we will most likely not live long enough to benefit directly from the ethical sublimation of our will.[42] Adrienne Martin makes the point that Kant's view of faith provides a form of "meta-confidence" that can reinforce an individual's sense of autonomy and agency, especially when faced with uncertain outcomes.[43] The motivational element provided by these postulates toward ethical behavior is itself part of the proof for the rationality of religious hopes. Pursing an ideal of moral perfection is rational and pragmatically necessary for both individuals and society in order to achieve an authentic state of happiness, but we can only hope that these pursuits will have real empirical payoffs in our lifetimes.

In the *Critique of Practical Reason* (1788), Kant continued to emphasize the correlation between beliefs in the immortality of the soul, hope for moral progress in history, and the importance of autonomy for the rational establishment of an ethical society.[44] In his later work *Religion within the Boundaries of Mere Reason* (1793), however, Kant further developed his view of hope in response to what he identified as the limits of reason. Hope is rationally justified insofar as it pragmatically assists in the task of overcoming fears that happiness and harmony may in fact be impossible to obtain in our lifetime.[45] Although it is almost impossible to imagine "something perfectly straight framed out of such crooked wood,"[46] our ability to conceive of such ideals gives rational grounding for retaining the ideal of a perfect Supreme Being.[47] Our hopes for harmonizing our instincts and our rational ability to educate ourselves to channel our "unsociable" instincts toward righteous behavior are only justified if linked to metaphysical ideals.[48] Only a Supreme Being could guarantee the eventual reconciliation between nature and morality; therefore only belief in a Supreme Being provides the rational grounding for the hopes of a virtuous person to achieve happiness in the afterlife.[49]

Although the standard reading of Kant is to see his reflections on hope as a way to make room for faith, it is also possible to read Kant as inverting the relationship between God and hope: The fact that we need to hope in order to maintain the pragmatic goal of striving after a moral society gives us reason to believe that there is a God who would provide this kind of inspiration despite the "crookedness" of our inclinations, which often bend toward evil. God becomes more of a pragmatic placeholder—an enabling ideal unknowable through synthetic knowledge—that allows us to hope for a correspondence between the civil realm and ideals of a supreme good.

Kant's philosophy of hope also developed out of his desire to straddle the divide between personal faith and the chiliasm of an eventual reconciliation between the individual's will (*Willkür*) and what he designated as religion's collective messianic aspirations for a *perpetual peace*.[50] In his works "Idea for a Universal History from a Cosmopolitan Point of View" (1784) and "Perpetual Peace" (1798), Kant set out to elaborate on his central thesis that individuals have a rational right to hope for moral perfection and happiness by daring to use their own reason. The role of a modern liberal state is to provide individuals with the rights and education necessary for the self-cultivation of the mind and body (*Bildung*).[51] Through reason individuals eventually arrive at the rational link between their own hopes for happiness and the need to live in societies dedicated to mutual recognition of each individual as an "end in themselves." Reflecting on the history of human "unsocial sociability" (*ungesellige Geselligkeit*), ironically our "crookedness" and proclivity for evil assists in the march toward universal peace and harmony by illustrating the perils of not striving for mutual affirmation.[52] Unfortunately, the horrors and mistakes of history can be our best teachers. The struggle between the egoism involved in individualization and collective demands for norms will always cause tension, but these tensions also carry the hope of pushing humanity toward realizing a greater cosmopolitan unity. Kant acknowledged that the unity between human inclinations, nature, and civic norms may never be experienced in our lifetimes, but an idealized hope provides the heuristic fantasy that enables us to imagine that such a unity is at the very least theoretically possible. And it is this hope that allows Kant to argue that it is pragmatically useful and constitutes a "rational belief" for us mere mortals to act "as if" moral perfection and a moral world order are possible. Hope is a necessary *transcendental illusion* for grounding morality, but as a *postulate,* it pragmatically motivates individuals to seek the liberation of all as the most rational path toward mutually assured happiness and harmony.

Kant also contributed to the modern disenchantment of redemptive hope, by removing any pretense of personal salvation connecting practitioners to an ideal of intimacy, dialogue, and personal experience of the divine. Synthetic knowledge may have been limited to make room for faith, yet the phenomenal world within Kantianism was devoid of the need for divine immanence or dialogue.[53] Faith in a law-giving Supreme Being may be rationally justifiable, but such a faith is not necessary so long as the ideals of moral perfection serve as a pragmatic heuristic device for inspiring hope in the possibility of achieving greater peace, harmony, and freedom. By effectively "rendering unto Caesar" (in the form of synthetic knowledge) Kant removed the noumenal ideals contained within the *postulates of pure practical reason* from having any real claim on our synthetic knowledge of the physical world. Kant consequently transformed the ideal of hope from the legacy of heteronymous ecclesiastical faith into an expression of the individual's autonomy and ethical commitment to the categorical imperative.

Kant's legacy of limiting the parameters of religious dialogue from infringing on the acquisition of synthetic knowledge had a profound effect on defining the contours of religious redemptive hope within liberal democratic societies. For example, Kant critiqued Judaism for lacking the necessary category of belief in an afterlife, a constitutive element of any *real* religion; nevertheless, he liberalized religious philosophy in regards to what specific redemptive narratives were needed in order to achieve a *kingdom of ends*.[54] A general disposition of hopefulness replaced dogmas over which particular expressions of faith are necessary for maintaining civic virtue. As long as one's God provided hope—a hope that provided the necessary resilience and incentives to be an upstanding citizen—the details of each particular faith doctrine were of less consequence.

Although Kant's defense of hope in rational terms had a profound effect on reconciling the redemptive components of religion to the Enlightenment's own liberatory politics, other intellectuals looked to the ideal of reason as a secularizing force for removing all vestiges of religious faith from dominating politics and philosophy. This intellectual shift contributed to what Karl Mannheim referred to as "the utopia of liberal humanitarianism" as a replacement for religious redemptive hopes.[55] Enlightenment-inspired thinkers increasingly embraced the notion that only reasonable assertions based on empirical evidence should determine which hopes are legitimate for the public realm.

Through the emancipation of the individual's reason (for philosophers), or the imagination (for romantics), progress toward new utopian horizons could replace humanity's premodern reliance on the saving grace of a vertically removed God. According to Strauss, the "peculiarity of modernity" is defined by the conviction "not to hope for life in heaven but to establish heaven on earth by purely human means."[56] For Strauss the shift during modernity toward a valorization of progress constituted a "secularization of biblical faith." Following Strauss, Jürgen Moltmann proposed that redemptive hope became in this period less about what we might expect in the afterlife and more about changing current conditions and consolidating a better future within our own lifetime.[57] In Moltmann's estimation, modernity is synonymous with the hubris in which individuals "no longer have to endure history unconsciously but must consciously create and control history."[58]

The impact of revolutions in North America and France at the end of the eighteenth century additionally contributed to these shifts in defining redemptive hope. At first, it appeared as if hope had suddenly been realized in praxis, and that a genuine new order would be established that could build a world of social justice, liberty, equality, and fraternity. The American and French Revolutions proved that emancipation and an ethical social order could be established through human struggle and hard work without overt religious sanction. These new redemptive narratives were additionally joined with romantic ideals of a new spirituality based on reconciling with nature and overcoming social alienation through unleashing the human imagination.[59]

SULTANS OF SUSPICION

In the wake of the humanist, romantic, and materialist revolutions that rocked Europe, later generations of intellectuals became more convinced that faith of any variety was itself a psychological impediment to fulfilling autonomous self-fashioning as an alternative hope for achieving liberation. Drawing on the tradition of Enlightenment critique, new champions of utopian revolutionary consciousness emerged within nineteenth-century Europe. Social critics of religion—such as Feuerbach, Marx, Nietzsche, and Freud—built on Spinoza's thesis that religious faiths had created a false reliance on superstitious hopes in future salvation as a form of psychological compensation and "enervating escapism" for individual suffering in the present.[60] The rise of the modern nation state also contributed to the marginalization of ecclesiastical power in favor of secular redemptive narratives rooted in the "general will" or "spirit of the people" (*Volksgeist*). Traditional religious narratives of redemptive hope were increasingly viewed as in fact performances of despair given their emphasis on the limits of human agency and dependency on divine transformation. The growing disenchantment with religious redemptive narratives created the demand for alternative forms of hope that could simultaneously provide a redemptive vision of greater harmony and fulfillment without assuming the same reliance on transcendental intervention.

Feuerbach's projectionist critique of religion during this period was one of many voices that came to define this shift away from institutionalized religious authority. Faith, according to Feuerbach, represents the externalization of hopes that rightfully belong to man's own ambitions for himself and society to actualize redemptive love.[61] Building on Feuerbach, Marx took the critique of the Young Hegelians even further by arguing against religious hope from a materialist position. Religious hope narratives do a service by giving voice to the "cry of the oppressed" and by providing "flowers on the chains of humanity."[62] Nevertheless, the great harm of religious narratives is that historically they have encouraged passive reliance on eschatological intervention, thus "rendering unto Caesar" by encouraging submission to the very social hierarchies and inequalities responsible for human alienation in the first place.[63] As Marx famously stated: "The call to abandon their illusions about their condition is a call to abandon a condition which requires illusions."[64] Religious redemptive narratives provide illusions because conditions of exploitation demand false hope in order to maintain the status quo. Consequently, religious hopes function as an "opiate," designed to enforce docility and acquiesce by providing the illusions of recompense in a world to come. Therefore, Young Hegelian concerns for the "illusions" generated by religious redemptive narratives is best addressed not just through better philosophy, but through changing the conditions that create the need for redemptive narratives that reinforce passive waiting for a world to come rather than on revolutionary praxis in this lifetime.

In contrast to Marx's redemptive aspirations for the proletariat, Nietzsche's philosophy represented a stark existentialist alternative. Nevertheless, as one of the other greatest philosophical prophets of his generation, Nietzsche's critique of hope shared with Marx a similar concern to redirect our vital energies away from "hope for the beyond" toward unmasking humanity's true desires lurking beneath the facade of social respectability.[65] Nietzsche warned that otherworldly hopes was one of many illusions humans have invented as part of an elaborate coping mechanism to distract from the harsh reality that we only have ourselves to rely on within a cold universe. Humanistic beliefs in infinite progress and optimism based on advances in science and the arts simply transferred biblical redemptive ideals into secular discourse. According to Strauss, Nietzsche sought to make the secular scientific world of his day face the hypocrisy of embracing ideals of technological progress and humanism while simultaneously claiming to remain committed to a biblically grounded ideal of morality.[66] If we have lost the moral foundations once provided by a biblical ideal of God through science and the "will-to-truth," as Nietzsche claimed, then there is no room for the groundless sentimentality that keeps Western society clinging to outdated social ideals of good versus evil. Redemptive hopes for accessing transcendental ideals prolongs our torments by keeping humanity from facing up to the existential task of becoming a self-reliant "dancing star" within the constellation of our lonely selves.

Nietzsche's writings reflected a tension between focusing on truth as merely a contingent form of social convention versus truth as a form of power that cuts through the façade of these very same conventions. Against most existential readings of Nietzsche, Rorty offered that there is a pragmatic streak within Nietzsche's thought that recognized the important poetic power within religious redemptive narratives, even if rooted in illusory hopes for future compensation and rectification of injustices. Similar to the redemptive power Marx posited in his analysis of dialectical materialism, Nietzsche's critique of religion paved the way for his own redemptive narrative rooted in the "will to power" of heroic individuals in overcoming social conventions. Conversely, and perhaps because of his religious upbringing, Nietzsche also saw in the "illusions" of hope narratives—both religious and secular—a source of inspiration that could be turned into a redemptive form of power. Nietzsche concluded the second treatise of his *Genealogy of Morality* with the following enigmatic and prophetic proclamation,

> Someday, in a stronger time than this decaying, self-doubting present, he really must come to us, the redeeming human of the great love and contempt, the creative spirit whose compelling strength again and again drives him out . . . when he again comes to light, he can bring home the redemption of this reality; its redemption from the curse that the previous ideal placed upon it. This human of the future who will redeem us from . . . the great disgust, from the will to nothingness; this bell stroke of noon and of the great decision that makes the will free again, that gives back to the earth its goal and to man his hope; this anti-Christ, and anti-nihilist; this conqueror of God and of nothingness—he must one day come . . . Zarathustra the godless.

The great irony in Nietzsche's writings is that the redemptive artistic ideal of Zarathustra represented an overcoming of redemptive ideals. Critics of Nietzsche failed to see how idealizing the overcoming of all metaphysical yearnings was not its own redemptive transcendental narrative. Scholars still debate whether Nietzsche's intention was to point to something completely beyond metaphysics or merely to restore vitalistic notions of truth. Nevertheless, what I find interesting is that both Marx and Nietzsche fundamentally changed the discourse on redemptive hope by providing new narratives more suited to social and material changes within the modern world. According to Marcel, the disenchantment induced by radical critique may have been necessary in order to reach a stronger form of existential hope.[67] The hermeneutics of suspicion developed during this period were imbued with an alternative "secularized eschatology" that looked to social critique as the new torch of truth that could help illuminate a path toward greater liberation.[68]

These and other secular utopian redemptive narratives also intensified expectations that were increasingly frustrated by what the Frankfurt School later identified as inherent contradictions within the legacy of the Enlightenment. In the words of John Gray: "The philosophers of the Enlightenment aimed to supplant Christianity, but they could do so only if they were able to satisfy the hopes it had implanted."[69] Replacing religious narratives with secular ideals of progress also contributed to a crisis of moral confidence among many intellectuals. The fundamental break with premodern foundations forever undermined, according to thinkers like Strauss, intellectual efforts such as Kant's to defend moral hopes of achieving an ethical world against either Machiavellian power politics or the amoralism of science.[70] Humanistic hopes in harmonizing individual desires for greater liberty to the social norms of the bourgeois state were increasingly questioned as inequalities became more pronounced and ideals of fraternity morphed into nationalist and imperialist belligerency.[71]

This combined breakdown of secular utopian hopes contributed to a renewal of interest among both Jewish and Christian intellectuals dedicated to the recovery of messianic narratives that could speak to the challenges of maintaining transcendental hopes within the modern world. In the next chapter I turn to efforts by late nineteenth- and early twentieth-century intellectuals to revive messianic narratives, which could speak to both the liberatory promises of Enlightenment politics and the pursuit of spiritual illumination.

2

REVIVAL OF MESSIANIC HOPE

For to him that is joined to all the living there is hope.
—ECCLESIASTES 9:4

Every man must be given what he needs for a really human life. . . . The hope for this hour depends upon the hopers themselves, upon ourselves . . . The hope for this hour depends upon the renewal of dialogical immediacy between men.
—BUBER, "HOPE FOR THIS HOUR" (1952)

HOPE AND IMMANENCE

The shock of World War I contributed to a crisis of reason and loss of confidence in the humanist foundations for modern secular utopianism.[1] For some, the ideal of material progress became synonymous with the creation of more efficient weapons of mass destruction. And for many artists, romantic yearnings to express the imagination were channeled toward a growing aestheticization of violence.[2] One of the consequences of this crisis in European culture was the renewal of interest among Jewish and Christian intellectuals in the history of apocalyptic and messianic hopes.[3] According to Gershom Scholem, an interest in the messianic has always emerged throughout Jewish history during moments of crisis and social upheaval. As Paul Mendes-Flohr points out, part of the appeal of recovering biblically based redemptive narratives was the theological consolation and foundational certainty they provided.[4] Perhaps most importantly, however, these narratives served as reminders for humanity's tragic inability to follow through on secular utopian aspirations. For modern religious intellectuals, the proven limits of unleashing human autonomy and liberty were cause for looking back to older narratives that could provide hope while countering what they saw as humanism's hubris in believing that man held all the resources for his own redemption.[5]

For Christian intellectuals during the late nineteenth and early twentieth century a recovery of Gnostic and apocalyptic narratives that emphasized cataclysmic transformation as the only solution to original sin also served to counter Enlightenment faith in the promise of technological progress.[6] For Jewish intellectuals during this same period, the challenges of Enlightenment emancipation and metaphysics were theological and political.[7] Rather than focus on humanity's fallenness, however, Jewish intellectuals increasingly saw the retreat from Enlightenment ideals of political emancipation and equality as a threat to their ability to partake in the liberatory ethos of modernity. Efforts to dismantle the West's cosmopolitan culture through a revival of repressed nationalist yearnings led some Jewish intellectuals to return to their own ethnic identity and the traditions discarded by previous generations of *maskilim* who were all too eager to reject what they viewed as superstitious and mystical elements within Judaism. Additionally, Jewish intellectuals increasingly looked to the recovering of messianic hope as providing an alternative model of redemption that could speak to the dialectics between moderate ideals of Enlightenment's civil emancipation and more revolutionary desires for total transformation.[8] In order to counter the despair over the failure of the Enlightenment's emancipatory politics to take hold—either in the form of liberal reformism or socialist revolution—European Jewish intellectuals also looked to recover messianic texts and history that could give consolation and meaning to the winds of change blowing across the West. Many Jewish intellectuals followed Franz Rosenzweig's demand for a *new thinking*, a new approach to ethics and politics that could merge discourses of messianic redemption with concrete praxis.[9]

MESSIANIC AND APOCALYPTIC HOPES

Writing in the midst of the political and cultural tempest sweeping the West, Martin Buber was acutely aware that a radical rethinking of religion, human relationships, and modern alienation was needed if the torch of messianic hope was to be kept alive for the future.[10] In contrast to the *maskilim* who engaged in the scientific study of Judaism (*Wissenschaft des Judentums*) in order to discard the ecstatic components (*Schwärmerei*) of Judaism, Buber looked to Jewish mysticism and messianism as a means for bridging the gap between romantic emotionalism and civic rationalism. The dialectical interplay between the legacy of Spinoza and the legacy of Hasidism were essential ingredients for generating a renaissance in Jewish communal life.[11] The political and cultural upheaval of his age was a major influence on Buber's decision to develop a philosophical anthropology capable of linking metaphysical questions with the social challenges of his day.[12] The three main influences that informed Buber's revivalist turn to prophetic hope were the Zionism of his youth, his early scholarly explorations of the Hasidic community, and his lifelong engagement with socialism (as introduced to him by his murdered comrade Gustav Landauer).[13] From all three sources Buber blazed new scholarly trails that skipped over most of Judaism's medieval and Talmudic heritage in order to weave together a unique political philosophy that mixed existentialist and mystical themes of direct encounter with a philosophical anthropology based on social solidarity.

In his early work on *The Kingship of God* (1932), Buber proposed that ancient Israelite political theology begins from a unique historical mission to create an alternative political system based on justice rather than pure power. The warning to the Israelites to "remember that it is the Lord your God who gives you the power" (Dt 8:18) served as an alternative model to the realpolitik of the ancient world whereby the earthly power of pharaohs and emperors was its own source of divine authority. The theological ideal of God's kingship over all the land and power structures radically shifts the position of the individual and national community in relationship to history and the divine. The redemptive hope that emerges in this period was based on the idea that the tyranny of kings could be replaced by the tyranny of God whose will could only be reflected through the righteous rather than the powerful.

Tensions between the idealism of a covenantal faith with the realism of ancient Near Eastern power politics lead to an early split between what Buber defined as "eschatological hope" and "historical hope."[14] Eschatological hopes represented precisely the type of docility that the nineteenth-century Jewish historian Heinrich Graetz had earlier identified with inner messianism and rabbinism's emphasis on waiting for God to redeem the world at the end of days. Graetz had argued that the development of what Weber characterized as inner-worldly asceticism and spiritualization of messianic hope by both the rabbis and early Christians also had the political consequence of transforming the fervor of messianic hope—especially after the disaster of Bar Kohba's rebellion in 132–135 CE—into an interiorized spiritual practice that could acquiesce to the imperial order of the Roman Empire.[15]

Following Graetz's distinctions, Buber proposed that eschatological hopes rely on a form of fatalism that diminishes the role of human agency within history. Conversely, the redemptive hope that Buber wanted to identify with the legacy of messianism and the prophets suggests a greater dialogic interaction between the divine and human within history. The main importance of this distinction in Buber's writings is that it raises questions about human agency and praxis in relationship to God's role in history. If redemptive hope is predicated on the notion of God directing history toward a final goal, is there any meaning to human freedom? Do humans have a role to play in history as partners in the redemptive process? For Buber the answers to these questions are found within the dialectics of humans reaching out toward the divine in search of recognition and dialogue. The notion of God's kingship reflects the distance between humans and the divine, but also the hope for intimacy with a divine presence within history and politics.

In *Prophetic Faith* (1942), Martin Buber further elaborated on the evolution of messianic hope by the Hebrew prophets. Prophets like Jeremiah and Isaiah refashioned the very purpose of ancient Israelite religious ritual and national identity so that it could serve to reinforce a basic universalistic hope in eventually uniting all of God's children in peace and justice.[16] The historical introduction of messianic hope represented the transformation of national group egoism toward a new universal solidarity. The holiness of a chosen few becomes the light of hope and promise that spreads to the entire world.[17] Not only will the Israelites become a "light unto the nations" (Is 49:6), but all nations will one day join in peace through worship on the Lord's mountain in Zion (Is 2:2–4). In contrast to the inculcation of devotion to ecclesiastical and social hierarchies represented by what Buber identified as the *priestly* principle, the prophets created an alternative devotional model to God and religion.

For his contemporary readers this prophetic ideal was also more amenable to Enlightenment ideals of autonomy and liberation. Following Herman Cohen's contrast between Plato's hope for power and the prophet's hope for justice, Buber maintains that the prophets also created a revolution within the history of religion by changing devotional intentions from a quest to access divine power through rituals toward a principle of protecting the weak and oppressed.[18] According to Buber, this switch from priestly religious concerns with maintaining power by overseeing cultic practice toward a prophetic emphasis on unifying all of creation within a transcendental moral order created the foundations upon which all subsequent narratives of redemptive hope were built.

Here Buber also elaborated on what he saw as a fundamental tension between messianic and apocalyptic faith.[19] Similar to the polarity in his earlier writings between religion and religiosity, the messianic for Buber helps to inculcate a spiritual sense of agency and praxis within the world.[20] Conversely, the apocalyptic embodies those qualities of religious faith that lead to an overdependence on God as an external force acting within history. Messianic yearnings to actualize a "new heaven and a new earth" (Is 65:17), were turned into an apocalyptic dependence on transcendental forces that only a small elite were capable of accessing by penetrating beyond the veils of illusions that define this worldly existence.

In *Two Types of Faith* (1945) Buber further distinguishes what he considered to be authentic Jewish faith (*Emunah*) as closer to a form of trust, and what later developed as Christian faith (*Pistis*) through Paulinism (and not, importantly for Buber, Jesus whom he identified with the legacy of Jewish messianism). As a consequence of this Pauline transformation of prophetic hope, Buber argued that a "soteriological hope replaced concrete Messianism," leaving individuals to place a greater emphasis on their own individual salvation rather than seeking broader social transformation.[21] Apocalyptic faith speaks to a fundamental human desire for a release from responsibility through radical acceptance of things that seem beyond human abilities.[22] Apocalypticism, Gnosticism, and even modern dialectical materialism, therefore, cater to our psychological need to believe that some eternal order is at work behind the scenes in achieving the final end of all history in which "time will no longer be."[23]

The temporal importance of messianic hope within Buber's work was deeply indebted to Hermann Cohen's earlier work on distinguishing between Jewish versus Hellenistic eschatological models in which the finite is submerged into the infinite.[24] Buber built on Cohen's designation of prophetic hope as a form of temporal opposition to actuality by linking messianism to the temporal dynamism of human solidarity. Buber grounded the prophetic praxis of shattering the present actuality identified by Cohen with messianic hope in the everydayness (*Alltagsleben*) of social interactions. In his essay "Plato and Isaiah" (1938), Buber gives a twist on Cohen's similarly titled essay by lauding the prophets for challenging philosophical privileging of individual flight into the ethereal realm of ideas and the contemplative life (*bios theoretikos*).[25] Buber adds an existentialist's twist, however, by linking personal soteriology with historical transformation.[26] From Cohen's neo-Kantian perspective, messianic transformation begins from the proper intellectual apprehension of the right idea, whereas for Buber it begins with the intersubjective encounter and the transformation of a self that can concretely respond to the needs of another person.[27]

In light of Michael Walzer's claim that the prophetic messianism of the biblical tradition lacks a basis for the type of revolutionary politics later derived by postbiblical interpreters, Buber's distinction between the messianic and apocalyptic is better understood within the polemical context of twentieth-century political theology.[28] Although Buber locates these tensions within their ancient historical context, his real purpose is to further his own polemical concerns to revive messianic hope as a viable source of inspiration in the modern world while avoiding an overdependence on the cataclysm of revolutionary violence (secularized by Hegel as "the cunning of reason") as a necessary stage for overcoming alienation.[29]

Distinguishing between the messianic and apocalyptic also allowed Buber to work out his conflictual attraction to the radical messianism of left-wing German politics (associated with his martyred friend Landauer and the utopian student movements involved in the Bavarian revolution of 1919). Although deeply attracted to both socialism and Zionism for their commitment to political transformation, Buber also wrote about messianism in order to warn against the dangers of actually trying to establish a new heaven and earth.[30] Buber's strategy for channeling the potentially harmful energy of messianic fervor was to present an interpretation of messianic hope that could speak to temporal and aesthetic experiences as a conduit for individual authenticity. For Buber the greatness of prophetic hope was its grounding in a phenomenology that combined political and ethical transformation. Prophetic hope does not fall into the traditional category of eschatology since, in his words, "the core itself does not belong to the margin of history where it vanishes into the realms of the timeless, but it belongs to the center, the ever-changing center, that is to say, it belongs to the experienced hour and its possibility."[31] However, it would be unfair to suggest that Buber's mixing of Hasidic notions of *teshuvah* with an interest in redemptive fervor signified merely a return to a form of inner-messianism. Nevertheless, his ambivalence over what it actually means to embody messianic ideals individually and communally is never fully presented in his writings.

The real issue here is the question of agency and freedom: apocalyptic eschatology suggests passive waiting, whereas the messianic for Buber is an extension of human existential freedoms experienced in each hour of decision and response to the call to help redeem the world. But, and perhaps most importantly, Buber kept his reflections within an existential framework so as to avoid the implication that messianic hope necessitates large revolutionary transformation of all society as modeled within the redemptive narratives of Marxist-inspired politics of his day.

One of Buber's other main contributions to discussions over the contemporary relevance of messianic narratives was his return to Hasidic and mystical models of redemptive temporality. The prophet represents an ideal of turning, of "inner transformation" (*teshuvah*) generated through the "everyday" sanctification of creation leading to redemption.[32] Similarly, just "as creation does not merely take place once in the beginning but also at every moment throughout the whole of time, so redemption does not take place merely once at the end, but also at every moment throughout the whole of time."[33] Messianism is not about looking forward to the day when desire ends, but rather represents a process in which the evil inclination (*yetzer ha-rah*) toward division within desire gives way to the inclination toward a unifying good (*yetzer ha-tov*). Messianic hope, therefore, is not just the "forward-thrust" that shatters the present actuality but also reflects the immanent sanctification of the prosaic and quotidian in the here and now into a greater unity.

The mutuality implied by human involvement in the redemptive process through *teshuvah* and acts of righteousness (*gemilut hasadim*) stands in contrast to what Rabbi David Hartman later identified as the "rupture paradigm" of apocalyptic faith.[34] Hartman's contrast between "a rupture concept of history" (introduced through the redemption of Israel at Exodus) in tension with "a covenantal concept of history" (introduced through the revelation at Sinai) helps illuminate Buber's distinction between redemptive models that either reinforce or undermine human freedom and agency.[35]

Halakhic hope affirms the power of human agency and partnership in moving the redemptive process forward, whereas radical hope places a greater emphasis on human dependency on outside forces—such as God's role in affecting the exodus from Egypt—for achieving redemption. Hartman's contrast between the halakhic hope of Sinai and the radical hope of Exodus is redolent of Buber's distinction between the passivity of apocalyptic faith versus the praxis of messianic hope expressed within everyday acts leading to redemption.[36] For Buber just as creation and redemption continue to unfold within every moment, so too the revelation from Sinai continues to reverberate within daily acts of righteousness.

Questions about the role of human agency within history continued to inform Buber's attempt to link religious and secular utopian redemptive narratives together. In his work *Paths in Utopia* (1947) Buber translated his polarities from ancient Israelite history into modern secular distinctions between social and political principles. The social principle relates to the solidarity of intersubjective relationships. Conversely, the political principle reflects the "priestly" impulse for institutional structures in which the "redemptive process has been fixed."[37] The desire for an "algebra of revolution" links secular utopian Socialism and Marxism with the history of both Gnosticism and apocalypticism.[38] Consequently, the fatalism within dialectical materialism and some versions of utopian socialism are merely secularized expressions of the same apocalyptic reliance on what Hegel initially identified in the laws of history as a substitute for individual responsibility. The idolatrous impulse to achieve "cosmological security" from the flux of time relieves individuals from what Buber saw as a sacred duty to engage directly in the temporal sanctification of everyday experience through dialogue.[39]

RESTORATION, UTOPIANISM, AND REDEMPTION

Gershom Scholem and Franz Rosenzweig were among Buber's most important twentieth-century interlocutors and critics, especially on the topic of redemption. Buber not only admired Hasidism's spiritualization of messianic fever—much more than either Scholem or Rosenzweig—he was also attracted to the possibility of actualizing these redemptive impulses within history. By contrast, Rosenzweig looked to engage messianic hope, mostly within the educational realms of philosophy and theology. In the polemical terms developed by nineteenth-century thinkers like Graetz, Rosenzweig's

Star of Redemption (1921) continued what could be interpreted as a form of Rabbinic "inner messianism." According to Rosenzweig, Judaism continues to serve redemptive hope while refraining from directly engaging in the revolutionary politics advocated by Jewish socialists and Zionists alike.[40] The great power and appeal of Judaism's redemptive tradition was precisely that it avoided the temptation to seek the actualization of divine perfection in the world, and thus also the implicit temptation toward imperialism (as with Christianity and Islam). By contrast, since the destruction of the Second Temple, Judaism managed to provide an alternative redemptive temporality enacted through procreation within the "blood community" and sacred rhythms of the liturgical calendar. The destruction of the temple and the end of political sovereignty had actually liberated Jews from having to live within political history and concomitant demands to ensure the sanctification of a holy space.

Although Christians lack the blood ties of belonging to the "eternal people," Rosenzweig proposed that Christianity's conquering of paganism and establishment of powerful political institutions also contributed to the fires that burn within the "star of redemption" by spreading the light of messianic hope throughout the world. Following on Maimonides's ecumenical appreciation for the role of Christianity within world history, Rosenzweig similarly affirms the role of Christianity in helping the world come closer to redemption.[41] The Jews, however, serve the eternal flame of redemptive hope by removing themselves from the task of perfecting the political realm to instead engage in the sanctification of cosmic temporality through life-cycle rituals and prayer.

Gershom Scholem famously differed with Buber's attempt to separate Judaism's redemptive traditions into separate spheres of influence. Scholem wrote and conversed within many of the same German-Jewish intellectual circles as Buber, but adopted a much more critical historical approach when evaluating Jewish messianic fervor and the role of mystical thought within Jewish communities. According to Scholem, all redemptive narratives within Judaism share in a dialectical tension between competing restorative, utopian, and revolutionary impulses.[42] The restorative desire for returning to the days of old or to the origins of creation will always stand in tension with the competing utopian impulse for a future redemptive horizon in which a completely new form of existence comes into being.[43] The dialectical interaction between violent imagery and political quiescence made it more difficult to clearly separate the history of messianism from apocalypticism. As Scholem states:

> It is precisely the lack of transition between history and the redemption which is always stressed by the prophets and apocalyptists. The Bible and the apocalyptic writers know of no progress in history leading to the redemption. The redemption is not the product of immanent developments such as we find in the modern Western reinterpretations of Messianism since the Enlightenment where, secularized as the belief in progress, Messianism still displayed unbroken and immense vigor. It is rather transcendence breaking in upon history, an intrusion in which history itself perishes, transformed in its ruin because it is struck by a beam of light shining into it from the outside source. . . . The apocalyptists have always cherished a pessimistic view of the world. Their optimism, their hope, is not directed to what history will bring forth, but to that which will arise in its ruin, free at last and undisguised.[44]

Following on conflicting biblical and Talmudic claims that redemption will result either from the collective merit of the Jewish people or their complete decline, messianic and apocalyptic visions of "transcendence breaking in upon history" are linked by their shared emphasis on an "outside source" as the foundation for maintaining redemptive hope.[45] As suggested by the prophet Isaiah, at the "end of days" (Is 2:2) there will be a "day of the Lord" (Is 2:12) when God's wrath will pour out on those who have caused the righteous to suffer. Isaiah's prophetic vision of restoration and recompense for the suffering of his righteous people combines the redemptive promise for eventual peace and reconciliation among all peoples of the world, as well as potentially violent reckoning by a divine judge and warrior.

Contrasting images of hope for peace with hope for violent vengeance on behalf of the oppressed righteous reflected the weaving together of conflictual attitudes regarding the meaning of human freedom. Psychologically, the redemptive hope that rises out of the ashes of apocalyptic destruction reflects, according to Scholem, competing libidinal impulses toward the future fulfillment of violent, antinomian, and masochistic desires. Our messianic impulses, therefore, are not just about hopes for justice and peace, but also reflect a desire to engage in the "redemptive sin" of tearing down and violating social conventions.[46] Messianism necessarily inspires a maximalist political disposition that can both keep the flame of hope alive in times of darkness, but also stimulate ecstatic fervor that resists pragmatic compromise. These destructive impulses, according to Scholem, are all too often ignored by those who draw on the fires of messianic hopes for inspiring modern utopian political projects like Zionism and socialism.

Scholem's writings demonstrate a unique attunement to the complicated role of despair and negation that informs the messianic tradition as the basis of his critique of Buber.[47] Although Scholem designates Maimonides and Herman Cohen as the main "liquidators of apocalypticism" in their reflections on Judaism, Buber is also implicated as part of the *Wissenschaft* legacy of insulating Judaism from the mercurial forces for doom, destruction, and radical transformation expressed through apocalyptic/messianic beliefs. Perhaps it was Scholem's witnessing of Buber's willingness to correlate the experience of war with mystical ecstasy at the beginning of World War I or his prescience that messianic nationalist politics might ultimately infect the Zionist project. Buber not only tried to privilege messianic hope as somehow exempt from these more destructive impulses, but also continued Graetz's and Cohen's thesis that alien influences were to blame for introducing apocalyptic fatalism into Judaism.[48] For Scholem, Buber's pointing to Persian or Gnostic influences merely deflected from the darker side of apocalyptic fervor mixed throughout the history of messianism.[49] Scholem also charged that this myopia in Buber's thought explained why he was attracted to the resoluteness of both religious and secular movements willing to translate some of these messianic hopes into contemporary politics.

Although he found the mercurial energies stirred up by messianic and apocalyptic fervor intellectually stimulating, Scholem was also disturbed by the appropriation of these very same energies by Zionists—particularly the Revisionist Party established by Vladimir Jabotinsky in 1925—in order to achieve what in Scholem's mind should be Zionism's more pragmatic and immediate goal of securing a defensible homeland for the Jewish people. He was deeply ambivalent over the extent to which messianic energies could play a constructive role in the concrete and immediate nationalist needs of the Jewish people in the twentieth century.[50] Part of what attracted Scholem to Zionism was precisely its realism in contrast to the "wishful idealism" within the Jewish messianic tradition.[51] Perhaps the real purpose of basing one's redemptive hope on a "transcendence breaking in upon history" is the perpetual "deferment" of actually having to achieve it.[52] If Zionism was to succeed it would have to resist the religious redemptive hope of radical transformation that had intoxicated failed messianic movements—like the Sabbatianism of the seventeenth century—throughout Jewish history.[53] For Scholem, the vitalistic core of all messianic movements was the subterranean "demonic anarchism" that harnessed redemptive hopes through the destructive joys of its own negation.[54] Part of the appeal of messianism, according to Scholem, was its power to subvert the staleness of institutionalization and social hierarchies. Yet, when linked to politics, history had proven that the antinomian fervor stirred up by messianic expectation could also become destructive. Consequently, similar to Leo Strauss during this same period, Scholem thought it best to address these anarchic messianic aspirations through the esotericism of scholarship, rather than use these redemptive hopes as a foundation for modern political philosophy.[55]

Whereas Scholem saw a greater value in distancing the ideal of messianism from a utopian ideal of political harmony within history, Buber saw a greater urgency to link the idealistic/utopian quality of messianism to endeavors of concrete actualization. Buber looked to the prophetic messianic tradition precisely as an inspirational alternative to the apocalyptic fatalism of "life lived in deferment." For Buber, the anticipatory qualities of messianism functioned as a reservoir of resilience and individuation: Rather than the apocalyptic reliance on a vertical "transcendence breaking in upon history," the distinctive alternative hope of messianism was located in the dialogic mutuality of finite human beings embodying a radical otherness capable of working in partnership to fulfill the task of reconciling with the infinite.[56] Messianism expressed a mutuality between the *infinite* and *particular* through which—in the words of Fackenheim—"God is God, and man is man; a veritable gulf separates the two: and yet they are immediately related."[57]

Yet, Buber also shared Scholem's more scholarly and cautionary concerns with embracing messianic fervor as part of a broader political platform.[58] Although Buber advocated for genuine encounters that would promote experiences of recognition and cosmic wholeness, he was equally cautious to temper against potential antinomian impulses that accompany religious attempts to further the process of redemption. For example, the messianic fervor of the Sabbatian movement's embrace of redeeming "holy sparks" through "sin performed in holiness as preparing the way for the Messianic world" represented a model for how messianic fervor will necessarily lead to its own spiritual negation.[59] Historically, Hasidism's "sublimation" of Sabbatianism's libidinal messianism created an alternative spiritual hope in which "man's service of the sparks takes place in everyday life."[60] For Buber, Hasidism's "redemption of the everyday" changed the focus from eschatological narratives that revolve around either a single redeemer or cataclysmic event toward the hallowing of everyday encounters through acts of loving-kindness.[61] Hasidism's sublimation of redemptive fervor provides a broader model for spiritually maintaining what Erich Fromm later referred to as the crouched tiger of messianic expectations, while simultaneously keeping redemptive fervor in check.

Buber elides what Strauss identified as the problem of power (namely that the exercise of political power is the precondition for community) in order to stake out the holiness of encounter. In Leo Strauss's terms, Buber oscillates between a *political theology* in which the point is to ground a conception of the good life in an externally justified divine source, versus a *political philosophy* based on humanity's horizontal reliance on addressing fundamental needs through the establishment of communities centered on dialogic intimacy. Following on the biblical ideal in Genesis that there is a fundamental goodness at the heart of creation (*ke tov kol ha-aretz*), Buber was much more willing to trust that something within dialogic relationships could serve to counter the "demonic anarchism" that may easily be unleashed by trying to live out redemptive hopes. The realm of encounter, however, is almost always intersubjective rather than political or institutional.

In the final analysis, Scholem and Buber shared an appreciation for the dialectic within the Jewish messianic tradition that fluctuated between the competing needs for actualization and a life lived in deferment. Parts of Buber's writings on spirituality, community, and education reflect a continuity of existential and mystical hopes that alienation can be overcome through the right effort (*kavanah*). It would be a mistake, however, to read Buber's rehabilitation of messianism as a continuation of his naïvely romantic view of politics as reflected in his earlier infatuation with Nietzsche and his mystification of war during the early days of World War I. Paul Mendes-Flohr makes the point that Buber was perhaps closer to Scholem's unease with the potentially explosive elixir of messianic and utopian anarchic politics than he acknowledged himself.[62] This unease might explain Buber's emphasis on intersubjective encounters rather than on a larger structural transformation as the basis for expressing redemptive hopes.

A PHENOMENOLOGY OF REDEMPTIVE HOPE

Within the history of redemptive hope narratives Martin Buber's philosophical anthropology of I-Thou relations was one of the first to suggest the possibility of messianic transformation through everyday intersubjective encounters. Buber's initially struggled to bridge the mystical and romantic ideals of ecstatic union (ideals derived from his youthful interest in Nietzsche's *Lebensphilosophie* and mystical experience) with his commitments to the political philosophy of socialist utopianism and Zionism. As he moved in Mendes-Flohr's famous formulation "from mysticism to dialogue," Buber brought these various interests together, transitioning from a focus on the "lived experience" (*Erlebnis*) to the experience of encounter (*Begegnung*). The shift in emphasis from the ecstatic experience of the *mysterium tremendum* meant turning toward an alternative spirituality grounded in ethical responsibility for the other person. Within the terms Buber developed in his seminal work *I and Thou* (1922) it is possible to imagine hope emerging from our commitment to transform our cognition of the world as comprised of mere objects to entities of *Thou-ness* with whom we can establish a reciprocal relationship. This hope for relationships begins with the self. However, unlike most post-Cartesian forms of subjectivity, our ability to develop into a healthy self is dependent on the strength of our commitments to other people. Subjectivity commences from our engagement with otherness. "I become through my relations with the Thou; as I become I, I say Thou."[63] Genuine encounter, therefore, requires the recognition of another Thou that both reinforces the identity of the subject, while creating a moment of presence with an other. Because "I-You can only be spoken with one's whole being," the boundaries of subjectivity break from the "experience" of subject/object dualism toward the mutuality of address and response to a Thou.[64]

Buber's book *I and Thou* had a profound influence on intellectuals who were similarly interested in linking intersubjective encounters with metaphysical concerns for transcendence and social transformation. Starting with his writings on the *phenomenology of hope* in the 1940s, the Christian social philosopher Gabriel Marcel was one of the first to combine a theory of intersubjective encounter with phenomenology.[65] Following Buber, Marcel proposed that existential meaning commences from human relationships.[66] In Marcel's terms, "I open my soul when I hope ... hope is essentially the availability of the soul ... the experience of communion."[67]

Meaningful interactions with others start from an inner spark of hope for genuine relationships. Experiences of communion conditions experiences of transcendence, creating a basis for mutuality and grounding against existential despair.[68] The phenomenology of hope thus unfolds through acts of solidarity with others. In the words of Aquinas, "being loved by someone generates hope in him, and then hope in him brings us to return his love."[69] We hope as individuals with our whole being, but our hopes are always tied to our relationships with other people.[70] Hope is both conditioned by and generated through our relationships with others. We hope for intersubjective encounters, and these encounters help to produce hope for further dialogue.

Marcel's use of the term *phenomenology* signifies the intersection of the transcendental with the broad range of spiritual, libidinal, and charismatic qualities that comprise social interactions. When we hope we reach out for the transcendence of the beyond while affirming the immanence of genuine recognition from those whom we encounter as a Thou. The "prophetic character of hope" that breaks social isolation allows us to overcome the impulse for security through what he referred to as "having," for example, the desire to exercise "power over" objects as reified extensions of egotistical self-affirmation.[71] By contrast, human need for encounter and recognition is what links a phenomenology of hope to religious promises for redemption through the temporal harmonization of past, present, and future.[72] A phenomenology of hope conditions the self toward encounters with other Thous in the present, and hope for the renewal of relationships in the future.

The phenomenological convergence of horizontal immanence with vertical transcendence in Marcel's work provides an alternative lens for rereading Buber's writings on messianic hope and intersubjective encounters. The first step in the phenomenology of hope that I read out of Buber starts from trust established in dialogic encounters: We enter into dialogue with the hope for encounter and understanding, while simultaneously, we have the potential to come away with a hope for future encounters. In the philosophical terms proposed by Martin, we have a "normative hope" based on the assumption that we can trust those with whom we have interpersonal relations to reciprocate our expectations for their behavior responsibly.[73] Where Martin puts the emphasis on the rational expectations involved when we invest hope in people, for Buber the phenomenological texture of intersubjective recognition is the essential quality that allows the emergence of the self to break the boundaries of a deterministic *egology*. With redemption as the end goal, each daily act of kindness, recognition, and justice on the intersubjective level serves as a catalyst for opening individuals to the hope contained within the messianic tradition. Dialogic encounters have the potential to provide experiences of mutual recognition that can justify working for larger redemptive hopes. The "eros of dialogue" generated through moments of reciprocal recognition between individuals provides the basis for imagining the possibility of one day living in a world organized around a "living center" based on reciprocity and mutual trust.[74] The phenomenology of hope generated through I-Thou encounters creates the necessary conditions from which larger messianic hopes become possible. Messianic hope is not an illusion or mere wishful idealism so long as it is rooted in the genuine solidarity that forms the basis of relationships and community.

Buber proposes an inductive model, starting with our first existential encounters with otherness, as the foundation for the future ascension toward redemption. For Herman Cohen, by contrast, I-Thou relationships begin deductively with God as the source from which all particular loves and relationships of recognition flow.[75] Our love for the principle of unity and uniqueness of God provides the foundations for recognizing the importance of uniqueness in others and for striving to realize an ideal of a unified humanity. Cohen also follows Kant in asserting that recognition of God creates the pretext for recognizing our duty, love, and moral commitment to our fellowman (*Mitmensch*).[76] Buber drew on Cohen's neo-Kantian idealism, but his focus was more anthropological. Rather than starting with the transcendental encounter with God as the basis for redemptive hope, for Buber we start with an I-Thou relationship and then build toward encounters with the "eternal Thou" and divine presence. "Only if and because I love this or that specific man," Buber states, "can I elevate my relation to the social idea of man into that emotional relationship involving my whole being which I am entitled to call by the name of love."[77] As in Kant, hope serves as a transcendental ideal that can help motivate us to strive for a kingdom of ends despite the "crookedness" of humanity. Unlike Kantian idealism, however, messianic hope begins from the intimacy of our encounters with other unique persons.

Rather than ground social and political authority in abstract categorical ideals that stand outside our human condition (à la Kant's postulates of pure practical reason), subjectivity and political theology come together for Buber within the complexity and intimacy of human relationships.[78] Additionally, the phenomenological quality of hope emerges through the recognition of one's responsibility for the other as the basis for subjectivity. "I cannot legitimately share in the Present Being without sharing in the being of the other; with the fact I cannot answer the lifelong address of God to me without answering at the same time for the other."[79] The encounter with otherness constitutes both our hope for self-knowledge (thus fulfilling the criterion of autonomy) but also hope for transformation, as expressed through messianism. Buber looked to the intimacy of intersubjective encounters as the initial basis from which messianic hopes are later justified.

> The faith of Israel in the redemption of the world does not signify that this world will be replaced by another; rather it is the faith in a new world on this earth. The here and the beyond does not exist in Hebrew. This hope including the whole world signifies that we cannot talk with God if we abandon the world to itself. We can only talk with God when we put our arms, as well as we can, around the world, that is when we carry God's truth and justice to all.[80]

Addressing other persons as Thou generates the pretext of hope from which it becomes possible to imagine addressing others, and perhaps someday the whole world, as a Thou. Following on his appropriation of Hasidic spirituality, each moment of hallowing and addressing the world as a Thou infuses the mundane, according to Buber, with sparks of redemption. Grand worldly redemptive hopes begin not with revelations in the desert or mountains, but within the everydayness of social interactions. The process of mutual recognition in I-Thou relations has the potential to create the concentric bonds that provide the psychological foundations upon which individuals can open themselves up to a larger redemptive hope for the entire world.

Yet Buber also suggests that our typical I-It consciousness significantly limits our ability to see other people as potential sources of hope. Humanity is afflicted by what Buber referred to as a "twofold I" that not only seeks the intimacy of an I-Thou relationship but simultaneously seeks to instrumentally grasp at the essence of a thing. Buber begins from the premise that humans at their core lean toward the good, but that the combination of our egoism and social pressures for conformity accentuate our impulses to objectify others for the purpose of security and control. We are fundamentally driven to transform others into objects that can be seized, controlled, and manipulated.[81] Although Buber resisted what he considered the Gnostic ontologizing of human fallenness, he did acknowledge that the "sublime melancholy of our lot" is to be forever pulled between hopes for communion and needs for autonomy through "standing at a distance."[82] Consequently, "every You in the world is doomed by its nature to become a thing."[83]

These same tensions between intersubjective openness and ego security are also reflected in the various religious discourses developed for relating to the divine.[84] The same idolatrous impulses that cause us to seek out God as something we can intellectually and physically grasp is the same impulse that leads us to reify other people as It objects that can be manipulated as means to our own egotistical ends.[85] Buber correlated the desire to externalize the infinite as a distinct power with the age-old metaphysical quest to penetrate through the realm of contingency and appearances to the realm of eternal truth. Philosophy and theology historically have been united by the "idolatrous" impulse to grasp something that we can "handle" and "spread out in time."[86] Buber's concern is that this "theomania," as suggested by Elliot Wolfson, has distorted the history of human and divine encounters.[87] Too often, according to Buber, theology replicates the same analytical approach established by a "detached self" capable of utilizing "the objectifying telescope of distant vision" in order to compartmentalize, co-ordinate, and subdue.[88] "Philosophical" thinking necessarily entails a knowing through compartmentalization and domination.[89] Because "vision is the first disengagement from the I-Thou relationship," Buber argues that the ocularcentrism of philosophers has led to a reification of the senses in which only that which we can objectify has legitimacy as a candidate for knowledge.[90] According to Buber:

> The tendency of the Greeks to understand the world as a self-contained space, in which man too has his fixed place, was perfected in Aristotle's geocentric spherical system. The hegemony of the visual sense over the other senses . . . the very hegemony which enabled them to live a life derived from images and to base a culture on the forming of images, holds good in their philosophy as well. A visual image of the universe [*Weltbild*] arises which is formed from visual sense-impressions and objectified as only the visual sense is able to objectify. . . . Even Plato's

world of ideas is a visual world, a world of forms that are seen ... a universe of things, and now man is a thing among these things of the universe, an objectively comprehensible species beside other species.[91]

Buber followed in the trend of affirming a rather simplistic division between the "God of the Philosophers" and the "God of Abraham, Isaac, and Jacob" as reflecting a fundamental choice between the distancing of ocularcentrism or the hope for genuine relationship. In contrast to what Buber referred to as "Mosaic man," "Socratic man" seeks "philosophical security" by detaching himself from the confines of the physical world.[92] Buber went on to charge that metaphysical thought "does not have the power to build up man's real life, and the strictest philosophical certainty cannot endow the soul with that *intimate certitude* that the world which is so imperfect will be brought to its perfection."[93] This desire to achieve "objectivity" contributes to a broader alienation from our own humanity and our willingness to trust that other finite humans are worthy of our efforts.[94]

In contrast to the metaphysical model of knowing through objectification, Buber proposed that there is an alternative model of knowing based on a biblical ideal of intersubjective encounter through one's whole being. Buber followed the trend among many Jewish intellectuals during this period in assuming that their own intellectual reflections were capable of avoiding what was widely viewed as the inherent imperializing qualities of the metaphysical tradition. Rather than experience the other as a "thing among things," the goal should be an encounter with the "wholeness of the person" in which the pretense of achieving what Hillary Putnam called the "archimedean perspective" of the "untouched observer" gives way to mutual encounter.[95] Buber points to the example of how "Adam knew his wife Eve" (Gn 4:1) as emblematic of an alternative "foundation for the religious world view." The verb *to know* in Hebrew implies direct relation through erotic encounter. Thus, when we read the statement, "Adam *knew* his wife Eve" Buber wants his readers to assume that what is implied is a different epistemological standard that, at the very least, cannot be comprehended by the metaphysics of objectification.[96] As Buber himself acknowledged, he is "pointing" at something within the "betweenness" of human encounters that is both real yet beyond the grasp of analytical definitions.[97]

Subjectivity in Buber's (anti)system is based on the premise that to *know* the *other*, is to *be* with the *other* in a way that breaks down traditional metaphysical dichotomies between the finitude of creation and a transcendental Divinity.[98] In contrast to the legacy of Platonic metaphysics there is "no world of appearance, there is only the world," and in this world, the only knowledge that can bring true comfort comes from the *eros of dialogue* that concretely connects us to the otherness of people and the world as both distinct from the self, yet capable of address and ultimate embrace.[99] Philosophy helps in the necessary process of establishing the power of an autonomous self, enraptured by the resoluteness of its own monologue. By contrast, the biblical ideal is one of reaching out toward others and the world in search of dialogue.[100] For Buber we exist at both a *distance* as a separate I, but also in *relation* so that alterity is not collapsed into the singular totality of the same.[101] Similar to the moment of reciprocal interdependence in Hegel's master/slave dialectic, Adam, as representative of all men, can only truly find the confirmation of existence through the female compliment represented by Eve.[102]

But how do we get from these intimate moments of intersubjective recognition to messianic hopes for worldwide redemption? Why should we assume that the concentric circles of care we have with family and friends can be extended to all peoples, even our enemies? Doesn't the phenomenology of hope that might emerge from intersubjective encounters depend on intimacy and exclusivity that cannot be translated into broad modes of civic and institutional association?

The answer I read out of Buber begins with our first moments of self-affirmation based on the trust created by being addressed and addressing others in moments of authentic recognition. "Man can become whole not in virtue of a relation to himself but only in virtue of a relation to another self."[103] Because our ability to establish our subjectivity is intimately and reciprocally dependent on our relationship to others, we can only fully actualize ourselves to the extent that we experience a phenomenology of hope that allows us to view the other as a Thou rather than as an It.[104] Following on Hegel's phenomenology of the master/slave dialectic, for Buber our initial moments of confrontation with otherness creates the first stage within the emergence of an authentic self. Contra Hegel, however, the first stage in moving from being a raw ego to a person starts from an individual's first moments of recognition and confirmation.[105] As Buber states, a "child says Thou before it learns to say I."[106] Norman O'Brown's statement that the "only grounds for hope for humanity are in the facts of human childhood" illuminates the Buberian insight that our redemptive hopes start inductively with our intersubjective encounters in our most vulnerable states as young children. Initially experiences of love and dialogic encounters with caregivers enable feelings of trust and courage to reach out in hope for further recognition and love. An ability to hold onto a redemptive vision of hope for the whole world, therefore, is always dependent on intersubjective experiences starting at a very young age.[107]

Buber's philosophical anthropology comes closer to a postmetaphysical position by bringing epistemology down from the heights of Platonic and Cartesian dualism into the relational terms of intersubjective encounter.[108] For Levinas and other phenomenologists, Buber's critique of modern subjectivity provided the foundations for an alternative redemptive ideal of intersubjective relationships. Particularly, Buber's critique of the "imperialist" qualities of a singular "I" that seeks to "objectify" otherness and the world as thing (*Ding*) locates him within the orbit of what Jean-François Lyotard famously defined as the postmodern condition.[109]

Conversely, Buber undeniably held onto an ethical grounding rooted in an ideal subject that put him at odds with most postmodernist critics of subjectivity, including Emmanuel Levinas.[110] Indeed, Levinas correctly argued that Buber's thought retained many of the dualistic components of a separate *self* in relation to an external *otherness* found within Cartesian, Kantian, and Hegelian versions of modern subjectivity. Although the other is essential for any authentic understanding of selfhood, Buber was unwilling to give up on the conviction that "the I is indispensable for any relationship."[111] The main difference that separates Buber from both modern and postmodernist camps is that both the I and the other are paradoxically, and perhaps mysteriously, constituted in their separateness through relationship—in much the same way that the infinite and finite are defined in reference to one another.

Although firmly rooted within the European existential tradition, the intersection of subjectivity and redemptive hope within Buber's thought emerged through his growing opposition to the monadological individualism of existentialists like Kierkegaard and Heidegger. Buber's interest in bringing the transcendental down into the hopes for becoming whole through a relation to another self put him at odds with Kierkegaard and Heidegger's emphasis on responsibility for otherness as a hindrance to individual authenticity.[112] For Heidegger, hope remains a part of the individual's quest for greater authenticity away from the social conventions of the crowd (*Das Man*). As he states in *Being and Time* (1927), "he who hopes takes himself with him into his hopes."[113] The elation we get when "hoping for something for oneself [*für-sich-erhoffen*]," according to Heidegger, is ultimately rooted in the temporality that emerges from the tension between our resoluteness in the present and future promise for authenticity away from the conventions of idle chatter (*Gerede*) and bourgeois social conformity.

What existentialist philosophers miss, according to Buber, is that *betweenness*, created between individuals through dialogue, is also the greatest form of self-affirmation.[114] The "primal hope of all history" is, according to Buber, grounded in our fundamental "drive for communion" (*Trieb der Verbundenheit*).[115] This drive that leads to moments of hope in encounters with otherness is the same drive that can inspire messianic hopes for a "new heaven and earth."

Existentialists' concerns to break free from the crowd or civic duties fail to recognize that we are most authentic when fulfilling our hopes for communion with others. Rather than concern ourselves with authenticity, humanity's real hopes are expressed through the desire to not feel alone and homeless within the world. The phenomenology of hope that defines human existence stems from the following fact:

> In an essential relation . . . the barriers of individual being are in fact breached, and a new phenomenon appears which can appear only in this way: one life open to another . . . the other becomes present not merely in the imagination or feeling, but in the depths of one's substance, so that one experiences the mystery of the other being in the mystery of one's own.[116]

Hope for shattering existential solitude comes from recognizing the mystery of one's own being within the mystery of the other.

A phenomenology of intersubjective hopes is the crucial bridge allowing individuals to cross over from their isolation toward a grander vision of messianic solidarity. Although the term *solidarity* rarely appeared in Buber's writings, the question of how best to stimulate sentiments (*Gesinnung*) of solidarity between individuals was a defining concern of Buber's from the earliest stages of his intellectual development. Drawing on his early interests in Hasidic communal structures, utopian socialism, and the early kibbutz movement, Buber saw in solidarity the linking of the transcendentalism of cosmic communion with the immanence of everyday encounters around a "living center."[117] According to Buber, "The spirit of solidarity can in truth only remain alive to the extent that a living relationship obtains between human beings."[118] The fundamental desire for "living relationship," stems from the fundamental "need of man to feel his own house as a room in some greater, all-embracing structure in which he is at home, to feel that the other inhabitants of it with whom he lives and works are all acknowledging and confirming his individual existence."[119] This sense of being imbricated within a broader cosmic structure is the first step for overcoming what Buber saw as the alienation of modern existence.

Like most Jewish intellectuals of his day, Buber also looked to Kant's "Kingdom of Ends" as the secular model for linking intersubjective recognition with a universal cosmopolitan ideal. In his essay "What is Man?" (1938), Buber credits Kant with limiting reason so that we can better appreciate the mystery of man as a creature uniquely defined by the act of hoping.[120] He breaks, however, with Kant's earlier focus on the importance of hope for immortality for Kant's later writings in which redemptive hope is directed toward the achievement of an ethical commonwealth. "We may come nearer the answer to the question what man is when we come to see him as the eternal meeting of the One with Other."[121] Idealism is only important if it translates into genuine encounters with others.

The other crucial nuance in Buber's elaboration on Kant's anthropology of hope was his emphasis on the mutuality between finitude and the infinite.[122] "Above and below are bound to one another."[123] We affirm our finitude because we also participate in infinity through our relationships with others, and thus we are given the revelation of what we may hope for, namely, dialogic recognition. "Our hope for salvation" is predicated therefore on the theological premise that "our human way to the infinite leads only through fulfilled finitude."[124] The "eternal Thou" is not accessed through directing one's intentions (*Kavannot*) vertically, but rather horizontally through bonds of solidarity.

Concrete relations of mutual trust between individuals creates the foundation for a more transcendental *trust of eternity* in which the cosmos itself takes on the personal characteristic of an "eternal Thou"—something that is similar enough to our personal selves so that we can establish a relationship, but also something larger than just a self so as to constitute a radical otherness.[125] "Trust is trust that there is meaning in the world; it is trust in the world as a world of potential Thou."[126] This trust creates "a bridge from self-being to self-being across the abyss of dread in the universe," that gives birth to the hope for a dialogic relationship with the entire world.[127]

The grounding of redemptive hope in intersubjective encounters also follows from Buber's controversial interpretation of revelation as a moment of presence (*Gegenwart*). Revelation is not about specific legislation handed down long ago at Mt. Sinai but rather lies in the *event* of presence as the *self* opens to *otherness*.[128] God's revelation to humanity is less about creating a correspondence to eternal laws that stand outside of the world, and more about understanding oneself as existing in dialogic partnership with the process of completing the work of creation within history.[129] The sense of presence generated in revelation is renewed through the hope created by each moment of recognition.[130]

Hans Ulrich Gumbrecht's discussion of the oscillation between *presence effects* and *meaning effects* is useful for reading Buber's controversial writings on revelation in relationship to a phenomenology of hope.[131] According to Gumbrecht, we first experience moments of presence from events, but these moments of encounter necessarily become meaningful through the process of allocating terms that help to translate moments of presence into a language that can be shared with others. Therefore, depending on our terms, specific qualities of presence will take on different meanings. For Buber the revelation of presence is the primary cause, making all specific attempts to create a correspondence through language or *Halakhah* (legislative interpretation of scripture) secondary.[132] In his famous retort to Rosenzweig, Buber challenged: "I do not believe that revelation is ever a formulation of law. It is only through man in his self-contradiction that revelation becomes legislation."[133] For Buber, Rosenzweig's interest in affirming the law (*Gesetz*) as a commandment (*Gebot*) can only occur through inner transformation and the intimacy of appropriation.[134] Revelation has to be experienced first as personally meaningful for each individual before it can take on a collective meaning through imposing terms and traditions that enshrine moments of presence within a common language.

Buber's emphasis on the experiential component of revelation also applies to messianic hope. Hope, like revelation, is an event that is experienced with one's whole being, never purely a sensational experience, nor purely intellectual, but rather entails the confluence of both a mental image of what is hoped for, coupled with an affective quality of what we imagine we will feel upon its actualization.[135] Also, like revelation, hope correlates to what Edith Wyschogrod referred to as "desire for presence" that creates a temporal continuity between memory, the "now," and the future.[136] The bridge Buber creates between metaphysics and anthropology is woven through revelation and messianic hope. This hope for presence—like revelation—can only be experienced through dialogic encounters. As Buber states in his essay "Hope for This Hour," (1952) written against the backdrop of the Cold War standoff between the totalitarian East and liberal West: "[M]an wishes to be confirmed by man as he who he is, and there is genuine confirmation only in mutuality. . . . There is no salvation save through the renewal of the dialogical relation . . . the overcoming of existential mistrust."[137] The temporality of "hope for this hour," just like revelation, is always contextually circumscribed to the contingency of the moment. The presence of the eternal creates an event, but the meaning of the event is dependent on the sense of dialogue generated through address and response. Presence is revealed in the moment, but we hope that such moments can turn into the basis for social transformation in which dialogical encounter spreads to include the whole world. Therefore, the redemptive hope that intersubjective encounters can be extended to the whole world still remains an open goal to strive for, but the path toward that redemptive horizon can only begin with the intimacy and love of genuine recognition. It may be wrong to assume that we can achieve messianic redemption on our own, yet we are made better by striving to experience a taste of redemptive hope in our everyday experiences.

This hope for establishing a link between personal moments of presence and broader social hopes for a better world were similarly shared by Ernst Bloch. Bloch's writings on hope and Marxism were deeply inspired by Buber's dialogic model of creating a conversation between ancient Israelite prophetic messianism and modern secular utopianism. Both thinkers' interests in messianic hope drew on anarchist impulses during the Weimar period that, in Rabinbach's terms, combined "radical, secular, and messianic" hopes with a new political spiritualism.[138] In Bloch's terms, recovering the "Utopian potency within the religious sphere" created new opportunities for bringing together the liberatory ideals within the Enlightenment and religious traditions.[139] In Chapter 3 I turn to Bloch's radical theology and the "school of hope" he helped inspire.

3

THE GOD OF EXODUS AND THE SCHOOL OF HOPE

> Thou shalt remember that you were once slaves in Egypt and the Lord redeemed you from there. Therefore I command thee.
> —DEUTERONOMY 24:18

> There is always an exodus in the world, an exodus from the particular status quo. And there is always a hope, which is connected with rebellion—a hope founded in the concrete given possibilities for new being.... The exodus begun by Job from the Caesar-like concept of God, when he placed mankind above all forms of tyranny—above the very questionable tyranny of righteousness from on-high and the neo-mythical tyranny of majestic nature—this exodus is ... the rebel who has trust in God, without believing in him.
> —ERNST BLOCH, *ATHEISM IN CHRISTIANITY* (1968)

BLOCH'S MESSIANISM OF THE "NOT-YET"

Within the history of modern Jewish redemptive narratives, Bloch played a central role in translating what he interpreted as the subversive metahistory within religion into the praxis of horizontal solidarity and revolutionary agitation. Ernst Bloch's great innovation was to infuse secular Marxist materialism with quasi-Kabbalistic mysticism and a metaphysics of contingency. This chapter is an exposition of those features within Bloch's writings that contributed to the post–World War II creation of a "school of hope" among theologians and critical theorists. Later theologians—both

Jewish and Christian—were drawn to Bloch's analysis because he also insisted that Marxism had missed the importance of religious redemptive narratives in subverting the idolatry of social hierarchies. Part of the appeal and controversy of Bloch's phenomenological approach was that it illuminated the common revolutionary core of both religious and secular redemptive narratives.[1]

Starting in his youthful days at the University of Munich (entering in 1905), Bloch followed many of his peers in the search for intellectual alternatives to the stifling bourgeois culture of his day. Like Buber during this same period, the vitalistic philosophy of life (*Lebensphilosophie*) of Nietzsche and Bergson pointed to the possibility of affirming a new Promethean kinetic spirit that could break through the stayed and conventional. Also like Buber, however, Bloch was always concerned to mix his interest in vitalistic impulses with concerns for social solidarity. With *The Spirit of Utopia* (1918–1923) Bloch shifted the conversation on the future of secular utopianism among his fellow Marxists away from a singular focus on dialectical materialism toward what he calls the "not-yet-conscious." Bloch's critical theory starts from a mystical appreciation for our "dream-like" ability to experience radical "amazement" as a basis for propelling history toward new possibilities.[2] To get from the *is* to the *ought*, the human ability to daydream about the *not-yet* creates a foundation for negating the idols of the status quo.[3] For Bloch, negating the idols of capitalism required a more mystical and nuanced appreciation for the metaphysics of negation and becoming. The greatness of Marxism was not its scientistic pretenses in providing laws for understanding material accumulation and class conflicts, but rather through updating human redemptive aspirations to achieve the not yet possible.[4] These liberatory aspirations that had come to define the modern age have always been a part of what Bloch identified as the underground dialectics of transgression and revolutionary agitation within the biblical tradition and religious mythology more generally.

Bloch's interest in illuminating a redemptive content out of both secular and religious narratives developed partially through his early friendship with Walter Benjamin. Bloch and Benjamin initially developed a mystical—perhaps psychedelic—relation to the ideal of hope as a substitute for the crass materialism and positivism of the Enlightenment.[5] Bloch and Benjamin also drew on Buber's appropriation of messianic hope as a paradigm for existential and social transformation. Drinking from a new elixir of messianic fervor, romanticism, and liberation politics, these Jewish intellectuals sought to incorporate Marx's theses on the need for material redistribution with the Romantic poet's emphasis on the importance of sublimely inspired social relations.[6]

Benjamin's construction of messianic hope was also notable for its Kabbalistic accents.[7] For Benjamin, hope emerges from the interaction of our social impulses with mystical illumination. We are given hope only through the brief illuminating moments of experiencing sublime aesthetics or authentic interactions with other individuals.[8] Rather than focus on the need for large-scale structural transformation of society, Benjamin's mystical aesthetics were based on the recovery of memory and an authentic temporality as the locus through which "chips of messianic time" would be revealed.[9] Benjamin saw in the ideal of memory the same powers to stimulate hope that Bloch posited in the future projection of consciousness.[10]

For Benjamin a proper relationship with memory provided the greatest grounding for propelling us toward a redemptive future.[11] In his famous essay "Theses on the Philosophy of History," Benjamin concluded that there "is no document of civilization which is not at the same time a document of barbarism."[12] But the past also contains clues and possible glimpses of redemptive hope that can carry us forward as well. "The past carries with it a temporal index by which it is referred to redemption . . . we have been endowed with a weak Messianic power, a power to which the past has a claim."[13] The redemptive potential of the historian—as a practitioner of memory—is to generate a "non-totalizing anamnestic solidarity" for the past which had the additional potential of "fanning the spark of hope" by reminding us of the historical costs of subjugation and human alienation. The anamnestic recovery—the memory—of what has been discarded to the slaughter bench of history by the "march of spirit" becomes the stepping-stone into the past—a past that can simultaneously pave the way forward toward the "gate through which the Messiah might enter."[14]

Despite some interest in a broader sense of solidarity, the ideal of hope nevertheless emerges in Benjamin's writing more as a desperate concept of apocalyptic faith than as something that can shatter solipsistic despair. Hope arises, paradoxically, precisely within the conditions that most negate its viability.[15] Despair and lack of hope, paradoxically, are precisely the conditions in which hope in the messianic promise for redemption can emerge. Drawing from Franz Kafka's mystical interplay between hope and despair, for

Benjamin the paradox and tragedy of the modern condition is that "there is an infinite amount of hope, but not for us."[16] Precisely the moment when the emotion of hope appears most absurd is precisely the moment of decision in which the negation of despair gives way to the phoenix of hope. Similar to Kierkegaard's conviction that despair is the well from which genuine faith emerges, so too despair in Benjamin's works resets the dialectic within consciousness toward the messianic gates of redemption.[17] As Walter Benjamin famously proposed, "hope is given to us only for the sake of those without hope."[18] We may not have much hope for ourselves, but we cannot lose hope for the sake of helping others. We have a right to hope because we cannot give up on our responsibility for others and believing in the possibility of making strides toward redemption. We have a responsibility to maintain our hope, so that we can participate in the process of redeeming the world.

Foreshadowing Theodor Adorno's later theory of "negative dialectics," Benjamin sees the negation of hope through an interiority of despair precisely as the condition for an apocalyptic destruction that makes every moment pregnant with the possibility of redemption.[19] The importance of maintaining this type of radical hope in the face of destruction is what I believe Adorno was later suggesting when he stated that the "only philosophy which can be responsibly practiced in face of despair is the attempt to contemplate all things as they would present themselves from the standpoint of redemption."[20] Although Adorno goes on to lament that gaining such a "standpoint" is impossible, there remains nonetheless a value in the illumination achieved when hopes are refracted through "messianic light." The utopianism of messianic illumination is perhaps the only island of hope within the flood of barbarism.

The moments of insight generated from these moments of redemptive illumination within the context of profound despair is where both Benjamin's and Bloch's narratives on hope converge. Experiencing the despair that something is missing—that the center is a void, a primordial *tohu-ve vohu* (Gn 1:2), a divine contraction—is the pretext from which true hope and creation can emerge. In a manner analogous to Heidegger's *Dasein*, hope functions as the open space where new constellations emerge for both personal and collective inspiration. In the same way that Chinese checkers commences with the opening up of an empty space so that movement can begin, so too the presence of hope among a people—or individual—creates the sensations of inspiration that serve as the catalyst toward the possible. Hope is how we begin to bridge the void from what Aristotle identified as *kata to dynaton* (what is possible) to *dynamei on* (what might become possible).[21]

After Benjamin's tragic death in 1940, Bloch went on to develop a broad historical narrative that placed hopes for the "not-yet" at the center of humanity's evolution toward greater freedom. Bloch's seminal work on the principle of hope (*Das Prinzip Hoffnung*) begins with the redemptive narratives of what he designates as the "Promethean rebellion" against the hierarchy of Greek gods and Judaism's rebellion against the tyranny of Pharaoh and subsequent empires. The same rebellious spirit recounted in the Greek and biblical traditions constitutes a continuous chain of transmission from the ancient period down to the modern secular versions found in Marxism and socialism.

In his early essay "Karl Marx, Death and the Apocalypse," Bloch sets out to both strengthen the link between prophetic hope and modern secular utopianism while also critiquing Marx's economic determinism which he thinks lacks an appreciation for the transcendental politics provided by ancient narratives. Marx's overemphasis on material conditions occludes the fact that "Man does not live by bread alone."[22] Marx was right, however, to embrace what Bloch viewed as an extension of the kabbalistic ontology of the infinite "*eyn-sof*" (forward-look) of consciousness. Marx's quasi-mystical insight that the modern world is defined by a social revolution in which "all that is solid melts into air" reflects, according to Bloch, an ontology of "becoming" as the basis for future hope. Marx was wrong, however, to embrace Hegel's thesis in *The Philosophy of Right* (1820) that the dialectical struggle between individual desire and collective norms would come to an end, but was right to side with Hegel's earlier thesis that the spirit of freedom is the driving force within history. There is, Bloch asserts, no end to freedom or desire, only the principle of hope that shatters conventional structures for the open horizon of the future.

In his seminal multivolume work, *The Principle of Hope* (1954–1959), Bloch further developed his metaphysical linkage between hope and the thrust of consciousness toward "venturing beyond."[23] Here consciousness is the process of our thoughts lurching toward the future through an infinite kinetic state of "becoming."[24] Following John Locke, the metaphysics of "becoming" has the sensory effect of creating a pleasurable image within our minds' eye of future fulfillment, which then stimulates feelings of physical elation in the present.²⁵ Hoping creates a temporal bridge between our present situation and projections of the self into the future. A consciousness of openness toward the future is why hope makes humans unique within the world. Consequently, we are most human when we hope.

The "not-yet" impulse within consciousness is the force that continues to negate the new idolatries within modern capitalism. This force of negation to existing idolatries is the essential metaphysical component within religion that makes it relevant to modern goals of liberation and freedom. Religion has always reflected an internal psychological and political struggle between our dependency on stable social conventions versus our anarchic impulses to imagine, and sometimes act out, the overturning of these very same norms. Although religion reflects a "priestly" concern for submission and docility, it also contains a subversive existential "fierce questioning" generated by the phenomenon of hope that historically bubbles up to shatter complacency in existing power structures.

In sum, religion gives us the "idols" of stability, conventionality, and mystification of social hierarchies, but it also gives us a transcendental appreciation of the forces of becoming and a prophetic hope that allow us to reach out for new utopian horizons.²⁶ Just as Buber acknowledged that every *Thou* gets turned into an *It*, so too Bloch proposed that every utopian hope to affirm a God of freedom turns into idolatry, dogma, and priestly hierarchies.²⁷ Yet, the principle of hope within humanity will always rise up to challenge what Erich Fromm was to later identify as our "flight from freedom" in the form of religious dogmas and proscriptions. For Bloch, the truth of religion is its ability to shatter its own idolatry.²⁸ Yearnings for the possible are the "features of religion" that persist even if it is no longer recognized as part of a distinct tradition. The essence of the religion, therefore, is not priestly focus on the "upward-look" toward an external metaphysical realm, but rather the hope that humans are in fact capable of achieving greater freedom through greater levels of solidarity.

Following on his youthful interests in mysticism and the psychedelic, Bloch elaborated on the kabbalistic thesis that redemption is something that is both utterly transcendent but also can take place through the "horizontal" and daily intimacy of negating despair by affirming the principle of hope. Hope represents a radical immanence within consciousness, while also pointing to a "transcending without any heavenly transcendence."²⁹ "The *forward-look* has replaced the *upward-look* . . . where there is hope there is religion, but where there is religion there is not always hope ... hope is able to inherit those *features of religion* which do not perish with the death of God."[30] To hope is to channel God within the world, and to find God all one is required to do is discover the inner reserves of hope within consciousness. God as the transcendental force for creating and opening up new horizons of possibilities can now be recognized within the immanence of human hopes.

Bloch defended his paradoxical metaphysics of "horizontal" redemptive hope by tracing competing models of divine power within the biblical tradition. Within Bloch's dialectical read of history, the ancient Israelites were torn between older models of God as a divine tyrant versus the prophetic discovery—starting with Moses—of the God of Exodus. The God of Exodus also represented a radical rupture from the contrasting static ideal of nature within paganism. Belief in the fixed laws of nature and fate were an extension of the ideological mystification of tyrannical social hierarchies by priestly "lords of opium."[31] Also in contrast to the later Hellenic ideal of static *Being* forever opposed to the carnal realm of mere *becoming*, the biblical God of hope liberates through freedom. The God of Exodus—like creation itself—is always in a state of becoming which gives meaning and direction to history.[32] The merging of the God of Exodus as a force of becoming within history introduces a new ideal of freedom and partnership between finite humans and the eternal. We do not become more divine by imitating static *Being*, rather humans become more like the God of Exodus by actualizing freedom within history by overturning the social hierarchies first represented by ancient Egypt.[33] The historical greatness of the prophets in later identifying this God of hope and temporal becoming is in their discovering of a force of freedom that allows the negation of the present for an infinite future.[34] The freer we become, the more we imitate the God of Exodus. And the more we become like the God of Exodus, the less dependent we are on a metaphysics of static *Being*. In essence, the monotheism introduced by the God of Exodus succeeded in killing off previous models of human dependence on God as tyrant and primary source of creation. And by extension, the force for freedom and hope that was once externalized as God is now properly recognized as located within humanity's ability to hope and express its own autonomy. Ironically, our freedom from the biblical conceptions of God is also an implicit affirmation of the God of Exodus who redeemed the Israelites and gave them freedom in the first place.

In his later controversial book *Atheism in Christianity* (1968), Bloch synthesized his earlier reflections on the dialectics of negation within the history of Judaism and Christianity by further using religious narratives to demonstrate the spirit of transgression and revolt against orthodoxies and social systems of repression.[35] Starting with the creationist accounts in the book of Genesis, "through the serpent, freedom came into the world."[36] The dialectical interplay between light and darkness, chaos and order from which creation emerges demonstrates the mystical force of negation as necessary for furthering the genesis of human consciousness. Bloch focuses selectively on characters and episodes in what he called the "underground Bible"—from "the serpent in the garden" down to Moses, Job, the prophets, and Jesus—as representing a hidden narrative of religious negation to religious orthodoxies. When read against the grain, the moment of disobedience recounted in the biblical tradition provides a counternarrative of humanity caught in the dialectics of challenging tyrannies while also fleeing from its own freedom.

According to Bloch, "the discovery of Utopian potency within the religious sphere" allows us to reread Jewish and Christian traditions as a story in which the "Caesar-like concept of God" as a distant tyrannical power over creation is gradually challenged.[37] The God encountered by Moses and the Israelites at Mt. Sinai—"a God who is himself not yet what he is: who is only in the future of his promise-to-be"—introduces a subversive ontology into history.[38] Unlike the cold and distant Olympian gods of fate, the God of Exodus can be argued with and turned (*teshuvah*) in accordance with our greatest hopes for rebellion against the idols of necessity. Paradoxically, to affirm the God of Exodus means cracking the edifice of religious belief itself. To embrace this is to become, in Bloch's terms "a rebel who has trust in God, without believing in him." The same force of hope that negates idolatry will also negate religion.[39] Once we arrive at the infinite openness of becoming through the principle of hope, there is no longer any need to hold onto the idolatrous conceptions of God born out of a history of human fears and slavery. Hope as a force for negation, therefore, refines religion down to its core revolutionary impulse to affirm human freedom. But as the cunning of history has taught, we need the idolatrous trappings provided by religion because embracing a metaphysical state of becoming is often too difficult.

The phenomenon of religion continually creating its own negation, however, never ends because competing impulses for the security of tyranny and freedom of exodus can never be fully reconciled. Hence, Bloch observes, "The best thing about religion is that it makes for heretics."[40] Elliot Wolfeson expands on this Blochian insight where he states that part of what defines our postmodern moment is a growing recognition between the "codependency of religion and idolatry."[41] The dualism and competing binaries that define the history of religious discourse partakes in a mystical and ontological dependency on precisely that which it seeks to negate or transcend, and thereby affirms the opposite in the attempt at transcendence. Religion is both challenged by heresies, but also dependent on the forces of renewal unleashed through these dialectical challenges. Adam and Eve could never have had a relationship with God as free beings without having encountered the serpent.

Religious traditions will always enshrine impulses for freedom and slavery, and therefore will always ensure conflict that brings about the next stage. We yearn for correspondence to principles of power—a prime mover—that can in turn provide a sense of stability and order. Yet, we also yearn for a *force-for-becoming* (God of Exodus) that can give hope and fortitude to brave uncharted waters toward the "not-yet." The brilliance of religion is that it captures competing human impulses to overthrow orthodoxies, while also fleeing from the abyss of our own freedom back toward the comforting image of gods, or God, as an all-powerful protector and "tyrannical father-ego," one who can be propitiated through displays of obedience and offerings.

The dialectics of desire and obedience—set in motion by Adam and Eve's desire to become like God through knowledge of good and evil—speaks to a deeper tension within the human psyche over the meaning of freedom. Bloch reverses the traditional narrative with its promise of subsuming human desire at the end of days in the ultimate embrace of God's love, to a new redemptive myth in which human freedom and rebellion—both theological and political—is the fulfillment of God's purpose in giving humanity the desire to initially seek freedom through knowledge.

Bloch's paradoxical thesis that "without atheism there is no room for Messianism" means that there is always a tension between hope and its negation.[42] In claiming to reflect eternal *Being*, religion sets into motion its own dialectics of negation by generating new narratives of becoming that end up shattering pretenses of "priestly" access to eternal *Being*. Each generation creates temples, priesthoods, idols, and other systems of power that then produce heresies based on the redemptive hope that justice and freedom can be actualized on earth. Through messianic hope, however, we open to the deeper truth that "nothing is complete; nothing is conclusive; nothing has a solid core" and therefore no human constructs will ever fully grasp the infinite.[43] The "serpent" and every "heresy" produced once this principle of negation has been unleashed, unsettles dogmas by illuminating the contingency of our condition and comprehension.

Atheism, therefore, is the most advanced expression of this dialectical movement within history toward greater freedom generated by religion's own redemptive impulses starting with the "God of Exodus." Paradoxically, atheism comes to fulfill the redemptive hope that defines the core of religious traditions.[44] Bloch therefore came to the controversial conclusion that "only an atheist can be a good Christian; only a Christian can be a good atheist" because the overcoming of authoritarianism is itself definitive of what it means to truly understand the redemptive spirit exemplified by religious radicals like Moses, the prophets, Job, and Jesus.[45] Thus, to affirm "a God who is himself not yet what he is: who is only in the future of his promise-to-be"[46] is not only a reflection of humanity's utopian impulses, but also an affirmation of "eschatological" inclination toward "overthrowing all things from their beginning to their end: the Exodus into God as man."[47]

This "Promethean" human impulse for freedom renews the ontology of becoming, thus setting into motion new forms of discontent with present orthodoxies. From these discontents, inner voices within the depth of consciousness rise up to haunt the psyche with the feeling that something profound is still missing, and a better future might just be over the horizon. From this sense of something missing religious narratives of hope emerge based on the promise that the lack we sense will be overcome when the future kingdom is established. And yet, we also experience ourselves as creatures forever "not-yet-being," not yet complete.[48] The idea that we will leave this life as yet uncompleted projects is existentially terrifying and a spur to both our greatest hopes and feelings of despair. Part of the impulse toward idolatry stems from a desire to imagine ourselves as self-sufficient, complete, and capable of escaping the realm of becoming for eternal *Being*. Religion addresses these unsettling feelings of incompleteness by providing teleological narratives based on the hope that someday there will be an end to the machinations of history and desire, when we will become resurrected from feelings of futility and dread resulting from our finitude. Yet, just as Elijah mocked the priests of Baal for their worship of mere wood and stone, consciousness never ceases to shatter our illusions. The lurching toward the "not-yet" is a reminder that the self will forever remain an unfinished project. We hope for a moment of culmination, a moment in which a coherent narrative will emerge that can give life and all its trials an ultimate meaning, but like Moses, we discover that the God of Exodus keeps us forever in the space of the "not-yet" on the boarders of the promise land. We strive to overcome this lack—to overcome this feeling that "all is vanity" (Eccl 1)— yet are forever reminded through the compulsion of desire that our will-to-become can never find true fulfillment within the kingdom of *Being*. We hope to one day become worthy of being redeemed from this history of struggle between orthodoxies and heresies, of prophets and priests, contentment with dwelling versus a sense of adventure, but in the attempt to actualize our hope of ending history we always reset the dialectic of history back on the kinetic path of eternal becoming. The metaphorical attainment of a promised land and building of a temple sets in motion a new foundation from which future generations will need to find liberation. In the terms offered by Buber, *religion* stems from the impulse of fathers to create temples and solid foundations upon which to create a legacy, and the fervor of *religiosity* inspires sons to tear them down.[49]

The discontent generated through our hope for the "not-yet" is both our greatest comfort and perhaps one of our greatest pathologies.[50] Bloch's emphasis on consciousness, always lurching toward the "not-yet" as a counter metaphysics to static *Being*, expressed a crucial revolutionary link between the God of Exodus and what commentators like Michael Walzer have identified as the liberatory history of exodus politics. For Bloch, we personalize the God of Exodus by affirming that something is missing, that we must always search for the exodus, the negation of the status quo and venturing into openness of hope. In our current century in which Fukuyama's end-of-history thesis has largely been accepted with regard to the limits of creating real alternatives to the global reach of capitalism, and given the almost apocalyptic fatalist acceptance of the inevitability of pending environmental collapse, Bloch's metaphysics of contingency serves as a voice of prophetic protest that still echoes for our own age. Bloch's ontology of becoming is a reminder that there are always alternatives for those who have the strength to hope.

Nevertheless, what is lacking in Bloch's account of hope was a clearly articulated understanding of what it means to replace an "upward-look" with a "forward-look." Why is the forward movement of consciousness in the form of negation necessarily a source of hope? Why should we assume a direct correlation between a metaphysics of "becoming" and the "new" (*novum*) as necessarily leading to a greater social good? Why is the future always better than the past or present? Can't living in a state of a "continual not-yet" induce neurosis as well as hope? Doesn't a singular focus on lurching toward the new undermine hopes for continuity and commitment?

Rabbi David Hartman made the important point that hope is not just about looking toward the future, but can also have roots in memory, particular collective memories of events like retelling the story of Exodus from slavery at the Passover Seder, thus linking "past salvation with future redemption."[51] If we are only focused on the future as a potential resource for hope, however, retaining a sense of covenantal continuity may be lost.

This same point applies to human relationships. If longing for the "not-yet" always entails negations of the old, what hope remains for longevity and commitment? If we accept Bloch's claim that, "human existence . . . means that which goes beyond," how do we make sense of our hopes for continuity, security, and loyalty?[52] How do we build meaningful relationships and communities if we are always afflicted with an "anticipatory consciousness" that constantly seeks to transcend the given for the possible?

Given the challenges we face in the twenty-first century with regard to excessive consumerism and environmental degradation, does Bloch's ontology of becoming help to slow down the abiding sense of dissatisfaction that too easily leads to excessive consumption? If we accept Bloch's view of consciousness as a force for negation of the present, we must then ask: is consciousness itself an enemy of our hopes for experiencing the present? How do we make sure that an abiding sense that something is missing as the force for negation leading to utopian speculation, as advocated by Bloch, doesn't itself reinforce a sense of discontent that requires illusions rather than sober solutions?

As a Marxist secular theologian, Bloch provided one of the best defenses of biblical redemptive narratives within the context of a secular metaphysics of praxis. Nevertheless, his emphasis on a metaphysics of becoming may in fact repeat the very transcendentalism that Marx's dialectical materialism hoped to overcome. Bloch's focus on the "forward thrust of consciousness" comes dangerously close to replicating the very negation of presence that has historically defined most critiques of hope.

In his *Theology of Hope*, Jürgen Moltmann sums up the countercritique to the negation of presence through an overemphasis on the transcendental qualities of hope in the following terms:

> The objection to hope arises from the religion of humble acquiescence in the present.... Hope casts him upon a future that is not yet. He remembers having lived, but he does not live.... He hopes to live, but he does not live. He expects to be happy one day, and this expectation causes him to pass over the happiness of the present. He is never, in memory and hope, wholly himself and wholly in his present.... Memories and hopes appear to cheat him of the happiness of being undividedly present. They rob him of his present and drag him into times that no longer exist or do not yet exist. They surrender him to the non-existent and abandon him to vanity. For these times subject him to the stream of transience—the stream that sweeps him to annihilation.[53]

Moltmann goes on to elaborate on Pascal's lament on hope from his *Pensées*:

> We do not rest satisfied with the present.... We scarcely ever think of the present; and if we think of it, it is only to take light from it to arrange the future. The present is never our end. The past and the present are our means; the future alone is our end. So we never live, but we hope to live; and, as we are always preparing to be happy, it is inevitable we should never be so.

For Moltmann the role of hope in sometimes undermining our ability and responsibility to be present is a serious theological problem. Although I attend to Moltmann's theology later, the problem of presence and transcendence here helps to highlight an equally important component of hope, namely the hope of achieving a sense of presence in the moment. Bloch's focus on hope as a force for prophetic negation of the idolatry of social conventions left out what Buber correctly identified as the importance of intersubjective encounters. By placing all his hopes on the power of consciousness to always reach for the "not-yet," Bloch's phenomenology leaves out the importance of intersubjective relationships necessary for grounding in the present, while also giving hope for the future.

Bloch's position within the history of redemptive hope narratives is nevertheless compelling by synthesizing the history of religious and secular redemptive narratives. After World War II, religious intellectuals increasingly drew on both Buber and Bloch's projects of rehabilitating messianic narratives for the purpose of addressing modern alienation and the failures of Marx's redemptive analysis.

EXODUS AND BEING

Enlightenment liberatory narratives based on an optimistic view of secular humanism continued to unravel as despair increased over the limits of Western liberalism to prevent the horrors of the early twentieth century (particularly mass genocides and threat of total nuclear annihilation).[54] Grand redemptive narratives, which looked to reason and material ideals of progress, contributed to what some scholars call a postutopian and post-ideological phase for many Western intellectuals.[55] Caught between realism and idealism, this postutopian moment after World War II was defined by the understanding that no single ideology or intellectual discourse could provide a grand theory for directing history.

For philosophers and theologians in this period who were still committed to the idea that intellectual reflection should be a source of hope and not just critique, the central challenge as they saw it was this: how to recover discourses of redemptive hope despite the shadow of despair cast by the recent horrors of Auschwitz and Hiroshima?[56] This phase of redemptive hope narratives functioned as a shibboleth for covertly talking about religious ideas and identities in vague neutral terms that could offer an account of meaning and purpose within history to increasingly secular audiences who were uncomfortable with grounding redemptive hope in pre-Enlightenment defenses of theology.

A group of intellectuals—most notably Jürgen Moltmann, Johannes Metz, Ernst Bloch, Walter Capps, and Emil Fackenheim—dedicated themselves to the task of creating what they referred to as the "school of hope." Inspired by Bloch's updating of Hegel's theory of history through the principle of hope, the religious intellectuals in this loosely defined "school of hope" tasked itself with the paradoxical challenge of affirming what was right with Marxism and nineteenth-century projectionist critiques of religion while also preserving the inspirational, transcendental, and ethical components of establishment theology.

At a 1968 symposium entitled *The Future of Hope*—hosted by the Department of Religious Studies at the University of California, Santa Barbara—

these intellectuals gathered together to explore the theological and philosophical challenges posed by the "harsh historical facts" of both mass human destruction of the recent past and the possibility of future devastation.[57] This forum on hope—later turned into a book with the same title—brought together the Marxist/messianic writings of Ernst Bloch and Jewish post-Holocaust philosopher Emil Fackenheim with some of the most important Christian theologians of hope. Although hailing from different religious and philosophical orientations these intellectuals were drawn together to form a "school of hope" that could revive a rigorous inquiry into the ongoing importance of religious redemptive hope narratives while simultaneously addressing the history of manipulation and exploitation of redemptive hope by religious institutions.

The writings and discussions recorded in *The Future of Hope* are noteworthy, not only in relation to the development of a post-Holocaust German Christian and Jewish dialogue, but also because they marked the emergence of what Walter Capps identified as a shift away from (Greek) metaphysics toward a recovery of an alternative radical Hebraic hope. In his introductory essay "Mapping the Hope Movement," Capps proposed that the "de-Hellenization of faith" signifies a shift toward a "*horizontal projection* instead of *vertical projection.*"[58] The importance of this move toward "horizontal projection," according to Capps, is that it helps counter the critique of religious faith by nineteenth-century theorists who correctly charged that "the perpetuation of the heaven syndrome" had turned transcendental redemptive hopes into a form of social quiescence to status quo politics and social hierarchies.

For all the thinkers involved in this project, Bloch's focus on reading religion as in conflict with its own competing impulses toward freedom and slavery, hope and fear, provided the lens for reinterpreting the competing redemptive voices within both Judaism and Christianity.[59] With the dissipation of a metaphysical "locus of permanence" within the contemporary era, Capps proposed that now "God becomes the *one who will be what I will be*, the world becomes the basis of affirmations and not a mere derivative of reality."[60] The "de-Hellenization of faith" allows for both Christian and Jews to shed Parmenidean conceptions of God as permanent and eternal, and embrace God as the force for "the *novum*" that challenges the status quo and demands the revolutionary transformation of all social structures.[61] Following Bloch, Capps saw the Exodus ideal of God as *Ehyeh Asher Ehyeh* as a necessary alternative to the Parmenidean ideal of sublation of all particulars into primordial *Being* (*Hen Kai Pan*, the *all* subsumed into the *one*) that dominated much of Christian theology.[62] To be committed to a God of impermanence—to the God identified as *Ehyeh Asher Ehyeh*—entails a commitment to striving for transformation, not just in the soul, but also in the real world.[63]

In this same volume and in his earlier classic work, *Theology of Hope: On the Ground and the Implications of a Christian Eschatology* (1964), Moltmann laid the groundwork for the transformation of Protestant Christian theology from an emphasis on future otherworldly compensation toward a prophetic hope in the power of praxis and solidarity. According to Moltmann eschatological hope stands opposed to the "rigidified utopia of positivistic realism" which commits the idolatry of clinging to "reality as it is." Furthermore, "hope alone is to be called *realistic*," because it brings to mind "possibilities of change . . . thus hopes and anticipations . . . are realistic ways of perceiving the scope of our real possibilities, and as such they set everything in motion and keep it in a state of change."[64]

Inspired by Buber's and Bloch's prophetic ideal of God as a force for promise and change, Moltmann distinguishes between "the God of Parmenides . . . epiphany of the eternal presence (*Parousia*) of being" and the God of Exodus that provides an eschatological promise of radical change and redemption that can reconcile the temporal divide between the present and future.[65] God is the force of becoming and negation to "every unfulfilled present." According to Moltmann, "that we do not reconcile ourselves, that there is no pleasant harmony between us and reality, is due to our unquenchable hope." The more we give into our redemptive hopes, the greater our discontent with the status quo.

Moltmann went on to credit earlier Jewish thinkers like Buber and Bloch for introducing into theology the opposition of the God of Exodus's "dynamos" that generates "the passion for the possible" in contrast to the "utopia of the status quo realism" resulting from the static logos of "Parmenides god."[66] Moltmann gives his own twist by affirming the importance of God as a moral force that stands outside the "realism" of existing power structures, while also bringing Christian theology closer to the prophetic demand to change the actual conditions within the world. "In promising the future . . . the *God of the Exodus* and of the resurrection 'is' not eternal presence, but he promises his presence and nearness to him who follows the path on which he is sent into the future."⁶⁷ Paul Ricoeur later was to elaborate on what he termed the "dialectical logic of hope" identified by Moltmann here as a distinction between *"promise* rather than *presence*; of a God that is *one who comes*, rather than the one who is."⁶⁸ Similarly, John Polkinghorne later sums up the distinction between the promise of biblical hope and Greek determinism as a distinction between "divine *chesed*" (loving kindness) and an "unchanging realm of ideas."⁶⁹

For Moltmann, the political consequences of this faith in the *"novum ultimum* of hope" is that "the man who thus hopes will never be able to reconcile himself with the laws and constraints of this earth. . . . Peace with God means conflict with the world, for the goal of the promised future stabs inexorably into the flesh of every unfulfilled present."⁷⁰

Although not formally part of the "school of hope," Walter Brueggemann later brought together Bloch's metaphysics of negation and Moltmann's theology of prophetic agitation in his works *Hope within History* (1987) and *Hopeful Imagination: Prophetic Voices in Exile* (1986). Redolent of Cohen and Buber's distinction between Plato and the prophets, Brueggemann goes on to define this orientation of "sacred discontent" in the following terms:⁷¹

> The issue of the juxtaposition of hope and knowledge is at the heart of the crisis now to be faced in our culture. The traditions of the scientific knowledge and power seem oddly alienated from the traditions of hope. The tradition of hope means a relinquishment of control over life. . . . This hope does not consist of losing control, but relinquishing it in trust. . . . The substance of biblical hope . . . a new world of justice, equity, freedom, and well-being. This hope has nothing to do with progress. . . . Hope keeps the present arrangement open and provisional. Hope reminds us that the way things are is precarious and in jeopardy. Hope reminds us not to absolutize the present, not to take it too seriously, not to treat it too honorably, because it will not last. . . . So what is the function of hope? . . . It is to provide standing ground outside the system from which the system can be evaluated, critiqued, and perhaps changed. Hopeless people eventually must conform, but hope filled people are not as dependent, not as fully contained and administered. Hope is an immense human act which reminds us that no system of power or knowledge can finally grasp what is true . . . hope gives reason not to submit to present power arrangements. Hope affirms . . . that the present well-established

power is not permanent and need not be taken with too much seriousness. It is endlessly suspicious and refuses to accept the orders of the day.... This "sacred discontent" is rooted in hope... Israel's hope is to keep us from becoming excessively contented with the ways things are.[72]

Here Brueggemann follows the same thread of prophetic praxis going back to nineteenth-century thinkers like Graetz and Cohen. Hope retains a mystical quality of being both immanently rooted in the world—in our interactions and bonds of trust with others—but also necessarily connected to some other transcendental source that is not correlated with the metric of secular optimism quantified by displays of material progress. For a postutopian age forever bent to the siren's call of cynical realism, only a God of hope can restore confidence that humanity was intended for exodus and not slavery.

For all the theologians inspired by the "school of hope," in the post-Holocaust/Hiroshima age, hope may lack rational justification, but nevertheless remains the only rational way for motivating individuals to have the audacity to prevent further global destruction.[73] This is what Moltmann means about hope being realistic, because without hope there is nothing rational to prevent us from embracing these demonic impulses toward despair or even nihilism. Thus, hope becomes the most realistic response to a world drifting toward its own self-destruction.

HOPE AND COMMANDMENT

In his entry on hope within the encyclopedic work *Contemporary Jewish Religious Thought* (1987), Charles Vernoff defines Jewish hope (*tikvah*) as spiritually rooted in a praxis-oriented anticipation of immediate transformation. Similar to Buber's distinction between faith and trust in *Two Types of Faith*, Vernoff proposed a distinction between hope as a form of praxis and agency versus what he referred to as the contrasting ideal of *faith* (*bitahon*) that, in his words, "inclines toward patient and passive waiting."[74] Although he does not take into account Scholem's counter claim that living in hope also entails living in a form of deferment, Vernoff's distinction is particularly noteworthy for its narrative compliance with Buber's earlier distinction.

After the Shoah, Jewish theologians increasingly asked if the type of waiting suggested by the messianic tradition had become simply untenable.

Although Buber was one of the first to delineate the theological importance of separating hope from faith, in the post–World War II period the Jewish philosopher Emil Fackenheim was the first to formulate a more praxis-oriented messianic hope that could speak to post-Holocaust concerns. Fackenheim contributed to discussions within the "school of hope" by grounding his reflections on hope in Jewish responses to collective tragedy and evil. In his essay "The Commandment to Hope," Fackenheim sharpened the tensions between hope as a demand for praxis and the sublimation of redemptive expectations by the rabbis into passive waiting for the Messiah.[75] After the Holocaust, however, a resolution to this dialectic within Jewish redemptive hope narratives became impossible. We simply have to learn to live with these tensions. For Fackenheim, traditional Jewish commitments to the righteousness of passive waiting for the Messiah—as exemplified by stories of singing about the coming of the Messiah while walking into gas chambers—are no longer fully viable. Conversely, the more praxis-driven forms of redemptive hope that lead many Jews to join the ranks of Marxist revolutionaries and other forms of secular utopianism are equally untenable. What this means is that we are now living in a post-Kantian period in which both religious and Enlightenment redemptive hope narratives have lost their rational credibility.

What to do when both God and humanity have failed? Where do we turn for hope? Fackenheim warns us that cynicism and despair are equally illegitimate responses. To embrace despair is to give in to the very nihilism that defines the fascist and social Darwinian *Weltanschauung*. This is where hope turns into a negation of its own negation. Rationally, according to Fackenheim, hope may not be justified, but rationality cannot survive the "revolutions of nihilism" responsible for the rise of Fascism. Therefore, the commandment to hope paradoxically affirms a rational defense against nihilism. Adorno famously wrote that there is no poetry after Auschwitz, likewise to hope after Auschwitz is perhaps our only rational defense against nihilism.[76] Hope and poetry are rationally impossible after Auschwitz, yet also impossible to live without. Kant's Enlightenment hope in the power of autonomous individuals to rationally affirm the good simply can no longer hold against the tidal wave of horror unleashed by Auschwitz and Hiroshima. Yet, we must continue to cling to the commandment to hope and write poetry even if we no longer have the same metaphysical grounding as our ancestors.

Ironically, the heteronomy implied by following a commandment is necessary to protect the ideal of humans autonomously choosing to reject nihilism by embracing redemptive hope. Fackenheim argued that the dialectics of Enlightenment have proven that the "slaughter bench of history" (Hegel) has crushed the secular liberal optimism once held in universal humanism. The answer can be found in a return to the heteronomy of commandment. In the face of the absurdity of any form of hope, hope becomes the supreme commandment, the only logical response in the face of a world so hopeless that it allows genocide and nuclear destruction. Rationally, despair may be the only legitimate intellectual response, yet our inner spiritual voices of freedom and hope must resist these inner destructive voices of nihilism. We may no longer be rationally justified, but humanity cannot endure without the commandment to hope.

Hope as an expression of autonomy over the forces of despair makes rational sense for Fackenheim, paradoxically, only through the heteronomy of seeing oneself as encumbered by a transcendental commandment. After the Holocaust the only way to affirm one's autonomy lies in the individual decision to return to a premodern ideal of obedience to a biblical notion of redemptive hope. This paradox leads Fackenheim to posit that we must learn to live with what he refers to as the "dialectics of work and wait."[77] We must *work* because we can no longer *wait* with the same type of faith that our ancestors did for the Messiah. As a Zionist, Fackenheim could barely hold back his scorn at the possibility that messianic faith may have contributed to the perceived docility of religious Jews in the face of their own destruction. As a theologian though, Fackenheim saw the importance of affirming the virtues of discipline and humility inculcated through faith in the waiting for the Messiah throughout the history of Jewish exile (*Galut*). Additionally, the ideal of waiting might also help to bring humanity back from the brink of technological devastation. Fackenheim seems to assume that somehow religion inculcates a form of humility that would have prevented the unleashing of nuclear destruction.

After the Holocaust we both need a transcendental grounding for our redemptive aspirations and, precisely because of the Holocaust, we can no longer simply wait for a supernatural intervention to save the world. Drawing on the rabbinic tradition, Fackenheim offers that faith in a God who acts in history to bring about redemption is necessary, but when confronted with life's challenges it is equally as necessary to act as if it all depends on us. Hope is necessary for both activities because both dispositions of *"working* and *waiting"* are no longer justified on their own given what we know about the history of the human propensity for destruction and cruelty. We can't simply wait, but neither are we expected to "finish the task" (*Pirkei Avot*) on our own.

Drawing on the traditional Jewish messianic dichotomy between contrasting perfectionist and antinomian ideals as equal catalysts for redemption, Fackenheim concludes his essay with a eulogy to both ideals of secular progress and religious faith.[78] Fackenheim points to the haunting image from Eli Wiesel's book *Night*, in which the hanging of an innocent child by the Nazis becomes symbolic of the death of God as a force within history. With this image in mind, Fackenheim quotes Wiesel's prophetic and Kafkaesque remark, "It is precisely because it is too late that we are commanded to hope."[79] Faith in a rupture and overturning of human nature may no longer be viable, but there are new opportunities for creating a basis for hope through the renewal and continuity of a covenantal community. Fackenheim's statement that we are commanded to "testify against the Devil (Hitler) by our very existence" brought Jewish theology closer to a horizontal naturalism in which the solidarity of community replaces the certitude of grace or miraculous redemption. Just as God dies with the slaughter of innocents, so too God's presence and hope must be reaffirmed through the covenantal continuity of Israel, with all the problematic ethnocentrism implied.

Fackenheim's essay continues to stand out from this period precisely because he resisted any easy resolution of dialectical tensions presented by holding onto traditional Jewish redemptive hope narratives in the post-Holocaust period.[80] His insistence that we live within the paradox of both needing to "work and wait" brings greater clarity to the tensions between realism and idealism. The commandment to hope becomes less about imagining an end to the tensions between reason and inclination, sin and grace, and more about appreciating the paradox that the sense of agency generated through the embrace of hope also has the potential to generate greater levels of nihilism. In such moments of despair, looking to history or to Enlightenment notions of human nature to find rational grounding for utopian aspirations is of little help. If we follow Spinoza in thinking that reason is mostly about self-preservation, then the commandment to hope is perhaps our only rational recourse for warding off debilitating despair when confronted with horrors of history. For Fackenheim, viewing oneself as commanded is the only way we can maintain solidarity with others standing against the dark.

THE PARADOX OF HOPE

In his writings on hope during this same period, the social theorist Erich Fromm similarly engaged the dialectics between work and wait. Although Fromm was not formally included in the "school of hope," he shared their interests in reconciling Marxist critique with religious eschatology.[81] The ideal of hope for Fromm challenged both the passivity of religious faith and modern secular optimism in technology as a solution for human alienation. Similar to Buber and Bloch, from an early age Fromm embraced utopian social projects through which authentic relations could emerge free from the alienation of a mass capitalist society.[82] Fromm also helped synthesize Buber and Bloch by elaborating on the tensions between hope as a horizontal prophetic principle for change in contrast to the vertical apocalyptic ideal of passive acceptance of the status quo.

In his book *You Shall Be as Gods* (1966), Fromm elaborated on the distinction between vertical passivity and the possibility for praxis that springs from horizontal solidarity. According to Fromm:

> In the post-prophetic period a change takes place in the meaning of the messianic idea, making its first appearance in the Book of Daniel around 164 B.C. While in the prophets the aim of human evolution lies in the *Yamin ha-baim*, in the "days to come," or *be-aharit ha-yamim*, "the end of the day," in Daniel and in the part of the apocalyptic literature following him the aim is *ha-olam ha-ba*, the "world to come." This "world to come" is not a world within history but an ideal world above, a world in the beyond. . . . There, in the prophetic world, the line of longing is *horizontal*; here—and this is the essence of the apocalyptic orientation—it is *vertical*. We find here the differentiation which is to become later the crucial difference between the Jewish and Christian development. The Jewish development emphasizes the horizontal, the Christian development emphasizes the vertical axis.[83]

Idolatrous impulses to identify with an all-powerful Father God in Heaven forever linked religion to ideologies of social hierarchies in which "the minds of the people had to be distorted in such a way that both the rulers and the ruled believed that their situation, as it existed, had been decreed by God, by nature, and by moral law." The greater the need for ideological illusions supporting social hierarchies down here on earth, the greater the emphasis on maintaining a "vertical axis" to a "world in the beyond." Within the history of Western redemptive narratives, only the prophets challenged what Bloch previously identified as the complacency of "opium priests" in ontologizing social exploitation. According to Fromm, the prophets "rob force and power of their moral and religious disguises" by stripping away the ontological illusions used by ruling elites throughout history to justify their regimes as a natural extension of the cosmos's sacred order. Similar to Bloch's God of Exodus, hope operates, according to Fromm, as a force for contingency against the dogmas of social conventions and power structures.

Writing in a postutopian age, however, Fromm was equally concerned with the uses and abuses of redemptive narratives, especially among secular left-wing radicals. In *The Revolution of Hope* (1968), Fromm anticipated Obama's concerns with "blind optimism" by warning against the "pseudo-radical adventurism" that can create unreasonable expectations.[84] The great paradox with hoping is that the moment of presence created by projecting into the future is both a form of anticipation and potential revolutionary praxis all in the very same moment. Following Scholem, Fromm argues that the paradox with redemptive narratives is that living a life of anticipation can also lead to the "deterioration of hope into a passive waiting."[85] Similar to Fackenheim's dialectic between work and wait, a supererogatory disposition of hopefulness can function like a narcotic, leading to either opiate passivity or intoxicating adventurism. Redemptive hopes are also paradoxical for creating idealized visions that are mostly impossible to actualize, yet are also essential for thwarting despair and maintaining a sacrificial readiness to strive for their actualization. This dual quality of hope is its own form of negation in the form of despair that resets a response of hope as a negation to the negative (in the form of despair), thus renewing the possibility of new openings. How to decide between the two remains the grand mystery for all critically reflective persons. The challenge from Fromm's perspective in the 1960s is the same question that has come to national attention in the age of Obama, namely: how do you maintain a messianic and utopian impulse for radical transformation while at the same time avoiding the "radical adventurism" that has often led to the perversion of these very same messianic impulses into a form of "blind optimism"?

The challenge of redemptive hope narratives, according to Fromm, is in the way they maintain a spark of utopian resistance to the status quo while also retaining sobriety and resilience that can protect against despair. On a personal existential level, individuals are defined by how they wrestle with these challenges. For Fromm, mature hope means a willingness to live with this paradox.

Yet, living with this paradox cannot be an excuse for accepting the status quo. As a Marxist-Jewish intellectual who lived through the failures and horrors of both right- and left-wing totalitarianism, Fromm was concerned to retain the "crouched tiger" of revolutionary expectation and resistance.[86] Fromm also was concerned that the culture industries had succeeded in castrating the progressive utopian openness to "that which is not yet born" by convincing the potentially revolutionary masses to embrace a "facile optimism" in consumerism and technological innovation. Bourgeois faith in material and technological progress has produced a facile optimism as a replacement for our deep hopes for love and human contact.[87] The "mechanization of society" inaugurated by the "worship of progress in modern bourgeois thought" has contributed to the "shattering of hope" in the modern era by increasing social alienation and psychological isolation.[88] The rise in an "average optimism" has lead to the resignation that vulgar forms of stimulation provided by the cultural industries can serve as a replacement for the hope stimulated through genuine interactions with other people.[89] The irony is that the optimism in technological innovations as a source of meaning protects individuals from facing the despair over the reality of modern alienation. The "optimism" of technology, according to Fromm, helps to obfuscate the disconnect most people experience in their daily interactions. But without the first step of despair, revolutionary fervor is increasingly negated. Sometimes despair is a prerequisite for reigniting the "crouched tiger" of genuine hope.

The challenge that Buber, Bloch, and Fromm raise is the question of religion in relation to what the "school of hope" identified as the "de-Hellenization of faith." What does it mean for Western redemptive narratives to be truly "de-Hellenized"? Is it possible to have religious redemptive narratives without any vertical hope, or is Bloch right that the transition toward hope in horizontal solidarity signifies the overcoming of the God of Exodus within history?

Recent scholarship—most notably Jeffrey Bloechl's *Religious Experience and the End of Metaphysics,* Santiago Zabala's *The Future of Religion,* and Gianni Vattimo's *Religion after Metaphysics*—propose that the twentieth century's *crisis with reason,* coupled with the proliferation of critiques of philosophy (generally subsumed under the name of postmodern theory) has created a space in which religious and theological issues, once marginalized by an overly rationalistic Enlightenment legacy, can now return to the Western democratic intellectual conversation.[90] Habermas sums up this postmetaphysical paradigm shift between philosophy and religion in the following terms:

> Viewed from without, religion, which has largely been deprived of its worldview functions, is still indispensable in ordinary life for normalizing intercourse with the extraordinary. For this reason, even postmetaphysical thinking continues to coexist with religious practice.... Philosophy, even in its postmetaphysical form, will be able neither to replace nor to repress religion as long as religious language is the bearer of a semantic content that is inspiring and even indispensable, for this content eludes the explanatory force of philosophical language and continues to resist translation into reasoning discourses.[91]

For Habermas, the turn toward "postmetaphysical thinking" is both a cause for concern and mixed optimism: his optimism lies ironically in the possibility of drawing on religious discourses to strengthen liberal democracy. Without the grounding provided by metaphysical forms of hope, Habermas joined in the chorus of concern over the very viability of liberalism to provide convictions and motivations necessary for maintaining the ideals of democratic citizenship.

In Chapter 4 I turn to Richard Rorty's neopragmatic answer to these tensions between hope, transcendence, and solidarity. Rorty's central contribution to post–World War II engagements with the ideal of hope is that he took what Capps identified as the "de-Hellenization of faith" a step closer to Bloch's argument for the necessary evolution from the transcendentalism of religion toward horizontal solidarity and Promethean freedom from authoritarian religious hierarchies. There we grapple with one of the most sophisticated attempts of the modern age to propose a postmetaphysical philosophy of hope.

4

RICHARD RORTY'S SOCIAL HOPE AND POSTMETAPHYSICAL REDEMPTION

> The secret things are God's, but the revealed things are ours and our children's forever.
>
> —DEUTERONOMY, 29:29

NEOPRAGMATISM AND REDEMPTION

At the turn of the twenty-first century, Richard Rorty put forward his vision for a new form of social hope, "the hope that life will eventually be freer, less cruel, more leisured, richer in goods and experiences, not just for our descendants but for everybody's descendants."[1] The first step toward this neopragmatic future requires a change in priorities in which "everybody thinks that it is human solidarity, rather than knowledge of something not merely human, that really matters."[2] This utopian task of "replacing certainty with hope" requires establishing a different kind of solidarity based on increasing individual happiness rather than establishing a correspondence between ourselves and the eternal.[3] Additionally, embracing the contingency of solidarity established through a free exchange of ideas among a liberal democratic citizenry involves putting "social hope in the place that knowledge has traditionally occupied." For Rorty, the utopian future of liberal democracy is itself dependent on the possibility of finally jettisoning the cultural ladders of Greek metaphysics that have provided the foundations for Western civilization.[4] Instead of vertical gazing toward the heavens, the social hope of expanding on Western democratic utopianism means we now consider "our conversation with our fellow-humans as our only source of guidance."[5]

The audacity of a neopragmatic redemptive hope is found through a willingness to embrace the radical contingency that our personal hopes are connected to our ability to mutually recognize, create dialogue with, and help actualize the hopes of our fellow citizens.[6] The intellectual energy once devoted to the metaphysical desire to "step outside our skins" by comparing "ourselves with something absolute" can now be directed toward intersubjective relationships.[7] "Whatever good the ideas of objectivity and transcendence have done for our culture can be attained equally well by the idea of community which strives after both intersubjective agreement and novelty."[8]

Giving up on transcendence as the only ground for social justice additionally allows us to strive for what Rorty called a "culture of hope" rather than "cultures of endurance."[9] Rorty points out that the ideals of the Enlightenment were historically situated between the quest for a vertical transcendence and the unconditional as key to unlocking human essence in contrast to a more pragmatic vision that looked horizontally to interpersonal solidarity. In an essay titled "The Continuity Between the Enlightenment and Postmodernism," Rorty stated that there were essentially "two Enlightenment projects—one political and one philosophical."[10] The Enlightenment's political agenda of "maximal freedom and minimal humiliation" still remains the right goal for society. The emancipatory hope radiating from the Enlightenment remains the hope of collectively establishing an "egalitarian utopia" through dialogue. Rorty's utopian hope for overcoming the metaphysical tradition is as much about moving beyond the pretense to *objectivity* within science and Enlightenment rationalism as about overcoming religious appeals to God. In a postmetaphysical world we may lose what Nietzsche referred to as the "metaphysical comfort" and existential grounding of epistemology, but here we gain the social hope that comes from the combination of a more emboldened sense of social solidarity, coupled with the freedom of an unfettered poetic imagination.[11]

SOCIAL HOPE: BETWEEN PRAGMATISM AND UTOPIANISM

Rorty's emancipatory ideals stem from a tension between his utopian conviction that pragmatism offered a way to finally overcome the West's metaphysical legacy, and his more ecumenical interest in reappropriating religious and philosophical discourses for the purpose of strengthening liberal democratic cultures. Rorty oscillated between a pragmatism in which the eudemonistic satisfaction of human needs is the highest good and a more utopian form of neopragmatism in which our central concern is the overcoming of humanity's transcendental impulses toward establishing a correspondence with something nonhuman. Having grown up surrounded by leftist intellectuals who had dedicated their lives to social change, Rorty reflects in his autobiographical essays on the tension he felt from an earlier age with regard to competing desires to reconcile encounters with the sublime within nature (such as wild orchids) with revolutionary demands for utopian transformation.[12] According to Rorty this is ultimately a challenge of trying to create enough coherence across discourses so that we can "hold reality and justice in a single vision." Although he came to the conclusion that achieving coherence between reality (as represented through sublime moments in the woods) and justice (as expressed by the progressive strivings for overcoming inequality) is a false metaphysical hope, Rorty nevertheless continued to ponder the importance of harnessing redemptive narratives that provided inspiration for achieving a reconciliation between private bliss and a public need for justice and civic solidarity. According to Rorty, Western culture has evolved from religion, to philosophy, and now literature as the means for enriching the human imagination. Rorty elaborated on his evolutionary view of Western culture in the following terms:

> As secularist politics gradually replaced theocratic politics in the West, it became more and more possible to substitute hope that there was something powerful on our side with simple hope that human beings would do certain things, that they could freely cooperate in certain ways.... Now that we have made politics secular, let us also make politics nonmetaphysical. Let us give up even secular ways of trying to assure ourselves that there is something larger and powerful on our side. Let us make progress simply through hope for cooperation with one another, rather than hope of achieving universal truth or contact with the transcendent.[13]

Although Rorty's views on the march of secularism are historically problematic, his utopian impulses lead him to present his own redemptive narrative for how Western culture might evolve. In his more utopist moments, Rorty advocated a complete overcoming of religious and philosophical redemptive narratives based on metaphysical transcendence for what he saw as literature's alternative promise for "redemption from insensitivity."[14] In contrast to the Platonic concern with linking philosophic wonder with a form of eternal power, Rorty encourages instead a new form of utopian liberalism premised on the courage to "substitute hope for the sort of knowledge which philosophers have usually tried to attain."[15] In his more pragmatic moments, however, Rorty embraced a principle of utilitarian tolerance.[16] Based on his readings of James, Mill, and Dewey, pragmatism represented the great ecumenical hope of reconciling human interests with transcendental discourses.

The great ecumenical appeal of pragmatism, according to Rorty's interpretation, was that it broke down all hierarchies between scientific and intellectual disciplines. The point of discourses is to serve various needs; therefore we should utilize the widest available vocabularies as part of a broad metaphorical toolbox for addressing different desires. The greater the number of discourses at our disposal the greater our chances for satisfying the widest variety of needs—both known and yet to be discovered—as the surest way to increasing human happiness.[17] "Every human need should be satisfied unless doing so causes too many other human needs to go unsatisfied."[18] Pragmatism allows for the continuous oscillation between moments of resoluteness and moments of compromise depending on conditions. There is simply no single template for determining when to seek discourses that provide a sense of continuity versus discourses that encourage radical rupture, innovation, and irony with regard to social conventions. Rorty famously proposed that the concepts of *contingency*, *irony*, and *solidarity* exist as part of a triangulation of competing and complimentary ideals; the point is not to become a pure ironist, nor to submit to the social conformism of solidarity, but rather, to establish a social equilibrium through which each ideal can be utilized for its strengths depending on the contingency of circumstances.

With regard to religious redemptive hope narratives, the ecumenical core of pragmatism means that religious discourses are no longer dismissed as simply irrational and superstitious but are instead rehabilitated for their inspirational value.[19] Because there is no single template for adjudicating between competing social goods of justice, freedom, and security we have to draw on as many competing discourses as possible. Therefore, from a pragmatic perspective, religious discourse should be viewed as one among a variety of tools garnered in order to motivate individuals toward greater horizons of self and communal fulfillment. In his essay "Failed Prophecies, Glorious Hopes," Rorty elaborates on his hermeneutics of recovery in the following terms: "Failed prophecies often make invaluable inspirational reading. Consider two examples: the New Testament and the Communist Manifesto.... Both sets of predictions have, so far, been ludicrous flops. Both claims to knowledge have become objects of ridicule."[20]

There is pragmatic good to both religious and Marxist narratives that allows us to imagine a greater sense of "we-ness" among a diverse citizenry. Both religious and secular Marxist narratives of liberation are still relevant so long as we ignore their predictive claims and just focus on their ability to inspire social hope. In a postmodern world we may no longer hold to an idealistic vision of justice or a transcendental supreme good. Yet, Rorty proposes, "hope for social justice is nevertheless the only basis for a worthwhile human life."[21] Marxist and religious redemptive hope narratives are therefore still relevant for social and existential tasks of making life worthwhile.

Once we relinquish the desire to dig down to the essence behind all phenomena, the great debate between science and religion is deflated into concerns of utility and felicity rather than the need for an accurate representation of some external reality. In contrast to the Platonic legacy of bifurcating the world into an irreconcilable dichotomy between matter and spirit, Rorty argues that the best solution for harmonizing science and religion is to allow for both vocabularies to operate simultaneously for the fulfillment of different needs. Because there is no way to determine ultimately whether a "carpenter's or the particle physicist's account of tables is the true one," Rorty claims that there remains a heuristic advantage in maintaining a distinction between the functions of "poets" (as reflective of traditional religious/romantic desires for personal perfection and relating to the sublime) and "plumbers" (as representative of mechanistic, predictive, and materialist utilization of phenomena for concrete ends). "Science enables us to predict and control, whereas religion offers us a larger hope, thereby something to live for."[22] Scientific explanations of causation provide the consolation of greater efficacy over the physical world, but the power of greater predictive control does not always contribute to the inspiration needed for human flourishing. "There are lots of things you want to do with human beings for which descriptions of them in nonevaluative, inhuman terms are very useful; there are others (e.g., thinking of them as your fellow citizens) in which such descriptions are not."[23] Once the criterion for justification switches from a concern for *ultimate truth* to a pragmatic criterion of *usefulness*, religious discourses are taken out of the controversial role of providing what Kant referred to as "synthetic knowledge." Rather, religious narratives become one of many poetic discourses in our toolbox for making meaning out of human experience.

The postmetaphysical implications of placing both science and religion on the level of complementary discourses for achieving human happiness, however, led to the criticism that Rorty's pragmatism contributed to ethical relativism. Rorty was particularly sensitive to the charge that his postfoundational pragmatism provided little incentive for those with power to obligate themselves toward social justice.[24] Rorty responded to the age-old ethical dilemma over "Why should I care about a stranger?" by suggesting that the best we can do is to offer a "long, sad, sentimental story" that will hopefully move individuals to expand their circles of care.[25] According to Rorty "I think of imagination and sentiment rather than reason as the faculties which do the most to make moral progress possible" by inspiring a greater sentimental ability to see others as "one of us."[26] Redemptive narratives that stimulate sentiments of solidarity through literature will have a greater democratic chance of making a demeaned *other* into a *we*, than analytical arguments claiming a privileged correspondence to an ultimate good.[27] According to Rorty, an "imaginative acquaintance with as many alternative final vocabularies as possible" leads to greater tolerance and freedom, thereby increasing our chances of enlarging our sense of whom to include as part of a collective *we*.[28] The less we insist that there is only one way to know the good, the more open we become to those who are different from us.

As a replacement for these metaphysical concerns regarding the true and timeless, all we really need is Judith Shklar's definition of liberalism as a concern with recognizing "a common susceptibility to humiliation" and respecting individual rights.[29] Part of Rorty's self-described "fuzzy" utopianism is based on the hope that democracies are actually made stronger and grow by inculcating a sense of vulnerability to both the potential contingency of our truth and to the possible pain of others. Rorty's claim that becoming open to the narratives of other people's experiences and pains is, I propose, itself a redemptive performance of opening toward creating new descriptions for turning an *other* into *one of us*.

In response to Levinas and Derrida who argued for a sense of "infinite responsibility" to a privileged ideal of *otherness*, Rorty retorted that pursuing the "unreachable" and "unrepresentable" might be useful for "our individual quests for private perfection," but might become a "stumbling-block to effective political organization" within the public arena.[30] For Rorty, progressive intellectuals across the spectrum share the same mistake of assuming that either finding the right metaphysical formulas for ethics (Kant) or perfecting the social critique of existing power dynamics (Marx) can serve as a substitute for providing hope and working toward concrete change for a better future.[31]

Despite the centuries of yearning for Platonist transcendence "beyond history and institutions," Rorty makes the salient point that, historically, the West's ontotheological tradition had little effect in preventing the atrocities committed in the heart of Western civilization's most scientific, most Christian, and most philosophical of all cultures.[32] Although idealists like Kant had developed rational arguments for ethics, Rorty proposed that the failure of European Christians to see Jews as "one of us" is not something that stronger appeals to categorical imperatives or other metaphysical ideals have solved.[33]

Rorty's interest in postfoundational ethics was shared by earlier Jewish thinkers who also challenged the moral relevancy of philosophy after Auschwitz. Adorno's claim that "there is no poetry after Auschwitz," Levinas's identification of philosophy with imperialism, and Fackenheim's insistence on a whole new commandment to confront the unique evil of Auschwitz, all shared a fundamental questioning of the efficacy of Western metaphysics with regard to social and ethical challenges. If a philosopher like Heidegger could commit the political "error" of joining and supporting the Nazi movement, then perhaps metaphysics itself was not a guarantor of ethics.

While sharing in this critique, Rorty's conception of social hope functions as a very different type of response to the horrors of history and the crisis of reason within Western culture. "No event—not even Auschwitz can show that we should cease to work for a given utopia."[34] We hope, not despite our natures, but simply because what we define as our "natures," or "species-being," is constantly evolving along with our understanding of what counts as genuine happiness. Thus, "to retain social hope, members of such a society need to be able to tell themselves a story about how things might get better."[35] Because what ultimately "binds societies together are common vocabularies and common hopes . . . the principle function of the vocabularies is to tell stories about future outcomes which compensate for present sacrifices." We should hope, not because we are commanded to do so, but because as humans we simply cannot imagine a world without heroes, without mountains to climb, and without hopeful narratives to live by and pass onto our children.[36]

Unlike most redemptive narratives, however, Rorty proposed that by dropping "revolutionary rhetoric of emancipation and unmasking in favor of a reformist rhetoric about increased tolerance and decreased suffering" we could instead focus on more local tasks of expanding bourgeois liberalism.[37] Transcendental quests for total transformation, therefore, should give way to local hopes for incremental improvements.[38]

POSTMETAPHYSICAL UTOPIANISM

The prophetic strand within neopragmatism is the hope that fallible humans are capable of building a New Jerusalem, a new City upon a Hill, without insisting on a "vertical relationship between representations and what is represented."[39] The "utopian hope" of neopragmatism is based on the premise that fallible human beings, on their own, are capable of "diminishing human suffering and increasing human equality" without being forced to direct their gazes vertically in order to garner, in Rorty's words, "backup from supernatural forces."[40] The utopian energies unleashed by giving up any "hope for the transcendental" allows us to stop asking the question "What are we?" and instead ask prophetic questions like "What might we try to become?"[41] The redemptive component within Rorty's postmetaphysical neopragmatism was premised on his utopian thesis that we will become motivated to expand the boundaries of solidarity with our fellow citizens so long as we relinquish our need for some transcendental referent. "We moderns are superior to the ancients—both pagan and Christian," Rorty tells us, because of "our ability to imagine a utopia here on earth."[42] Desires for "knowledge of the eternal" and for "another world" should give way to new efforts at generating innovative "images of the future" in this world.[43] For Rorty, the attainment of a "perfect secular utopia" is one in which social hope replaces fears for rewards and punishment in the next life.[44] Western civilization has matured enough that we can now move beyond "cultures of endurance" toward new "cultures of social hope" in which the quest for novelty through generating new descriptions and solidarity replaces the quest for epistemological certainty.[45]

Religious hopes once directed toward "union with God" can give way to the avant-garde ideal of novel self-fashioning and what Rorty referred to as "redemption from egotism."[46] In such a "democratic utopia tolerance and curiosity, rather than truth-seeking, are the chief intellectual virtues." With regard to Habermas's concerns for the ability of secular Enlightenment culture to maintain the virtues of sacrifice and civic responsibility, Rorty offered that we no longer need to keep ascending the same "vertically" oriented metaphysical ladders used by our ancestors.[47] It should be possible to motivate citizens toward the liberal ideal of greater inclusiveness while protecting private idiosyncratic loves and convictions from a test of empirical verification.

In what Cornel West described as his more "demythologizing" moments, Rorty proposed that philosophy and religion historically have shared in the same metaphysical project of providing discourses that speak to a psychological dependence on a "desperate hope for a non-contingent and powerful ally" in order to compensate for feelings of powerlessness.[48] The main problem with so-called supernaturalism is the desire to conflate idiosyncratic loves with a universal power, thereby transforming that which should remain subjective to an objective status worthy of public recognition.[49] "To give up the idea that there is an intrinsic nature of reality to be discovered either by the priests, or the philosophers, or the scientists, is to disjoin the need for redemption from the search for universal agreement, but this substitution is no reason to give up the search for a single utopian form of political life—the good global society."[50]

Because "self creation and human solidarity are equally valid, yet forever incommensurable," we can only maximize the potential for the greatest amount of freedom to bloom if individuals are allowed to cultivate their own private pursuits.[51] Once we give up the Platonic desire to hold "reality and justice in a single vision," our task changes to determining what is needed for the public realm to flourish versus those discourses and behaviors better sequestered in the private realm.[52] The discourse we use for private esoteric encounters with the sublime or romantic self-fashioning should not be subject to the same rational scrutiny demanded in the public arena. "People have the same right to idiosyncratic forms of religious devotion as they do to write poems or paint pictures that nobody else can make sense of, so we should extend to others the tolerance we enjoy; individuals are free to make up their own semi-private language games as long as they do not insist that everybody else plays them as well."[53] Increasing tolerance and freedom represents an alternative redemptive narrative based on the idea that there is an inherent good to stimulating greater complexity and novelty.

The utopian possibility of consensus from dialogue is possible only if citizens relegate discourses that transgress evidential criteria to the private realm. The disjoining of "political deliberation from projects of redemption" depends on those "issues that you must resolve cooperatively with others and issues that you are entitled to resolve on your own."[54] Rorty's proposal for the bifurcation of the public from the private is predicated on the "Jeffersonian compromise" that we are capable of separating private pursuits of the sublime from our public deliberations.[55]

Rorty singles out religious appeals to God as posing a special difficulty for the public square. Terms like *God* and *consciousness* have enjoyed the unique status of being presumed to exist beyond the type of predicates we use for defining other concepts.[56] As a self-described verificationist, Rorty challenged the legitimacy of using discourse to describe a concept that is "ineffable" and therefore, by definition, exists outside the realm of all discourse.[57] For a discourse to be included within the civil realm it must be comprised of terms shared in common. But the infinite, by definition, cannot be fully comprehended through terms derived through synthetic finite understanding. Further, Rorty asked, "can a descriptive term have a sense of its application if regulated by no public criteria?"[58] If Wittgenstein was correct that "the limits of language mean the limit of my world," Rorty concluded that appeals to the infinite can only function as a private signifier for demarcating where public discourse ends and personal sentiment or experience begins.[59] We can only know a subject through ascribing it predicates ($S=P$). Consequently, "metaphysical questions like does God exist . . . are undiscussable" because there is "no list of neutral canonical designators" that exists outside the predicates needed to translate moments of presence into rational terms that can be shared with others within the public arena.[60]

Projects pertaining to the need for social cooperation by definition depend on intersubjective rational consensus, whereas projects involving self-development and pursuit of the sublime do not.[61] Therefore, a standard of rationality for establishing consensus is necessary for facilitating public projects, but should not be applied to those idiosyncratic projects that pertain to private pursuits for meaning.[62] When individuals wish to transfer their private redemptive fervor into civic proposals, Rorty agreed with liberal theorists like Habermas that standards for civic discourse "must be translated into generally accessible language before they can find their way onto the agendas of parliament, courts, or administrative bodies and influence their decisions."[63] In the spirit of the US Constitution's establishment clause, Habermas further argued that because "the exercise of political authority must be neutral toward competing worldviews," secular public institutions should not support one version of redemptive hope against another.[64] The only way to maintain the civic right of tolerance and neutrality in the public arena is to insist that individuals who fail to translate their redemptive narratives into "generally accessible language" are required to keep their esoteric convictions sequestered to the private realm.

POSTMETAPHYSICAL SOLIDARITY

According to Rorty, the march of democracy follows the cadence set by taking "certain distinctions less seriously than our ancestors." Recognizing the contingency of our norms has the social consequence of viewing "traditional differences as unimportant," and therefore, allowing for greater plurality.[65] Moral progress advances, according to Rorty, when "a people's imaginative ability to identify with people whom their ancestors had not been able to identify with" takes hold.[66] Embracing a sense of commonality with others is more important than establishing epistemic conditions for when we are justified in including others. Once we "stop asking for universal validity" through a "willingness to live with plurality" a greater number of people once considered alien can now be included as part of the liberal democratic sense of *we*.[67]

Concerns for establishing "universal validity" within both religious and secular humanistic traditions overlook the importance of "smaller and more local" sentiments when including, or excluding, others from the solidarity embodied in concepts like "one of us."[68] In his essay "Justice as a Larger Loyalty," Rorty proposed that we drop a metaphysical ideal of justice that stands outside of history and circumstance and reinterpret justice as "the name for loyalty to a certain very large group."[69] The tension between our local loyalties and our ideal of global justice largely revolves around the very difficult task of determining how much we are willing to view the stranger as deserving of the same bonds of care we expect from our local, familial, and tribal or nationalists associations. Drawing on Michael Waltzer's political philosophy, Rorty argues that the relevant "thickness" or "thinness" of our loyalties boils down to the "detailed and concrete stories you can tell about yourself as a member of a small group" versus those "relatively abstract and sketchy stories you tell about yourself as a citizen of the world."[70] The more we can tell stories that break down ontological polarities between social conventions of *higher* and *lower* within the civil realm, the more expansive our circles of care.[71]

Both universal justice and local loyalties represent social goods that often exist in perpetual tension with one another, thus we are constantly faced with the dilemma of whether or not we should "contract the circle for the sake of loyalty, or expand it for the sake of justice. . . . The moral tasks of a liberal democracy are divided between *agents of love* and *agents of justice*."[72] Agents of love are devoted to generating creative, penetrating, and thick cultural venues for enriching our social relations in ways that cannot be addressed by large liberal institutions. Conversely, agents of justice are more concerned with satisfying the bare minimum of cultural identity so that a maximal number of people can receive justice through state institutions while infringing upon the least number of freedoms.

Living within large diverse democratic cultures, according to Rorty, we are often required to sacrifice local sentiments of love for more abstract notions of justice. Nevertheless, universal notions of justice that strip individuals of their thicker identity affiliations have the benefit of extending the boundaries of basic human rights. In his essay "On Ethnocentrism: A Reply to Clifford Geertz," Rorty proposed that the type of critical theory both Geertz and Foucault employ as "agents of love" overlooks the crucial benefit of having liberal institutions based on a quality of thinness that, theoretically, allows a larger group of individuals to have their basic needs addressed.[73] Liberal institutions based on the thinness of abstract ideals like protecting the boundaries of civil rights and protection of autonomy may mean that we end up expecting less from our interactions from our neighbors but what we gain is the possibility of greater tolerance.[74] The advantage of the mandarin's focus on procedures of *statecraft*—to the exclusion of prophetic concerns for *soulcraft*—is that, arguably, a greater diversity of personal pursuits can flourish without social interference while extending to social groups and individuals previously viewed as foreign—if not as enemies—rights and services that might otherwise be denied.[75]

The greatness of modern disenchantment and secularization, following Rorty, is that it has become increasingly difficult to use religious redemptive narratives in Western societies to justify the oppression and hatred of others as being less holy or somehow inherently degenerate. By loosening the links between social distinctions and metaphysical ideals, "it has become increasingly easier for the weak and the poor to see themselves as victims of the greed of their fellow-humans rather than of Destiny, or the gods, or of the sins of their ancestors."[76]

For liberal theorists like Rorty insisting that no single redemptive hope narrative dominates the public arena helps to undermine authoritarian impulses toward forcibly unifying or synthesizing all hopes into a single comprehensive doctrine. Liberal tolerance is the only political model capable of ensuring social dynamism by keeping "the pendulum swinging between moral dogmatism and moral skepticism."[77] The pragmatic turn away from the ontotheological tradition also creates the opportunity for a new polytheistic solidarity based on the plurality and tolerance for our neighbor's right to have different private redemptive hopes, while retaining a common concern for protecting against the pain and humiliation of others.[78] The more we recognize the contingency and ineffability of our spiritual narratives, the more ironic we become with regard to all comprehensive doctrines. To "both equalize opportunities for self creation, while also leaving people sufficiently alone to actualize or neglect their opportunities on their own," there is a fundamental looseness or "weakness" required with regard to all redemptive hope narratives. Consequently, the principle of neutrality compliments the principle of tolerance by allowing the greatest amount of private aspirations to blossom. Embracing a perspective of irony and humor with regard to one's own comprehensive doctrines also encourages greater polytheistic tolerance and compassion for the struggle of others to find existential meaning and resoluteness in terms that best suit their conditions.

The type of polytheistic tolerance championed by liberal political philosophers also contains an element of subversion.[79] The alternative redemptive ideal implicit within principles of tolerance and neutrality is the hope that the seriousness directed toward absolutist convictions can be replaced with a more ironic appreciation for the contingency of all comprehensive doctrines. The more citizens adapt to tolerating a variety of different comprehensive doctrines, the harder it becomes to insist on the supremacy of any one particular hope narrative at the expense of all others. Liberalism has always revolved around championing the individual's freedom from having to share the same redemptive hopes as their fellow citizens.[80] Maintaining the boundaries that protect the individual's right to have different beliefs from their neighbor is perhaps one of the greatest achievements of the Enlightenment.

In addition to standards of tolerance, insisting on a standard of rationality based on terms shared in common is essential for protecting against the encroachment of fanaticism in the public sphere. Concerns for maintaining a standard of rationality within public debate led Rorty to famously break with the ecumenism of pragmatism in his essay "Religion as a Conversation Stopper."[81] Because the concept of God is beyond all predicates, appealing to the divine in order to justify one's position makes conversations between opposing positions impossible. The problem of inexplicability is unique to religious discourses and thereby makes all religious discourse uniquely problematic for any civic conversation. Rorty's position initially shared Robert Audi's concern that in the public arena it is important to insist that religions adopt a "civic voice" that relies on a communicative rationality that maintains a "principle of theo-ethical equilibrium."[82] Consequently, arguments that rely on God as their foundation for evidence have no place within public debate because invoking the authority of God makes liberal democratic deliberations impossible since there are no neutral signifiers that can appealed to as justificatory evidence for civic claims made except that they are deeply felt.[83]

For many of Rorty's lifelong interlocutors and critics, however, the sacrifices made in order to maintain the idea of a public sphere predicated on premises held in common are both pragmatically questionable and spiritually undesirable. Additionally, Rorty's emphasis on the intersection between hope and solidarity creates internal contradictions within his utopian proposal for overcoming metaphysics.

POSTMETAPHYSICAL HOPE AND ITS DISCONTENTS

Critics of Rorty charged that his utopian desire to achieve a final overcoming of metaphysical discourses violated the very ecumenism that defines the legacy of American pragmatism. If the praxis and utilitarian ethos within pragmatism is predicated on the thesis that we have the best chance of actualizing all our needs to the extent that we develop, in Andrzej Szahaj's terms, "a surplus of potentially useful truths" within our hermeneutical toolbox, then religious discourse should be viewed as one more tool for satisfying a civic need for inspirational narratives of common purpose and greater meaning.[84] Consequently, it makes no sense to categorically dismiss potential "tools" from being included.

Nicholas Wolterstorff points out that within Rorty's "atheistic utopia" religion is singled out as inherently preconditioned to cause social ills in ways that do not affect other political and poetic discourses.[85] Wolterstorff charges Rorty not only with an erroneous belief in the possibility of achieving a pure separation of the public and private, but also with relying on a faulty ideal of a public arena shaped by "premises held in common" that, according to his own liberal democratic values, can only be determined through dialogue and debate. Since liberal ideals of freedom and equality are just as transcendental and contentious as religious interpretations of the civic good, the very point of a democratic public arena is for all discourses to compete with one another.[86] To set criteria that categorically exclude religion, therefore, perpetuates the same fallacy Rorty critiques with regard to the positivist's appeal to objectivity or religious appeals to the ineffable.

Similar to Wolterstorff, Jeffrey Stout challenges that Rorty's secular utopianism contradicts Rorty's own antiessentialism.[87] Additionally, the exclusion of religion in the name of protecting liberal debate does more damage to the liberal ideal of pluralism and tolerance than it does to protect these very ideals. Accordingly, Stout voiced the concern that "the policy would itself be a conversation stopper," since "political discourse of a pluralistic democracy . . . needs to be a mixture of normal discourse and conversational improvisation."[88] Rorty's contractarian liberalism erroneously assumes that our need for integrating our personal and public selves can be satisfied by a public square devoted to merely safeguarding the ideals of justice and equality alone.[89] Further, Stout argues that Rorty's utopian impulse to rid liberal democratic civic discourse of theism's "spectatorial conception of knowledge" follows from an ideal of "discursive purity"[90] that replicates the very same impulse of theocrats to see secularism merely as a tool of domination. Both theocrats and secularists end up mirroring the other by seeking to determine the terms of public deliberation by insisting on a "discursive purity" that favors their position. A more pragmatic and democratic solution, Stout proposes, is an ideal of democratic dialogue in which "citizens of various kinds hammer out their differences with one another as they go along."[91]

Martin Jay follows with a more phenomenological argument by challenging Rorty's offensive against experiences of the inexplicable. Jay asks Rorty, "Why not admit that there are also responses that are non-linguistic as well?"[92] To exclude experiences that border on the inexplicable as irrelevant to public discourse entails excluding a wide range of criteria used for justifying convictions that are not easily translatable into already established terms shared by the general public.

Jay's point is particularly relevant when considering Rorty's defense of Western liberal values as relying on decisions and commitments made in moments of conviction that cannot always be translated into terms held in common.[93] Breaking from his characteristically ecumenical sensibility, Rorty endorsed an exceptional Western ethnocentric position that not all cultures and traditions should be preserved just because they are considered to represent some privileged form of otherness. In contrast to Habermas's reliance on the internal coherence of rational debate, for Rorty there comes a certain moment within all debate when dialogue might have to give way to enforcement, especially with regard to protecting liberal democratic society from the threat of violence and terrorism.[94]

Rorty's view follows on John Rawls's principle of self-preservation: the "right of self-preservation" allows liberal democratic societies to not "stand idly by while others destroy the basis of their existence."[95] Whereas we may have an obligation to follow a principle of tolerance with other citizens, liberal democratic standards of justice do not obligate us to sacrifice the right of self-preservation for those who fail to reciprocate in upholding the principle of tolerance.

Following Rawls's claim that the *right to self-preservation* trumps the *right of tolerance*, for Rorty some people simply will not agree and must be stopped for the sake of preserving liberal democratic society for the greatest number of citizens. "I do not think that there is anything self-contradictory in the Nazi's refusal to take me seriously. We may both have to reach for our guns."[96] Sometimes liberals are placed in the paradoxical situation of stopping discussions and using violence for the very sake of preserving a procedural republic based on freedom of speech. Public dialogue only works for those committed to the procedures that ensure discussion and consensus as the basis for determining public action.

The willingness to use illiberal means to defend liberal institutions raises the question of which regulative ideals do we appeal to for determining when we have reached the point of needing to "reach for our guns" rather than continuing to search for greater consensus?[97] If we jettison all metaphysical standards, thinkers like John Horton ask, "What is there for the ironist to worry about?"[98] Recognizing the inherent dignity of human beings in the form of inalienable rights rests on metaphysical foundations that ironists undermine. If from a neopragmatic view all rights are inherently contingent, then why adhere to metaphysical ideals of equal protection or liberty for all? Why should we expand the circles of care to those who might pose a threat to our security?

Despite his critique of religion's reliance on the inexplicable or unrepresentable, when it comes to dealing with fanatics who might threaten liberal democratic society, Rorty's own neopragmatism is paradoxically beholden to inexplicable existentialist convictions. His focus on the importance of realizing the contingency and "relative validity of one's convictions and yet stand for them unflinchingly" implies a priority of sentiment over discursive exchange that is hard to distinguish from taking a leap of faith.[99] When it comes to knowing when we should give up on discursive exchanges with fascists or terrorists and instead "reach for our guns" Rorty seems to be suggesting that we will have to mostly rely on our intuitions and make a gut call.

Rorty came remarkable close to embracing a similar reliance on sentiment and inexplicable transcendentalism when discussing the redemptive importance of metaphors for creating new utopian horizons.[100] Rorty surprisingly invoked a quasi-mystical language for describing the function of metaphors to help break through "the crust of convention" (Dewey). According to Rorty, metaphors are "agents-of-change" by rupturing social conventions in order to create greater openness toward new ways of relating to phenomena.[101] Metaphors function like "lightning bolts which blaze new trails" by "producing effects on your interlocutor" that open up new horizons of meaning.[102] New metaphors give voice to something "not already within us."[103] Metaphors signify the "realm of possibility as open-ended," like "a voice from outside logical space" that provides an alternative vision for how to "change one's language and one's life, rather than a proposal about how to systematize them."

Rorty's quasi-mystical description of metaphors as a "voice from beyond" and "striking like lightning bolts" suggests holistic experiences between people that exceed the boundaries of linguistic practices.[104] There is an interesting analogy here to how Ricoeur defined metaphors as possessing the "power to refer to a reality outside of language." In Rorty and Ricoeur's thought both hope and metaphors provide the inspirational ingredient that allows us to imagine new descriptions for desires and needs previously unimagined.[105] Hope can give us the courage to generate new metaphors, and, conversely, we look to generate new metaphors based on our hopes for novelty and increased solidarity.

Additionally, as Frankenberry notes, new metaphors in Rorty's thought also hold a liberatory promise of furthering social emancipation.[106] Progress should be viewed, according to Rorty, as "a history of increasing useful metaphors rather than of increasing our understanding of how things really are." A cultural willingness to entertain different metaphors has allowed Western civilization to take important conceptual leaps and to imagine new utopias beyond our inherited norms and terms.

Nevertheless, Rorty's terminology for describing the social role of metaphors is strikingly redolent of the very transcendentalism and nonlinguistic affect that he previously argued stops conversations within the public sphere. His praise of metaphors for their ability to "send shivers down our spine, non-sentential phrases which reverberate endlessly, change our selves and our patterns of action," shares in the same physiological affect that comes with ineffable or transcendental experiences.[107] Without this quality of transcendence it is hard to imagine how new metaphors are possible. As Aboulafia suggests, at the very least, Rorty's concern with "cosmopolitanism" and "individual self-determination" necessarily involves a form of transcendence over the "given."[108] What separates the "shivers" we may get from new metaphors from other types of spiritual experience?

For many of Rorty's critics his utopian aspirations to jettison all vestiges of transcendental discourse from the public arena constitutes the Achilles heel in his postmetaphysical social hope.[109] For Derrida it is not only impossible to achieve a neutral public sphere, but also the opening generated by a messianic commitment to "transcendental questioning" of social conventions and inequalities is essential for fulfilling Enlightenment's own goals of emancipation.[110] Without the transcendence of a messianic hope that commands justice and "infinite responsibility" toward the *other*, it is hard to imagine how social hope can sustain itself merely on the solidarity of mutual tolerance and exchange of resources.[111] The philosopher Richard Bernstein similarly opined that it is impossible to advocate for a vision of how to improve human interactions—as an ironist or liberal—without relying on a discourse imbued with transcendental signifiers.[112] Following the chorus of critics, John Conway charged that Rorty's "transitional praxis" is predicated on "harnessing the metaphysical fire of utopian theorizing" while simultaneously trying to extinguish the metaphysical flames from which social hope springs.[113] Conway rightly questions if social hope is at all possible without some form of "metaphysical fire."[114] Without this "metaphysical fire" it is hard to imagine historically how individuals would have been motivated to have taken the risks and make the sacrifices necessary to create the liberal societies of today. The motivational challenge that William James correctly identified in his essay "The Moral Equivalent of War" (1910) still remains for finding the right balance between inspiring redemptive hopes without slipping into fanaticism.

From a pragmatist perspective, because we can no longer "heed a heavenly voice," Rorty proposed that we are now left on our own to summon the courage "to realize the relative validity of one's convictions and yet stand for them unflinchingly."[115] But is this enough? Once one realizes the "relative validity of one's convictions" is one really inspired to make the sacrifice of jumping into a trench in order to defend liberal democratic principles? Additionally, is it possible to have "beliefs worth dying for" premised on "nothing deeper than contingent historical circumstance" as Rorty suggests, without levels of love and demands for synergy that will necessarily spill over into the public arena?[116] Adrienne Martin presents the challenge in terms of the possibility of creating what she refers to as a "secular faith."[117] For Martin, the challenge for secularists is to express hope commitments that are capable of motivating and sustaining commitments without appealing to the transcendental foundations traditionally associated with religion. Are there resources within secularism that can provide a sense of hope in moments of profound despair? Following on Martin's line of inquiry, the question additionally becomes one of whether religion and philosophy, as suggested by Rorty, are similarly dependent on some transcendental source for sustaining their claims to hope. Perhaps more importantly from a political perspective, do concerns for the civic good triumph concerns for foundational certainty, thereby obviating the binary tensions created by assigning a value to motivations as either secular, religious, or even metaphysical? To return to Stout's proposal, shouldn't we focus more on the political implications of what is being proposed when engaged in civic discourse than concern ourselves with the ontotheological terms of any one particular discourse?

Rorty's embrace of these binary distinctions between the secular and religious in his more utopian writings complicates the issues. Further, the political implications of assuming a strict divide between a public and private self also obfuscate the problems of political ideology. John Pettegrew shares Conway's concerns by warning that Rorty's compartmentalization of the bourgeois liberal subject between a socially respectable and purely private sphere smacks of accomodationlism to the social and economic imperatives of the status quo.[118] Pettegrew further charged that Rorty's commitment to the private sphere reflects the larger "end of ideology" zeitgeist (brought into vogue during the 1980s) in which bourgeois intellectuals decided to wallow in postutopian despair and the "consumerist schizophrenia" reflected in the "hegemonic escapism" of the ironist rather than striving to revitalize revolutionary transformation. The bourgeois solution of dividing our personhood between a seemingly incompatible private libidinal self versus a socially acceptable one, is a solution born out of the larger economic and historical imperatives of advance capitalism.

Habermas also argued that it is impossible to advocate for improving social conditions without relying on discourses infused with transcendental signifiers. Without a "rational motive for expanding the circle of members," Habermas questions whether Rorty's attempt to undermine all metaphysical foundations undermines his ethics as well.[119] For Habermas, all postmodern and postfoundational discourses are dependent on the very modernist ideals they intend to replace. Rorty falls into the same trap of assuming that it is possible to "opt out of the game" of using transcendental signifiers while arguing for social hope.

Habermas counters that we should not concern ourselves categorically with religious narratives, but rather with how these narratives might contribute to supporting liberal democratic values. Habermas shocked many fellow secularists in his essay "On the Relation Between the Secular Liberal State and Religion" by arguing that liberal political philosophy can be strengthened by recovering concepts within religious narratives (e.g., all humans are all created in the image of God) that provide comprehensive doctrines for grounding human rights.[120] Habermas essentially came around to sharing Derrida's position that it is nearly impossible to maintain virtues of courage and self-sacrifice within secular liberal societies without the resources of messianic narratives.[121] Accordingly, secular liberal intellectuals should embrace "saving translations" of religious discourse in order to recover the motivational narratives needed to maintain a commitment by individual citizens to the public square.[122] Similar to Christopher Lasch's defense of hope against secular "progressive ideology," Habermas thinks liberalism is itself dependent on "prepolitical ethical convictions" that provide narratives of hope and motivation for its own survival.[123] Rorty's emphasis on modes of procedure that resist appeals to ideals or sensations that do not lend themselves to rational linguistic description may provide some useful guidelines for a liberal procedural republic, nonetheless the utopianism of achieving a pure form of secularism is not only unattainable but also violates the principle of tolerance at the heart of America's pragmatic tradition.

Similar to the boundaries between the sacred and profane within religious discourse, the boundaries between our private and public selves require negation and reaffirmation, suggesting greater levels of fluidity and contingency within the pretense of distinction making. Sacred/Profane and public/private dichotomies rely on human hopes for creating cosmos out of chaos. As mystics and ironist remind us, however, these hopes for hard distinctions melt away in the face of contingency and the infinite. Therefore, for Rorty to claim the possibility of making a hard distinction between the religious and the secular is to assume an ontological dichotomy in contradiction to his own recognition of the force of contingency and the exercise of hope through *redescriptions*.

To his credit, Rorty acknowledged toward the end of his career the mistake in categorically dismissing religion as a conversation stopper and embraced a more ecumenical pragmatism.[124] Rorty returned to the ecumenical tolerance for religious narratives found in William James and John Dewey. Rather than the dogmatism of atheism which perpetuates metaphysical assumptions of a core self by trying to purge all vestiges of religious false consciousness, Rorty went on to propose a more pragmatic distinction between affirming a "God of love" as distinct from a "God of power."[125] Additionally, Rorty agreed with critics like Wolterstorff that it is ultimately "best to keep the conversation going without citing unarguable first principles, either philosophical or religious."[126] As already noted in the introduction, in the end Rorty even went so far as to put forward his own theory of redemption and "novel-reading as a spiritual exercise."

Rorty's appeal to the teaching of literature as "spiritual exercise" for maintaining intellectual openness also applies to what Patrick Shade referred to as "habits of hope."[127] Steve Fishman's work on applying Dewey to a theory of hope is also helpful in this regard.[128] Dewey's concern to shift the meaning of "living in hope" from concerns with otherworldly salvation toward "this-worldly social reform" is where religious concerns for transcendental meaning and civil concerns for inculcating commitment to social praxis come together. "Hope—the ability to believe that the future will be unspecifiably different from, and unspecifiably freer than, the past—is the condition of growth."[129] Viewing redemptive hope narratives as an exercise for the imagination, rather than as a search for metaphysical foundations, also helps liberate religious texts and metaphors from the burden of empirical verification.[130] Drawing on Dewey's legacy, Rorty's proposal for reading secular and religious redemptive narratives for their inspirational value is another way to inculcate "habits of hope" as a "spiritual exercise" for furthering Western liberal "cultures of hope."

The combination of solidarity and hopes for generating novel discourses championed in Rorty's thought also suggests what I propose is a form of *horizontal transcendence*. To get beyond what Rorty characterizes as the ontotheological conception of "truth as a vertical relationship between representations and what is represented," horizontal transcendence is useful for characterizing the immanent and transcendental components involved in a phenomenology of hope.[131] Horizontal transcendence reflects the desire to be a part of something larger than oneself, but—instead of directing these desires for greater meaning upwards—directs them horizontally by inspiring us to look to other people as sources for hope and fulfillment. Rorty's "God of love" and proposal for redemption from "insensitivity" and the "self-satisfaction of egotism" grounds this type of horizontal transcendence in the union of hope and solidarity.[132]

Rorty's ambivalent and controversial appeal to separating the secular from the religious, however, was less relevant to his overall vision of social hope based on reconciling notions of contingency to solidarity. The hope of a social solidarity that could also make room for the contingency and ironies of avant-garde aesthetics suggests an elective affinity with Ernst Bloch's atheism and ontology of contingency. Both Bloch and Rorty were critical of religious appeals to transcendence grounded in static notions of eternal being, but nevertheless affirmed the solidarity derived from the horizontal transcendence inspired by a God of love and infinite becoming. Rorty and Bloch's atheism made it difficult for them to fully account for the transcendental nature of these ideals, yet both saw the force of contingency and becoming playing a redemptive role within history.

The relation of transcendence to utopianism and social hope also raises larger questions concerning the motivation required for stimulating solidarity. As mentioned in the introduction, once we have jettisoned the search for a fixed truth, we are nevertheless faced with the difficult task of providing narratives for what it means to stand together against the dark. Rorty provides a compelling narrative for how to imagine liberal solidarity premised on social hope. Nevertheless, his critics also make a compelling case for the limits of achieving a postmetaphysical social hope. In my last chapter I return to Buber and the challenges of redemptive hope in the twenty-first century.

CONCLUSION: BETWEEN PRAGMATIC AND MESSIANIC HOPES

> *Roman General:* Rabbi, tell me the meaning of the whole Torah while standing on one leg!
>
> *Rabbi Hillel:* Love thy neighbor as thyself, all the rest is commentary. Now go and learn.
>
> —PIRKEI AVOT

HOPE AND ENCOUNTER

Theodore Gericault's Romantic era painting *Le Radeau de la Méduse* (1816) shows a group of castaways desperately clinging to a raft in the midst of chaotic seas. The contrast between some castaways in a state of deep despair and other castaways frantically trying to hail what might be a passing ship in the far distance is a fitting image for the combination of despair and hope within Rorty's appeal to "human beings clinging together against the dark."[1]

For those who yearn for traditional metaphysical foundations, Rorty's claim that there is "no foundation except shared hope and the trust created by such sharing" is similar to being placed on a raft adrift within a tempestuous ocean.[2] Without some type of transcendental foundation, how can we be expected to navigate the chaotic challenges of life? For others, Rorty's postmetaphysical appeal to social hope is a fitting tribute to the Enlightenment's emancipatory efforts to create new discourses of autonomy and self-fashioning. Keeping with Gericault's image of precariousness mixed with hope, Nancy Frankenberry similarly analogizes the pragmatic approach to truth in the following terms: "[K]nowledge or belief is more like a *raft* than a *pyramid*. We can pull up and repair or scrap any or all the planks on the raft, although not all at once, for we must at least provisionally stand on one or another."³ Keeping with Frankenberry's metaphor, the challenge is to figure out which planks can be discarded and which planks will keep us afloat. Rorty proposes that how we answer this question will always depend on the contingency of our condition, but the important thing is to affirm the moment of solidarity that comes from realizing that we are all committed to the same task of staying afloat as we are "muddling through toward happiness as best we can."⁴

For his admirers, Rorty's privileging of hope and happiness over foundational certainty undoubtedly opened up new democratic vistas for the twenty-first century. Yet, what about Kant's concern for becoming *worthy* of our hopes and happiness? And perhaps more importantly, do we need a more elaborate shared narrative capable of binding divergent religious, ethnic, economic, regional, and religious communities together? John Rawls characterizes the dilemma in the following terms: "How is it possible that there may exist over time a stable and just society of free and equal citizens profoundly divided by reasonable though incompatible religious, philosophical, and moral doctrines?"⁵ Part of the dilemma is that, as Mittleman reminds us, liberal democratic societies cannot survive without inculcating hope in, and civic commitment to, social institutions among the citizenry at large.⁶ When Martin Luther King Jr. spoke about the importance of "infinite hope" in the "power of redemptive love" to transform society, or when Senator Obama first moved many Americans to embrace the audacity of genuine change, these narratives reached for a vision of solidarity that inclined toward what King famously referred to as the "arch of the moral universe."⁷ If these narratives of "radical hope," however, must always be reined in by concerns for "wishful idealism," then what does this mean for the future of solidarity among diverse groups of citizens within liberal democratic societies? How do we motivate and inspire citizens to take the risks involved with opening up resources to those who might be experienced as different and perhaps even threatening? Is the polytheistic toleration proposed by Rorty sufficient to sustain the flourishing of liberal democratic ideals in the twenty-first century?

Rorty may be right that we can get by without the same metaphysical foundations as our ancestors. Nevertheless, Rorty also recognized in his latter works that without larger shared narratives of hope it is impossible to achieve and secure the social solidarity needed to advance liberal democratic cultures.[8] Rorty was too reluctant, however, to elaborate on a vision for how to imagine solidarity taking root among individuals. What is missing in Rorty's turn to solidarity as an alternative foundation for social hope is a holistic account of how individuals should go about establishing the social bonds and intersubjective relationships necessary for postmetaphysical democratic liberalism to flourish. Although Rorty claimed to have given up the Enlightenment's privileging of subjectivity, he failed to provide an alternative "plank" for standing together or explanation for how social interactions can serve as a basis for social hope.[9] How are we to imagine such hopes arising? Exactly what about postmetaphysical solidarity justifies larger hopes in humanity?

There are no easy answers to these challenges. For those who share an appreciation of Rorty's neopragmatism, and yet cannot accept a purely postmetaphysical notion of hope, Buber's account of intersubjective encounters provides a much richer poetry for imagining what it means to find solidarity as we "cling against the dark" on rafts of hope. We start with an ability to say "Thou" to another person, and from these moments of mutuality come the courage and hope to reach out to others, even the stranger. "Only men who are capable of truly saying Thou to one another can truly say We with one another."[10]

According to Buber, liberalism's emphasis on laws and procedures can't fully address the profundity of human needs for the "wholeness" that comes from a cosmic sense of being located within an "all embracing structure."[11] Adumbrating Habermas's concerns, according to Buber the civil structures of bourgeois society are largely incapable of embracing "concrete persons in a concrete way" needed to sustain loyalty to the social institutions that make up the public square.[12] The modern liberal state has increased certain forms of security, but it has also contributed to a deepening of existential "homelessness."[13] Because "man is not a bundle of separate autonomous providences of the soul," the liberal "cleavage" between the public and private spheres cannot substitute for experiencing a sense of "home" within a meaningful cosmos.[14]

It is important to note, however, that Buber's political philosophy does not lend itself to a complete collapse of the public into the personal, or the sacred into the secular. Buber was pragmatic enough to acknowledge also that religious and existentialist demands that all social interactions abide by a standard of spiritual "wholeness" or "authenticity" are simply impossible, and perhaps undesirable.[15] Part of our condition is that we always have to switch between I-Thou and I-It relationships depending on our needs. Every *It* can be transformed into a *Thou*, and every *Thou* is destined to become an *It* because our needs change pragmatically in relation to our circumstances.[16] Sometimes our ability to respond to *Thou-ness* is situationally dependent on the security provided by experiences of *It-ness*. At other times, we need the depths of encounter that Buber's philosophical anthropology correctly identifies as the basic human need to feel imbricated within an "all embracing structure."

This pragmatic sensibility to seek out the middle ground also defined his views of the liberal state. "No more State than is indispensable," according to Buber, and "no less freedom than is allowable."[17] The middle path Buber forged from his selective reading of Hasidism also served as a model for his other writings on eschatological and secular redemptive narratives. Politically, sometimes we have to be satisfied with achieving, in Buber's words, "as much as one can."[18] Our twin needs for just institutions and for personal connections within the civic arena represent complementary, yet also at times antagonistic, principles of hope. Sometimes we need to be recognized by "agents of love" (Rorty), and sometimes we need the "veil of ignorance" (Rawls) that allows for unencumbered forms of justice.

For Buber, the redemptive thread running through socialist utopianism, Zionism, messianism, and even Enlightenment thinkers like Spinoza, can only be appreciated dialectically: all have something to contribute, and all become dangerous when taken to the extremes. Anticipating Rorty's appeal to contingency, Buber goes on to state: "There is no once-for-all: in each situation that demands decision the demarcation line between service and service must be drawn anew—not necessarily with fear, but necessarily with that trembling of the soul that precedes every genuine decision."[19] For Buber, our souls are trembling precisely because of the contingency involved for each individual as he or she struggles to make a decision with their entire selves to the demands of each situation. In such moments we may intuit a presence, but the decision for what prescription is merited to meet the demands of our situation, both personally and collectively, is left to us. This is not to disregard Buber's concern for what he termed the potential for relativizing within practical pragmatism. Nevertheless, Buber's affirmation that each situation demands decisions that require a "trembling of the soul" suggests a fluidity of norms that brings his views on revelation and religious law closer to pragmatism.

Buber's emphasis on the importance of intersubjective encounters and Hasidism's everyday redemption placed him on the divide between modernist conceptions of subjectivity and postmodernist critiques of metaphysics.[20] The combination of immanence and transcendence throughout all of Buber's writings on self-and-other relations makes it difficult to squarely designate his thought within either modernist or postmodernist camps. As Buber himself acknowledged, his thinking draws on metaphysical discourses while suggesting a path away from the metaphysical quest to create a correspondence with something not merely human.[21]

For scholars who see a natural affinity between Judaism and a critique of metaphysics, Buber's subjectivity is a fitting complement to postmodernist moves toward presenting Judaism—and religion in general—as a fortress of particularism against the totalizing discourses of the West's homogenizing "master narratives."[22] For other commentators, however, the suggestion of postfoundationalism in statements like "revelation is not legislation" suggested an ethical deficit within Buber's overall thinking.[23] Buber's claim that "no prescription can lead us to the encounter, and none leads from it," raises fundamental ethical concerns.[24] For example, why dignify personal experiences of ultimate presence with normative religious terms like *revelation* and not just personal epiphany?[25] If "it is not to be proved; it is only to be experienced," as Buber claims, what happens, his critics ask, when the intensity of our feelings dissipate, or we are faced with competing emotions and social goods?[26] Additionally, how do we adjudicate between our loyalties to those with whom we have had I-and-Thou encounters and our obligations to those on the farthest outskirts of our concentric circles of care?

Jewish philosophers like Emil Fackenheim were part of a chorus of critics who argued that Buber's only response to these ethical challenges was further existential and mystical statements like there is "no way other than standing in the relationship and enduring its risk."[27] But can we afford to jettison concerns for security and take the risk that enough existential and spiritual "trembling" will lead to the right convictions? Also, given the human propensity for evil, even if we have moments of encountering others as a *Thou*, is this enough to provide a sense of hope that can keep us afloat in turbulent times?

Following Fackenheim, Steven Schwarzschild similarly charged that Buber's appeal to wholeness as a standard for social relations leaves a lot of important political and social quandaries unanswered. Schwarzschild asked the same question of Buber that many asked of Rorty: "What are the criteria by which determination is to be made?"[28] If it is impossible to legislate or prescribe how intersubjective encounters should affect the public realm, what does it mean to take seriously Buber's plea for applying I-Thou relationships as a standard for social relations?

Scholem's sardonic retort to Buber that the dialogue between Cain and Abel led to murder is also a fitting reminder that our encounters with otherness can be experienced as a threat as well as a form of self-affirmation.[29] The leap in the dark required for seeing other people as a sufficient source of hope after Auschwitz and Hiroshima lends credence to Moltmann and Fackenheim's claim that redemptive hopes in one day "loving thy neighbor as thyself" have to be tied to a sense of commandment or faith in a supernatural providence.

Buber answered these types of charges, not with arguments, but with further appeals to existential reflection and trembling as the best we can do in any given situation. Echoing Rorty's veneration of contingency, Buber argued that, "community should not be made into a principle; it, too, should always satisfy a situation rather than an abstraction. The realization of community, like the realization of any idea cannot occur once and for all time: but always it must be the moment's answer to the moment's question, and nothing more."[30] If any regulative ideal bequeathed by culture and society does not confirm our "concreteness" in this "historic hour," then little good comes from appealing to formulaic imperatives, either within religious communities or within liberal society more generally.[31] The theological-political challenge essentially boils down to a standoff between prophetic hope and the quest for metaphysical certainty: either you trust the hope you experience in those genuine moments of dialogic encounter, or you don't. The rest, according to Buber, is commentary.

PRAGMATIC AND EXISTENTIAL SOLIDARITY

Buber and Rorty's shared dialogic turn to solidarity forms the basis for a fruitful comparison of their thought. The ongoing scholarly discussions around Buber's work and postmetaphysical philosophy have already furthered the conversation over Buber's dialogic philosophy and American pragmatism.[32] Buber's interest in theological discourse is nevertheless impossible to reconcile with Rorty's neopragmatic critique of transcendence. Although Buber was no neopragmatist, his emphasis on intersubjective encounters and community as the starting point for our redemptive hopes, however, provides a complementary model for exploring the tensions and correlations between these redemptive narratives. Their perspectives are brought closer by their shared conviction that the ethics of strengthening communities should always trump the desire for epistemological certainty. Critics of Buber's lack of solid metaphysical foundations for his philosophical anthropology suggests a point of continuity with Rorty's later postfoundational social hope. Buber combines, I propose, Rorty's appreciation of contingency with the existentialist and mystical sense that social relations are designed not only to provide the satisfaction of basic needs, but also to create a sense of presence between individuals. It is this sense of presence and wholeness between individuals that makes Buber's philosophical anthropology an indispensable complement to Rorty's own redemptive vision for a postmetaphysical social hope.

A shared critique of vertical transcendence provides an intersection between Buber's philosophical anthropology, the post–World War II "school of hope," and the social hope of Richard Rorty. Both Rorty and Buber suggest different approaches to identify and appreciate the role of the *transitional praxis* and *horizontal transcendence* within the phenomenology of hope. The immanent transcendence that Buber identifies with the prophetic legacy helps us view our fellow humans as comrades in the struggle for redemption. Similarly, Rorty's emphasis on the utopian initiatives of the social reformer, the intellectual entrepreneur, and in some cases, the liberal ironist, combines the transcendence of utopianism with the horizontal bonds of solidarity, respect for individual freedoms, and the importance of the imagination.

Rorty and Buber shared the conviction that what matters most is not an ability to transcend our humanity, but rather our ability to foster greater depths of hope and, by dialoguing with others, to make a better world. The depths of encounter and trust established through genuine dialogue in Buber's thought provide a foundation for messianic hope. Community is always dependent on the contingencies of our ability to address and respond to others from a position of *Thou-ness*, not our ability to penetrate through the realm of appearance to eternal being. In less spiritual terms, for Rorty, the importance of dialogue lies in the solidarity it generates through the possibility of establishing a sense of consensus and the coming together of divergent interests. What for Buber entailed a phenomenological openness to *otherness*, for Rorty entailed liberal tolerance for different perspectives. This openness defined for Rorty what it means to achieve "redemption from egotism." In one of his rare direct references to Jewish thought, Rorty cites the literary "openness" reflected in Rabbi Tarphon's famous statement from *Pirkei Avot*, "It is not necessary for you to complete the work, but neither are you free to desist from it." In contrast to the "hope for certainty" and "philosopher's desire for completeness," according to Rorty this rabbinic maxim suggest an alternative solidarity based on the renewing of self and community through the work of continuous dialogue.[33] This alternative model of redemption strives to "enlarge oneself" through open dialogue with others and the radical transformation of self made possible through new experiences and perspectives. It is this common vision for how to root our hopes for relationship and redemption in our intersubjective encounters that forms the intersection between phenomenology and social hope.

The different approaches to redemptive narratives covered in this book are not intended to sooth but rather to further illuminate the challenges of reconciling religious and secular liberal redemptive narratives within democratic cultures. Conversely, the thinkers covered in this book also help to weaken a strict divide between secular and religious redemptive narratives in the modern period.

For Rorty, religion's emphasis on the importance of personal reenchantment and poetic pursuits of the sublime serves as an alternative to the critical unmasking and skepticism of the Enlightenment tradition. Yet, Rorty's neopragmatism neuters the fervor and intensity of conviction that often comes from living a life infused with religious hopes or revolutionary politics. Rorty's pragmatic version of social hope provides the necessary boundaries for liberal democratic tolerance, while Buber's writings provide the content for reimagining the "ultimate intimacy" and "wholeness" of I-Thou encounters that can help ground social hopes in real moments of genuine intersubjective relationships. The "resigned optimism" Fromm associated with modern bourgeois society helps keep what Buber identified as the "Eros of dialogue" in check and the boundaries of individual autonomy intact.

Buber's philosophical anthropology serves as an appealing complement to some of the gaps in Rorty's neopragmatism. But Buber's mix of sociology, mysticism, and philosophy are problematic from the point of view of liberal ideals of tolerance and freedom. While demanding that our "whole beings" become actualized within everyday encounters, Buber ignored some of the problems with invoking a criterion of "wholeness" for liberal societies. Buber was simply too confident that the type of "wholeness" and "inner-transformation" he imagined will always be compatible with the secular progressive and socialist ideals he valued.

Rorty's liberalism provides a necessary prophylactic against the potential excesses of living in hope that Gershom Scholem warned about in his writings on messianic antinomianism and the dark side of the apocalyptic imagination. There is a critical distancing, a shell of cynicism within Rorty's domestication of social hope that serves to shore up individual boundaries by undercutting any messianic expectations for having the whole human being actualized within civic institutions or the public arena. Rorty's insistence on maintaining a distinction between the public and private not only protects individuals from the infringement of other people's hope, but it also helps inoculate individuals against the possible despair that can set in when our rafts of "wishful idealism" are dashed on the rocks of realism.

An overemphasis on security and ego preservation through "distancing," however, is precisely what Buber hoped we can overcome.[34] "In its highest moments dialogue reaches out even beyond these boundaries."[35] The reciprocal dynamic Buber championed provides the crucial bridge between a phenomenology of intersubjective relations and a larger vision of messianic hope. In contrast to Rorty, Buber brings his readers closer to the phenomenological texture that surrounds our encounters with others, and thus, most importantly, closer to imagining how hope can emerge from such moments of intersubjective recognition. Buber teaches us that each act of kindness, recognition, and justice on the intersubjective level generates the context of hope for believing in the eventual triumph of justice in the world. Without these intimate moments of recognition it is hard to imagine maintaining the motivation necessary to sustain broader social hopes.

Those with strong religious or communitarian affiliations often chafe at the liberal boundaries between the public and private realm precisely because it is so hard to sequester personal doctrines from broader redemptive hopes involving all of society, if not the whole world.[36] A belief that no one should go hungry because all are created in the image of the divine is hard to sequester only to the private arena. For many religiously identified individuals, their religious convictions inform the totality of their existence and they cannot artificially sever private convictions from public obligations.[37] Many of these individuals find their meaning and sense of worth not from laws that promote mutual toleration or neutrality, but from being what Michael Sandel referred to as an "encumbered self," embedded within webs of community and family often structured around narratives of salvation.[38] Additionally, Rorty's understanding of private autonomy in tension with institutionalized religion reveals a protestant bias that relies too heavily on the notion that religious identity can be contained to a set of beliefs rather than actions or rituals that must be performed in public. For many individuals the radical hope that can come from being committed to a religious identity speaks to their whole being and not just a set of beliefs.

Inculcating an appreciation for radical hope also has important existential implications that necessarily impact on the public arena. Thomas Nagel, in his essay "The Absurd," proposes that when we reflect on the totality of our lives (what he refers to as the "process as a whole") "in a million years nothing we do now will matter"—yet, we have to take certain activities seriously in order to have meaning and perform daily functions.[39] This tension between the "unavoidability of seriousness" and the "inescapability of doubt" means we are destined to "pursue our lives with varying degrees of sloth and energy." Too much reflection on the absurdity of existence, doubt, and contingency, however, can threaten the personal and social good that comes from the resoluteness of taking some things seriously. Part of being serious about one's projects is the larger existential hope of being able to look back on the larger totality of personal activities and commitments and see how all our endeavors might be linked to a larger sense of self that can make meaning out of the process as a whole. The "audacity of hope" suggests precisely this type of resoluteness to take one's self seriously in the face of the existential absurdity of our efforts with reference to our finitude. Consequently, the personal and collective value of warding off the spirals of despair brings the idealism of Obama's original soaring rhetoric on the "audacity of hope" closer to a form of civic realism.

The tension Nagel identifies between needing seriousness of convictions and moments of recognizing "the absurd" perhaps goes back to the very origin of redemptive narratives in the Bible. To return to Rabbi David Hartman's distinction between halakhic and radical hope, the Exodus narrative and revelation at Mt. Sinai offer two sources for navigating these existential challenges. According to Hartman, the Exodus model of liberating the Israelites from slavery through "divine eruption" (contra Bloch) created the historical precedent for human dependency on God's intervention.[40] Conversely, the giving of the law at Mt. Sinai "reveals divine confidence in man" based on the "belief that man has the capacity to implement right behavior in his life." Thus, according to Hartman, the covenantal model of trust and reciprocity affirms human autonomy and partnership as an essential compliment to the redemptive process.[41] Rabbi Joshua Abraham Heschel perhaps best summed up this partnership ideal given by the Mt. Sinai model when he wrote: "[T]he whole hope of messianic redemption depends on God and on man. We must help Him. And by each deed we carry out, we either retard or accelerate the coming of redemption."[42] The Mt. Sinai model affirms both human freedom and responsibility within the *telos* of creation.

Hartman's distinction between the Exodus and revelation at Mt. Sinai may illuminate Nagel's dilemma of recognizing "the absurd" while taking life seriously. In moments when despair eclipses hope, remembrance of the Exodus narrative provides an important source of comfort that redemption is not ultimately dependent on human agency and resilience. The power of a God who can liberate from slavery, who only requires obedience and faith in the promise of a redemptive past, creates a precedent of hope for the future. Conversely, a Mt. Sinai model affirms the audacity of hope that through our commitments and resoluteness we can work toward redemption. To ward off personal despair over the absurdity of human existence, the Exodus model of an all-powerful God may be an appropriate form of personal comfort, but within the civic realm the contractual model of Sinai is more amendable to a liberal procedural republic based on individual autonomy. Therefore, within the realm of civic education, the Mt. Sinai model of self-reliance, competence, and autonomy is more constructive.

EDUCATING FOR THE FUTURE OF HOPE AND DEMOCRATIC SOLIDARITY

In the end, I do not think that an intellectually honest way to reconcile competing redemptive hope narratives exists, nor that the questions raised about the role of these narratives in the public arena can be solved. Yet, education can play a crucial role in strengthening the bonds of compassion, solidarity, and courage necessary for maintaining collective and personal hope in the face of despair.[43] The realm of education is a fitting place to conclude, since both Rorty's and Buber's models for bringing together hope and solidarity looked to education as the realm best suited for continuing conversations over how best to reconcile public and private hopes.

Buber reminds us that each individual's fundamental desire to be recognized and "confirmed in his being" as a "whole person" may not be applicable as a "political principle," but certainly has a role to play within education.[44] Based on the spiritual model that each day and every encounter can become a moment for igniting sparks of messianic hope, Buber argued that formal education was best suited for incrementalist efforts at building toward I-Thou encounters.[45] Accordingly, "biblical humanistic education," when interpreted correctly, emphasizes the "fulfillment of the one in the other."[46] Learning to be present and to sympathize with the plight of others creates the grounds from which redemptive hopes grow.

But education is also essential for providing individuals with a greater sense of competence as a means for strengthening their autonomy. Within the realm of education, according to Rorty, science does a better job of addressing our needs for prediction, whereas literature—both religious and secular—has the potential to stimulate new descriptions and hopes for expanding our sense of a common *we*, creating the solidarity needed for taking on serious projects together.[47] We still need to learn about the redemptive narratives of our ancestors, not in order to predict the future, but to learn to be inspired so we can create our own narratives for how to draw the world closer to "God as love." To learn how to gain "redemption from egoism" requires both recognizing the contingency of what we have inherited, but also the courage to create new narratives of social hope for future generations.

Another way to overcome what Buber suggested is part of the idolatry of egoism is to avoid the impulse toward forcing a resolution to the dialogic process. Buber's religious existentialism and Rorty's postmetaphysical pragmatism give us different perspectives for appreciating the importance of redemptive hope narratives while also warning us of the potential idolatry that comes from assuming that any one narrative can justify trying to bring all dialogue and history to an end. Rorty may have been wrong to single out religion for ending civic dialogue, yet his concern for narratives that tend to shut down dialogue still serves as a legitimate warning against those redemptive hopes predicated on arriving at a final resting place for all discourse. Those who imagine a revolutionary overcoming of history are often all too willing to engage in apocalyptic violence. Just as we should give up the hope for finding a final resting place for thought, so too we must relinquish redemptive narratives that promise a final overcoming of all desire or end to the human quest for wholeness. Giving up on the hope for ending all narratives depends on an alternative redemptive narrative based on embracing our condition of forever becoming.

Buber warned that part of the appeal of apocalyptic thinking is that it helps to exculpate individuals from having to face up to the personal challenge of finding hope through daily interactions within the world and people around us. Following Buber, I do not believe that faith in redemption can serve as a substitute for the hard work of generating hope within everyday contexts. The task of affirming hope requires daily redemptive acts of renewing commitments, responsibility, and compassion for others. Along similar lines, Rorty warned against the metaphysical temptation to avoid the work of establishing solidarity with other fallible human beings by taking flight into metaphysical speculations. How to avoid feelings of futility and being overwhelmed by the immensity of the challenges we face and take the task of inspiring hope in others seriously can only be answered by each individual as they stumble through life. Given the economic and ecological challenges ahead, an ability to address these concerns together may be our best source of hope. Thus, to engage in the phenomenology of hope is to wrestle with the hourly task of overcoming despair and fear by striving to see other people as possible sources of hope: to affirm that we are not alone as we stand against the dark and stumble toward greater fulfillment, never to be fully realized, but also never to be abandoned, for ourselves and future generations.

NOTES

INTRODUCTION

1. See Russell Jacoby, *The End of Utopia: Politics and Culture in an Age of Apathy* (New York: Basic Books, 1999) and *Picture Imperfect: Utopian Thought for an Anti-Utopian Age* (New York: Columbia University Press, 2005).

2. See Roger D. Hodge, *The Mendacity of Hope: Barack Obama and the Betrayal of American Liberalism* (New York: HarperCollins, 2010); Charles R. Kesler, *I Am the Change: Barack Obama and the Crisis of Liberalism* (New York: HarperCollins, 2012); Henry A. Giroux, *Politics After Hope: Obama and the Crisis of Youth, Race and Democracy* (St. Paul, MN: Paradigm Publishers, 2010); and Vincent Harding, *Hope and History: Why We Must Share the Story of the Movement* (Maryknoll, NY: Orbis Books, 2010).

3. See Joanna Macy and Chris Johnstone, *Active Hope: How to Face the Mess We're in without Going Crazy* (Novato, CA: New World Library, 2012). As ecologists Macy and Johnstone warn: "We can no longer take it for granted even that our civilization will survive or that conditions on our planet will remain hospitable for complex forms of life" (ibid., 1). See also Daniel Innerarity, *The Future and Its Enemies: In Defense of Political Hope* (Stanford, CA: Stanford University Press, 2012).

4. Richard Rorty, *Consequences of Pragmatism: Essays, 1972–1980* (Minneapolis: University of Minnesota Press, 1982), 166.

5. I am indebted to the following texts for informing my use of the term *transcendence*: Regina Schwartz, *Transcendence: Philosophy, Literature, and Theology Approach the Beyond* (New York: Routledge, 2004); James E. Faulconer, *Transcendence in Philosophy and Religion* (Bloomington: Indiana University Press, 2003); and Alan M. Olson, *Transcendence and the Sacred* (Notre Dame, IN: University of Notre Dame Press, 1994).

6. For further discussion of the relationship between Rorty's neopragmatism and pragmatism, see Cornel West, "The Politics of American Neo-Pragmatism," in

Post-Analytic Philosophy, ed. John Rajchman and Cornel West, 266–267 (New York: Columbia University Press, 1985) and *The American Evasion of Philosophy* (Madison: University of Wisconsin Press, 1989), 203. See also Charley D. Hardwick and Donald A. Crosby, *Pragmatism, Neo-Pragmatism, and Religion: Conversations with Richard Rorty* (New York: Peter Lang, 1997).

7. Gabriel Marcel, *The Philosophy of Existentialism* (New York: Citadel Press, 1962), 32.

8. See Martin Luther King Jr., "Pilgrimage to Nonviolence," in *Strength to Love* (Minneapolis, MN: Fortress Press, 1981), 153.

9. Richard Rorty, *Philosophy and Social Hope* (New York: Penguin Books, 1999), 120.

10. Richard Rorty, *Contingency, Irony, and Solidarity* (Cambridge: Cambridge University Press, 1989), 176.

11. Emmanuel Levinas, *Existence and Existents* (Pittsburgh: Duquesne University Press, 1978), 93.

12. For the distinction between restorative versus utopian models of redemptive hope, see Gershom Scholem, *The Messianic Idea in Judaism and Other Essays on Jewish Spirituality* (New York: Schocken Books, 1980), 3.

13. See Mordecai Kaplan, "The Belief in God," chap. 10 in *The Future of the American Jew* (New York: Reconstructionist Press, 1967). For more on Kaplan and redemptive hope, see my "Otherness and Liberal Democratic Solidarity: Buber, Kaplan, Levinas and Rorty's Social Hope," in *Thinking Jewish Culture in America*, ed. Ken Koltun-Fromm, 31–70 (Lanham, MD: Lexington Books, 2013).

14. Peter L. Berger, *The Sacred Canopy: Elements of a Sociological Theory of Religion* (New York: Anchor Books, 1990), 114.

15. Midrash in Shemot Rabbah, on Parashat Yitro.

16. For further discussion on hope and psychology, see Jerome E. Groopman, *The Anatomy of Hope: How People Prevail in the Face of Illness* (New York: Random House, 2004); Anthony Scioli and Henry Biller, *Hope in the Age of Anxiety* (New York: Oxford University Press, 2009); and C. R. Snyder, *Psychology of Hope: You Can Get Here from There* (New York: Free Press, 2003).

17. See James L. Muyskens, "The Phenomenology of Hope," in *The Sufficiency of Hope: Conceptual Foundations of Religion* (Philadelphia: Temple University Press, 1979), 20–36.

18. Martin Jay, *Songs of Experience: Modern American and European Variations on a Universal Theme* (Berkeley: University of California Press, 2005), 4.

19. J. P. Day, "Hope," *American Philosophical Quarterly* 6, no. 2 (1969): 89.

20. Adrienne Martin, *How We Hope: A Moral Psychology* (Princeton, NJ: Princeton University Press, 2014), 11.

21. Ibid., 69.

22. Joseph Godfrey, *A Philosophy of Human Hope: Studies in Philosophy and Religion* (Boston, MA: Academic Publishers, 1987), 55.

23. Ibid., 30.

24. David Hartman, "Sinai and Exodus: Two Grounds for Hope in the Jewish Tradition," *Religious Studies* 14, no. 3 (September 1978): 373.

25. See Arthur Cohen, "Redemption," in *Contemporary Jewish Religious Thought*, ed. Cohen and Paul Mendes-Flohr (New York: Free Press, 1988), 417–422.

26. See Alan Mittleman, *Hope in a Democratic Age* (New York: Oxford University Press, 2009), 7; David Novak, "Jewish Eschatology," in *The Oxford Handbook of Eschatology*, ed. Jerry Walls (New York: Oxford University Press, 2008), 114; and Jacob Taubes, *Occidental Eschatology*, trans. David Ratmoko (Stanford, CA: Stanford University Press, 2009).

27. For further discussion of the rise of secular utopianism, see Edward Rothstein, Herbert Muschamp, and Martin Marty, *Visions of Utopia* (New York: Oxford University Press, 2003); John Gray, *Black Mass: Apocalyptic Religion and the Death of Utopia* (New York: Macmillan, 2008); Susan Buck-Morss, *Dreamworld and Catastrophe: The Passing of Mass Utopia in East and West* (Cambridge, MA: MIT Press, 2002); Karl Mannheim, *Ideology and Utopia: An Introduction to the Sociology of Knowledge* (New York: Houghton Mifflin Harcourt, 1985); and Marcel Gauchet, *The Disenchantment of the World: A Political History of Religion* (Princeton, NJ: Princeton University Press, 1997).

28. See Mark Lilla, *The Stillborn God: Religion, Politics, and the Modern West* (New York: Random House, 2008); James M. Byrne, *Religion and the Enlightenment: From Descartes to Kant* (Louisville, KY: Westminster John Knox Press, 1997); and Peter Gay, *The Enlightenment: An Interpretation* (New York: Norton, 1977).

29. See Reinhold Niebuhr, "Optimism, Pessimism, and Religious Faith," in *The Essential Reinhold Niebuhr: Selected Essays and Addresses*, ed. R. McAfee Brown (New Haven, CT: Yale University Press, 1986), 12.

30. See Cornel West, *Restoring Hope: Conversations on the Future of Black America* (Boston, MA: Beacon Press, 1999), xii. In the words of West: "Optimism adopts the role of the spectator who surveys the evidence in order to infer that things are going to get better. Yet we know that the evidence does not look good.... Hope enacts the stance of the participant who actively struggles against the evidence in order to change the deadly tides of wealth inequality, group xenophobia, and personal despair. Only a new wave of vision, courage, and hope can keep us sane.... To live is to wrestle with despair yet never to allow despair to have the last word" (ibid.).

31. Muyskens, *Sufficiency of Hope*, 25.

32. See Jonathan Lear, *Radical Hope: Ethics in the Face of Cultural Devastation* (Cambridge, MA: Harvard University Press, 2009), 104.

33. Martin, *How We Hope*, 106.

34. See Bart Schultz, "Obama's Political Philosophy: Pragmatism, Politics, and the University of Chicago," *Philosophy of the Social Sciences* 39, no. 2 (2009): 127–173.

35. Judith Butler, Jürgen Habermas, Charles Taylor, and Cornel West, *The Power of Religion in the Public Sphere*, ed. Eduardo Mendieta and Jonathan Van Antwerpen (New York: Columbia University Press, 2011), 100. See also Roger D. Hodge, *The Mendacity of Hope: Barack Obama and the Betrayal of American Liberalism* (New York: HarperCollins, 2010).

36. See Cornel West, "Last Words on the Black Prophetic Tradition in the Age of Obama," in *Black Prophetic Fire* (Boston, MA: Beacon Press, 2014), 161–165.

37. Barack Obama, *The Audacity of Hope: Thoughts on Reclaiming the American Dream* (Newe York: Crown, 2006), 356–357.

38. Barack Obama, "Remarks at a Victory Celebration in Chicago, Illinois," November 7, 2012, www.gpo.gov/fdsys/pkg/DCPD-201200873/pdf/DCPD-201200873.pdf.

39. Ibid.; emphasis added.

40. Muyskens, *Sufficiency of Hope*, 41.

41. Ibid., 137.

42. Ibid., 100.

43. See Day, "Hope," 90. According to Day, "hope involves emotion," but does not necessarily count as an emotion itself.

44. Godfrey, *A Philosophy of Human Hope*, 180.

45. Martin, *How We Hope*, 141.

46. For more on Strauss's interpretation of Plato's "noble lie," see Martin Jay, *The Virtues of Mendacity: On Lying in Politics* (Charlottesville: University of Virginia Press, 2012) and Peter Minowitz, *Straussophobia: Defending Leo Strauss and Straussians against Shadia Drury and Other Accusers* (Lanham, MD: Lexington Books, 2009).

47. Butler et al., *Power of Religion in the Public Sphere*, 14.

48. For further discussion of the challenges of reconciling religious redemptive narratives with liberal democratic cultures, see Richard Landes, *Heaven On Earth: The Varieties of the Millennial Experience* (New York: Oxford University Press, 2011) and Tzvetan Todorov, *Hope and Memory: Lessons from the Twentieth Century* (Princeton, NJ: Princeton University Press, 2003).

49. For many nineteenth- and early twentieth-century Jewish intellectuals, viewing the legacy of Jerusalem as perennially distinct from the legacy of Athens was a central component of self-understanding. Nevertheless, although I draw on the history of this dichotomizing, I would not want readers to assume that I am endorsing the lack of nuance or fluidity reflected in the sharp distinctions between a mythologized Athens and Jerusalem. Recent scholarship has helped to problematize and contextualize why these categories are inadequate for capturing the full

complexity of the very discourses and communities they purport to represent. For further discussion, see Elliot Wolfson, *Giving Beyond the Gift: Apophasis and Overcoming Theomania* (New York: Fordham University Press, 2014); Martin Kavka, *Jewish Messianism and the History of Philosophy* (Cambridge: Cambridge University Press, 2004); Jonathan A. Jacobs, *Judaic Sources and Western Thought: Jerusalem's Enduring Presence* (New York: Oxford University Press, 2011) and *New Directions in Jewish Philosophy* (Bloomington: Indiana University Press, 2010); Leora Batnitzky, *How Judaism Became a Religion: An Introduction to Modern Jewish Thought* (Princeton, NJ: Princeton University Press, 2011); Willi Goetschel, *The Discipline of Philosophy and the Invention of Modern Jewish Thought* (New York: Fordham University Press, 2013); Gillian Rose, *Judaism and Modernity: Philosophical Essays* (Hoboken, NJ: Blackwell, 1993); and Kenneth Seeskin, *Jewish Philosophy in a Secular Age* (Albany: State University of New York Press, 1990).

50. See J. W. Burrow, *The Crisis of Reason: European Thought, 1848-1914* (New Haven, CT: Yale University Press, 2002) and Ariel Roshwald, *The Endurance of Nationalism: Ancient Roots and Modern Dilemmas* (Cambridge: Cambridge University Press, 2006).

51. See George L. Mosse, *German Jews Beyond Judaism* (Bloomington: Indiana University Press, 1985); Jehuda Reinharz and Walter Schatzberg, *The Jewish Response to German Culture: From the Enlightenment to the Second World War* (Lebanon, NH: University Press of New England, 1985); George L. Mosse, *Confronting the Nation: Jewish and Western Nationalism* (Lebanon, NH: Brandeis University Press, 1993); Zygmunt Bauman, *Modernity and the Holocaust* (Ithaca, NY: Cornell University Press, 2001); David G. Roskies, *Against the Apocalypse: Responses to Catastrophe in Modern Jewish Culture* (Syracuse, NY: Syracuse University Press, 1999); Henning Tewes and Jonathan Wright, *Liberalism, Anti-Semitism, and Democracy: Essays in Honour of Peter Pulzer* (New York: Oxford University Press, 2001); and Michael Löwy, *Redemption and Utopia: Jewish Libertarian Thought in Central Europe: A Study in Elective Affinity* (London: Athlone Press, 1992).

52. Martin Buber, *Israel and the World: Essays in a Time of Crisis* (Syracuse, NY: Syracuse University Press, 1997), 102.

53. See Neil Gross, *Richard Rorty: The Making of an American Philosophy* (Chicago: University of Chicago Press, 2008); Judith M. Green, *Pragmatism and Social Hope: Deepening Democracy in Global Contexts* (New York: Columbia University Press, 2008); and Colin Koopman, *Pragmatism as Transition: Historicity and Hope in James, Dewey, and Rorty* (New York: Columbia University Press, 2009).

54. Walter H. Capps, *The Future of Hope: Essays by Bloch, Fackenheim, Moltmann, Metz, Capps* (Minneapolis, MN: Fortress Press, 1970), 93. For further discussion on the theology of hope movement, see Godfrey, *A Philosophy of Human Hope*. See also Miroslav Volf and William H. Katerberg, eds. *The Future of Hope:*

Christian Tradition Amid Modernity and Postmodernity (Grand Rapids, MI: William B. Eerdmans, 2004).

55. Capps, *Future of Hope*, 14.

56. Ibid., 75.

57. See Richard Rorty, *An Ethics for Today: Finding Common Ground between Philosophy and Religion* (New York: Columbia University Press, 2010). Rorty states: "The notion of redemption presupposes a distinction between the lower, mortal, animal parts of the soul, and the higher, spiritual, immortal part. Redemption is what would occur when the higher finally triumphs over the lower, when reason conquers passion, or when grace defeats sin. In much of the ontotheological tradition, the lower-higher distinction is construed as a distinction between the part that is content with finitude and the part that yearns for the infinite" (ibid., 13).

58. See Rorty, "Redemption from Egotism: James and Proust as Spiritual Exercises," in *The Rorty Reader*, ed. Christopher J. Voparil and Richard J. Bernstein (Hoboken, NJ: Wiley-Blackwell, 2010), 389.

59. Ibid., 405.

60. For further discussion of the relationship between Judaism and postmodernism, see Steven Kepnes, *Interpreting Judaism in a Postmodern Age* (New York: New York University Press, 1995) and *Reasoning after Revelation: Dialogues in Postmodern Jewish Philosophy* (New York: Westview Press, 2001); Jeffrey Bloechl, *Religious Experience and the End of Metaphysics* (Bloomington: Indiana University Press, 2003); Eugene B. Borowitz, *Our Way to a Postmodern Judaism: Three Lectures* (San Francisco: University of San Francisco, 1993); Susan A. Handelman, *The Slayers of Moses* (Albany: State University of New York Press, 1983); and Edith Wyschogrod, *Saints and Postmodernism: Revisioning Moral Philosophy* (Chicago: University of Chicago Press, 1990).

61. For more on Buber as an edifying philosopher, see Laurence J. Silberstein, *Martin Buber's Social and Religious Thought: Alienation and the Quest for Meaning* (New York: New York University Press, 1989), 19. See also Paul Mendes-Flohr, *Martin Buber: A Contemporary Perspective* (Syracuse, NY: Syracuse University Press, 2002), 8.

1. REDEMPTIVE HOPE AND THE CUNNING OF HISTORY

1. For further discussion, see Heinrich Graetz, "The Stages in the Evolution of Messianic Belief," in *The Structure of Jewish History and Other Essays* (Jersey City, NJ: Ktav Publishing House, 1975), 72–73; and Hermann Cohen, "The Social Idea as Seen by Plato and by the Prophets," in *Reason and Hope: Sections from the Jewish Writings of Hermann Cohen* (Cincinnati, OH: Hebrew Union College, 1993), 66–77.

2. Saint Augustine, *The City of God*, trans. by Marcus Dods (New York: Modern Library, 1993).

3. Karl Barth, *The Epistle to the Romans*, trans. Edwyn Clement Hoskyns (New York: Oxford University Press, 1950), 157.

4. Saint Augustine, *City of God*, 698–699.

5. See Thomas Aquinas, *Summa Theologiae: A Concise Translation* (Allen, TX: Christian Classics, 1991). In Aquinas's words: "Hope is a virtue, we said, because it embraces the highest standard of human behavior: embraces God as the primary agency on which it relies and the ultimate goal in which it seeks happiness. Having God as object in this way defines it as a theological virtue" (ibid., 345).

6. Aquinas writes: "The virtue of hope has as its ultimate goal eternal happiness, and the primary agency on which it relies is God's help" (ibid., 344).

7. Ibid., 346.

8. Aquinas states: "What is impossible can't be hoped for . . . in relation to what we hope for, we must strike a balance between presuming to achieve inappropriate things and despairing of not achieving even what is appropriate" (ibid., 345).

9. Mittleman, *Hope in a Democratic Age*, 51.

10. For further discussion of Aquinas's philosophy of hope, see Muyskens, *Sufficiency of Hope*; Godfrey, *Philosophy of Human Hope*; and Mittleman, *Hope in a Democratic Age*.

11. For further comparative analysis on hope in Aquinas and Albo, see Mittleman, "The Virtue of Hope," chap. 2 in *Hope in a Democratic Age*. For more on medieval Jewish approaches to redemption, see Menachem Lorberbaum, *Politics and the Limits of Law: Secularizing the Political in Medieval Jewish Thought* (Stanford, CA: Stanford University Press, 2001). See also Joseph Sarachek, *The Doctrine of the Messiah in Medieval Jewish Literature* (New York: Hermon Press, 1968).

12. In his *Mishneh Torah* Maimonides states: "Let no one think that in the Days of the Messiah anything of the natural course of the world will cease or that any innovation will be introduced into creation. Rather, the world will continue in its accustomed course. The words of Isaiah: 'The wolf shall dwell with the lamb and the panther shall lie down with the kid' (Isaiah 11:6), are a parable and an allegory which must be understood to mean that Israel will dwell securely even among the wicked of the heathen nations who are compared to a wolf and a panther. For they will accept the true faith and will no longer rob or destroy. Likewise, all similar scriptural passages dealing with the Messiah must be regarded as figurative. Only in the Days of the Messiah will everyone know what the metaphors mean and to what they refer. The sages said: 'The only difference between this world and the Days of the Messiah is the subjection of Israel to the nations'[Sanhedrin 91b]" (quoted in Scholem, *Messianic Idea in Judaism*, 28–29).

For Maimonides, one of the most important hallmarks of redemption will be political changes regarding Israel's subjugation to other nations. Menachem Lorberbaum points out that there is a distinction within Maimonides's thought between his views on the future messianic polity, in which political power remains the main determinant, and his more utopian speculations in his *Guide for the Perplexed*, in which the quest for divine perfection supersedes the political. This might suggest a form of human transformation does in fact occur within the messianic age. See Lorberbaum, *Politics and the Limits of Law*, 78.

13. As Maimonides states in his *Mishneh Torah*: "In that [messianic] era there will be neither famine nor war, neither jealousy nor strife. Blessings will be abundant, comforts within the reach of all. The one preoccupation of the whole world will be to know the Lord. Hence Israelites will be very wise, they will know the things that are now concealed and will attain an understanding of their Creator to the utmost capacity of the human mind, as it is written: 'For the earth shall be full of the knowledge of the Lord, as the waters cover the sea' (Isaiah 11:9)" (quoted in Lorberbaum, *Politics and the Limits of Law*, 85).

14. See Ephraim Urbach, *The Sages: Their Concepts and Beliefs* (Cambridge, MA: Harvard University Press, 1979).

15. For more on messianic redemption as a moment of rupture versus gradual transformation, see David Hartman, "Learning to Hope," chap. 7 in *From Defender to Critic: The Search for a New Jewish Self* (Woodstock, VT: Jewish Lights Publishing, 2012). For further discussion of rabbinic concerns to restrain messianic enthusiasm, see Michael Wyschogrod, *The Body of Faith: God and the People Israel* (New York: Rowman and Littlefield Publishers, 1996), 255.

16. See Scholem, *Messianic Idea in Judaism*, 35–36.

17. For more on Maimonides's antiapocalyptic views on messianism, see Scholem, "Toward an Understanding of the Messianic Idea in Judaism," chap. 1 in *Messianic Idea in Judaism*.

18. See Jonathan Lear, "Radical Hope versus Mere Optimism," in *Radical Hope: Ethics in the Face of Cultural Devastation* (Cambridge, MA: Harvard University Press, 2009), 113. See also Patrick Shade, *Habits of Hope: A Pragmatic Theory* (Nashville, TN: Vanderbilt University Press, 2001), 139; and Jeffrey Stout, *Flight from Authority: Religion, Morality, and the Quest for Autonomy* (Notre Dame, IN: University of Notre Dame, 1987).

19. For more on the transformation of religious ideas during the Enlightenment period, see Jonathan I. Israel, *Enlightenment Contested: Philosophy, Modernity, and the Emancipation of Man 1670–1752* (New York: Oxford University Press, 2006); Terry Eagleton, *Culture and the Death of God* (New Haven, CT: Yale University Press, 2014); David Sorkin, *The Religious Enlightenment: Protestants, Jews, and Catholics from London to Vienna* (Princeton, NJ: Princeton University Press, 2008); Ernst Cassirer, *The Philosophy of the Enlightenment* (Princeton, NJ: Princeton University Press, 1951); Byrne, *Religion and the Enlightenment*; and Gay, *Enlightenment*.

20. For more on Spinoza's political philosophy, see Leo Strauss, *Spinoza's Critique of Religion* (New York: Schocken Books, 1965); Steven B. Smith, *Spinoza*,

Liberalism, and the Question of Jewish Identity (New Haven, CT: Yale University Press, 1998); Yirmiyahu Yovel, *Spinoza and Other Heretics*, vol. 1 (Princeton, NJ: Princeton University Press, 1992); Étienne Balibar and Warren Montag, *Spinoza and Politics,* trans. Peter Snowdon (Brooklyn, NY: Verso, 2008); J. Samuel Preus, *Spinoza and the Irrelevance of Biblical Authority* (Cambridge: Cambridge University Press, 2001); and Susan James, *Spinoza on Philosophy, Religion, and Politics: The Theologico-Political Treatise* (New York: Oxford University Press, 2012).

21. See Richard Mason, *The God of Spinoza: A Philosophical Study* (Cambridge: Cambridge University Press, 1999); Rebecca Goldstein, *Betraying Spinoza: The Renegade Jew Who Gave Us Modernity* (New York: Schocken, 2006); and Steven Nadler, *Spinoza's Heresy: Immortality and the Jewish Mind* (New York: Oxford University Press, 2001).

22. For a compelling critique of Spinoza's equation of hope with desire, see Gabriel Marcel, "Desire and Hope," in *Readings in Existential Phenomenology*, ed. Nathaniel Morris Lawrence and Daniel Denis O'Connor (Englewood Cliffs, NJ: Prentice-Hall, 1967), 277–285. For a more pragmatic critique of Spinoza on hope, see Isaiah Berlin, "From Hope and Fear Set Free," in *The Proper Study of Mankind: An Anthology of Essays*, ed. Henry Hardy and Roger Hausheer (London: Chatto and Windus, 1997), 91–118. For further discussion of Spinoza's critique of hope in relation to Nietzsche and Freud, see Paul Ricoeur, "Freedom in the Light of Hope," in *The Conflict of Interpretations: Essays in Hermeneutics* (Evanston, IL: Northwestern University Press, 1974), 408.

23. Spinoza, *Ethics*: part 4, Proposition 47. For more on Spinoza's critique of hope in the Ethics see Steven Nadler, *A Book Forged in Hell: Spinoza's Scandalous Treatise and the Birth of the Secular Age* (Princeton, NJ: Princeton University Press, 2011).

24. Benedictus de Spinoza, *A Theologico-Political Treatise and a Political Treatise* (New York: Dover, 1951), 3.

25. For more on Spinoza's critique of religious hope, see Emil Fackenheim, *Encounters between Judaism and Modern Philosophy: A Preface to Future Jewish Thought* (New York: Basic Books, 1973); Stuart Hampshire, *Spinoza and Spinozism* (New York: Oxford University Press, 2005); and Preus, *Irrelevance of Biblical Authority*.

26. See Leo Strauss, *Jewish Philosophy and the Crisis of Modernity: Essays and Lectures in Modern Jewish Thought*, ed. Kenneth Hart Green (Albany: State University of New York Press, 1997). Strauss summed up Spinoza's position in the following terms: "The philosopher lives in a state above fear and trembling as well as above hope . . . whereas biblical man lives in fear and trembling as well as in hope" (ibid., 109).

27. Moses Mendelssohn, *Jerusalem: Or on Religious Power and Judaism*, ed. Alexander Altmann (Lebanon, NH: Brandeis University Press, 1983), 43. See also

Allan Arkush, *Moses Mendelssohn and the Enlightenment* (Albany: State University of New York Press, 1994); Shmuel Feiner, *The Jewish Enlightenment* (Philadelphia: University of Pennsylvania Press, 2002); David Sorkin, *The Transformation of German Jewry 1780–1840* (New York: Oxford University Press, 1987); Jeffrey S. Librett, *The Rhetoric of Cultural Dialogue: Jews and Germans from Moses Mendelssohn to Richard Wagner and Beyond*, Cultural Memory in the Present (Stanford, CA: Stanford University Press, 2000); Alexander Altmann, "Moses Mendelssohn as Archetypal German Jew," in Reinharz and Schatzberg, *The Jewish Response to German Culture*, 17–31; and Michah Gottlieb, *Faith and Freedom: Moses Mendelssohn's Theological-Political Thought* (New York: Oxford University Press, 2011).

28. See Amir Eshel, "Cosmopolitanism and Searching for the Sacred Space in Jewish Literature," *Jewish Social Studies* 9, no. 3 (Spring/Summer 2003): 121–38. Eshel points out that Mendelssohn's intention of writing Jerusalem was in part born out of the dialectics throughout Jewish history between what Eshel identifies as the polarities of cosmos versus *makom* (sacred space). According to Eshel, Mendelssohn sought the "liberation of the idea of Jerusalem from the city's actual locus" as part of his overall endeavor to present a Judaism that could serve as vanguard for Enlightenment ideals. See also Leora Batnitzky, *Idolatry and Representation* (Princeton, NJ: Princeton University Press, 2000) and Gideon Freudenthal, *No Religion without Idolatry: Mendelssohn's Jewish Enlightenment* (Notre Dame, IN: University of Notre Dame, 2012).

29. Mendelssohn, *Jerusalem*, 132.

30. See Moses Mendelssohn, "The Right to Be Different (1783)," in *The Jew in the Modern World: A Documentary History*, ed. Paul Mendes-Flohr and Jehuda Reinharz (New York: Oxford University Press, 1995), 68–69. As Mendelssohn states: "Let everyone be permitted to speak as he thinks, to invoke God after his own manner or that of his fathers, and to seek eternal salvation where he thinks he may find it, as long as he does not disturb public felicity and acts honestly toward the civil laws, toward you and his fellow citizens. Let no one in your states be a search of hearts and a judge of thoughts.... If we render unto Caesar what is Caesar's, then do you yourselves render unto God what is God's! Love truth! Love peace!" (ibid., 69).

31. See Rorty, *Contingency, Irony, and Solidarity*, 30. See also Rorty, *Consequences of Pragmatism*, 146.

32. See Curtis H. Peters, *Kant's Philosophy of Hope* (New York: Peter Lang, 1993) and Godfrey, *A Philosophy of Human Hope*, 243. See also Christopher McCammon, "Overcoming Deism: Hope incarnate in Kant's Rational Religion," in *Kant and the New Philosophy of Religion*, ed. Chris L. Firestone and Stephen Palmquist (Bloomington: Indiana University Press, 2006), 79–89.

33. Immanuel Kant, *Critique of Pure Reason*, in *The Cambridge Edition of the Works of Immanuel Kant*, ed. Paul Guyer and Allen W. Wood (Cambridge: Cam-

bridge University Press, 1998), A 805/B 833. See also Allen W. Wood, *Kant's Moral Religion* (Ithaca, NY: Cornell University Press, 1970); Philip J. Rossi and Michael J. Wreen, *Kant's Philosophy of Religion Reconsidered* (Bloomington: Indiana University Press, 1991); Yirmiyahu Yovel, *Kant's Practical Philosophy Reconsidered* (New York: Springer, 1989) and *Kant and the Philosophy of History* (Princeton, NJ: Princeton University Press, 1980); and Matthew Alun Ray, *Subjectivity and Irreligion: Atheism and Agnosticism in Kant, Schopenhauer, and Nietzsche* (Surry, UK: Ashgate Publishing, 2004).

34. See Paul Ricoeur, "Hope and the Structure of Philosophical Systems," in *Figuring the Sacred: Religion, Narrative, and Imagination*, ed. Mark I. Wallace (Minneapolis: Fortress Press, 1995). Ricoeur sums up Kant's position in the *Critique* as moving toward an existentialist demand that between "hope and absolute knowledge we have to choose. We cannot have both" (212). See also Ricoeur, "Freedom in the Light of Hope," in *The Conflict of Interpretations*, 402–424.

35. Kant, *Critique of Pure Reason*, A 805/B 833.

36. Ibid.

37. Ibid.

38. Ibid., A 811/B 839. For further commentary on Kant's correlation of hope with rational morality, see Jürgen Moltmann, *Theology of Hope: On the Ground and the Implications of a Christian Eschatology* (London: SCM Press, 2002), 48.

39. Kant, *Critique of Pure Reason*, A 809/B 837.

40. See Peters, *Kant's Philosophy of Hope*, 32.

41. In his book on *Religion* Kant argued that the "reasonable grounds for hope" is found in an afterlife where we can continue to pursue the "goal of perfection." Immanuel Kant, *Religion within the Boundaries of Mere Reason*, ed. Allen W. Wood and George di Giovanni (Cambridge: Cambridge University Press, 1998), 86.

42. Kant states: "Thus without a God and a world that is now not visible to us but is hoped for, the majestic ideas of morality are, to be sure, objects of approbation and admiration but not incentives for resolve and realization, because they would not fulfill the whole end that is natural for every rational being and determined a priori and necessarily through the very same pure reason" (*Critique of Pure Reason*, A 813/B 841).

43. Martin, *How We Hope*, 106.

44. Immanuel Kant, *Critique of Practical Reason* (New York: Cambridge University Press, 1997), 5:124.

45. Kant, *Religion*, 6:68.

46. Ibid., 6:100.

47. Kant, *Critique of Practical Reason*, 5:125.

48. Kant, *Religion*, 6:32.

49. Ibid., 6:68.

50. Ibid., 6:34. For further discussion of Kant's chiliastic views, see Jürgen Moltmann, "Progress and Abyss: Remembrances of the Future of the Modern World," in Volf and Katerberg, *Future of Hope*, 10–11.

51. See Allen W. Wood, *Kant's Ethical Thought* (Cambridge: Cambridge University Press, 1999), 297.

52. For more on Kant's philosophy of hope and radical evil, see Martin Beck Matustik, *Radical Evil and the Scarcity of Hope* (Bloomington: Indiana University Press, 2008).

53. For more on Kant's rationalization of religion, see Nathan Rotenstreich, *Jewish Philosophy in Modern Times: From Mendelssohn to Rosenzweig* (New York: Holt, Rinehart, and Winston, 1968), 8.

54. For more on Kant's views of Judaism, see Fackenheim, *Encounters between Judaism and Modern Philosophy*; Paul Lawrence Rose, *German Question/Jewish Question: Revolutionary Antisemitism from Kant to Wagner* (Princeton, NJ: Princeton University Press, 1992); Arnold M. Eisen, *Rethinking Modern Judaism: Ritual, Commandment, Community* (Chicago: University of Chicago Press, 1998); F. Tomasoni, *Modernity and the Final Aim of History: The Debate over Judaism from Kant to the Young Hegelians* (New York: Springer, 2003); and Yovel, *Kant and the Philosophy of History*.

55. Karl Mannheim, *Ideology and Utopia*, 219. See also Hans Jonas, "Utopia and the Idea of Progress," in *The Imperative of Responsibility: In Search of an Ethics for the Technological Age* (Chicago: University of Chicago Press, 1984), 160–177.

56. Strauss, *Jewish Philosophy*, 82.

57. See Moltmann, "Progress and Abyss," 11.

58. Capps, *Future of Hope*, 110.

59. See Isaiah Berlin, *Political Ideas in the Romantic Age: Their Rise and Influence on Modern Thought* (Princeton, NJ: Princeton University Press, 2006).

60. Ernst Bloch, *The Principle of Hope* (Cambridge: MIT Press, 1986), 1:3. For more on the development of a hermeneutics of suspicion, see Paul Ricoeur, "The Critique of Religion," in *The Philosophy of Paul Ricoeur*, ed. Charles E. Reagan and David Stewart (Boston, MA: Beacon Press, 1978), 214. See also Gauchet, *Disenchantment of the World*.

61. Ludwig Feuerbach, *The Essence of Christianity* (Amherst, NY: Prometheus Books, 1989), 247–248. For more on Feuerbach's critique of religion in relation to the hermeneutics of suspicion, see Van A. Harvey, *Feuerbach and the Interpretation of Religion* (Cambridge: Cambridge University Press, 1997).

62. Robert C. Tucker, *The Marx-Engels Reader*, 2nd ed. (New York: W.W. Norton), 54.

63. Berger, *Sacred Canopy*, 90.

64. Tucker, *Marx-Engels Reader*, 54.

65. Friedrich Nietzsche, "The Antichrist," in *The Portable Nietzsche*, ed. and trans. by Walter Kaufman (New York: Penguin Books, 1976), 591.

66. Strauss, *Jewish Philosophy*, 99. See also Mittleman, *Hope in a Democratic Age*, 107.

67. Marcel states: "It remains true, nevertheless, that the correlation of hope and despair subsists until the end; they seem to me inseparable. I mean that while the structure of the world we live in permits—and may even seem to counsel—absolute despair, yet it is only such a world that can give rise to unconquerable hope. If only for this reason, we cannot be sufficiently thankful to the great pessimists in this history of thought . . . they have prepared our minds to understand that despair can be what it was for Nietzsche . . . the springboard to the loftiest affirmation" (*Philosophy of Existentialism*, 28).

68. Jonas, *Imperative of Responsibility*, 16.

69. John Gray, *Black Mass*, 24.

70. According to Strauss: "A religious man who is sure on the basis of divine revelation that this will be the future, namely, that the messianic age will come, then he is consistent if he believes in the face of all evidence to the contrary. But someone who bases his hopes not on divine revelation must show some human grounds for it. And I think you cannot show any" (*Jewish Philosophy and the Crises of Modernity*, 333).

71. See Isaiah Berlin, "The Decline of Utopian Ideals in the West," in *The Crooked Timber of Humanity: Chapters in the History of Ideas* (New York: Vintage Books, 1992), 20–48.

2. REVIVAL OF MESSIANIC HOPE

1. See Burrow, *Crisis of Reason*.

2. See Martin Jay, *Refractions of Violence* (New York: Routledge, 2003).

3. See Richard Wolin, "Reflections on Jewish Secular Messianism," in *Jews and Messianism in the Modern Era: Metaphor and Meaning*, ed. Jonathan Frankel (New York: Oxford University Press, 1991). In his essay Wolin states: "The proliferation of secular messianism on the eve of, and during, the First World War undoubtedly derived from an analogous historical dynamic. As hopes for Jewish equality in Central Europe were crushed, with prospects for an imminent, historical, and secular solution to the Jewish question in deadlock, only a recrudescence of messianic sentiment appeared to offer new hope" (ibid., 193).

4. Paul Mendes-Flohr, *Divided Passions: Jewish Intellectuals and the Experience of Modernity* (Detroit, MI: Wayne State University Press, 1991), 219–20.

5. See, for example, Lilla, *The Stillborn God*. According to Lilla, "the liberal deity turned out to be a stillborn God, unable to inspire genuine conviction among those seeking ultimate truth" (ibid., 301).

6. See Josef Pieper, *Hope and History* (San Francisco: Ignatius Press, 1994); Anthony Kelly, *Eschatology and Hope* (Maryknoll, NY: Orbis Books, 2006); and

Raymond Plant, *Politics, Theology and History* (Cambridge: Cambridge University Press, 2001).

7. See Mosse, *German Jews Beyond Judaism*. See also Mosse, "Jewish Emancipation: Between Bildung and Respectability," in Reinharz and Schatzberg, *The Jewish Response to German Culture*, 1–16; as well as Tewes and Wright, *Liberalism, Anti-Semitism, and Democracy*.

8. See Michael Brenner, *The Renaissance of Jewish Culture in Weimar Germany* (New Haven, CT: Yale University Press, 1996); Jonathan M. Hess, *Germans, Jews, and the Claims of Modernity* (New Haven, CT: Yale University Press, 2002); Pierre Birnbaum, *Geography of Hope: Exile, the Enlightenment, Disassimilation* (Stanford, CA: Stanford University Press, 2008); Martin Kavka, "Verification (*Bewährung*) in Martin Buber," *Journal of Jewish Thought and Philosophy* 20, no. 1 (2012): 71–98; and Rose, *Judaism and Modernity*.

9. See Stephane Moses, *System and Revelation: The Philosophy of Franz Rosenzweig* (Detroit, MI: Wayne State University Press, 1991); Bruce Rosenstock, *Philosophy and the Jewish Question: Mendelssohn, Rosenzweig, and Beyond* (New York: Fordham University Press, 2009); and Leora Batnitzky, *Idolatry and Representation*.

10. For more on the development of Buber's thought in relation to the crisis of reason and Western bourgeoisie culture brought on by World War I, see Paul Mendes-Flohr, *From Mysticism to Dialogue: Martin Buber's Transformation of German Social Thought* (Detroit, MI: Wayne State University Press, 1989); and Steven E. Ascheim, *Culture and Catastrophe: German and Jewish Confrontations with National Socialism and Other Crises* (New York: New York University Press, 1996).

11. See Buber, "The Foundation Stone" and "Spinoza, Sabbatai Zvi, and the Baal-Shem," in *The Origin and Meaning of Hasidism* (Atlantic Highlands, NJ: Humanities Press International, 1988). See also Asher D. Biemann, *Inventing New Beginnings: On the Idea of Renaissance in Modern Judaism* (Stanford, CA: Stanford University Press, 2009).

12. For further discussion on the link between Buber's personal life and his social philosophy, see Maurice S. Friedman, *Martin Buber: The Life of Dialogue* (New York: Routledge, 2002), *Encounter on the Narrow Ridge: A Life of Martin Buber* (New York: Paragon House, 1991), and *Martin Buber's Life and Work: The Early Years, 1878–1923* (New York: Dutton, 1981).

13. Rivka Horwitz, *Buber's Way to "I and Thou": The Development of Martin Buber's Thought and His "Religion as Presence" Lectures* (Philadelphia: Jewish Publication Society of America, 1980); and Mendes-Flohr, *From Mysticism to Dialogue*.

14. See Martin Buber, *Kingship of God* (Highlands, NJ: Humanity Press, 1990), 14. Buber states: "For the eschatological hope—in Israel . . . is first always historical hope; it becomes eschatologized only through growing historical disillusionment. In this process faith seizes upon the future as the unconditioned turning point of

history, then as the unconditioned overcoming of history . . . the eschatologization of those actual-historical ideas includes their mythicization" (ibid.).

15. Scholem was to later to continue Graetz's line of thinking by proposing that the "interiorization of redemption" that defines Christianity marked a stark departure from Judaism's ideal of redemption that "produces a totality that knows nothing of such a division between inwardness and outwardness" (*Messianic Idea in Judaism*, 17).

16. See Martin Buber, *The Prophetic Faith* (New York: Harper and Row, 1960), 48. Buber states, "through a holy event there comes into existence this category, decisive from the point of view of the history of faith, of the *holy people*, the *hallowed body of the people*, as image and claim; at a later time, after the people had broken the covenant again and again, this category [the holy people] changed and was replaced by the Messianic promise and hope" (ibid.).

17. Buber, *Israel and the World*, 255.

18. See Martin Buber, "Jewish Religiosity," chap. 5 in *On Judaism* (New York: Schocken Books, 1996).

19. Paul Arthur Schilpp and Maurice S. Friedman, eds., *The Philosophy of Martin Buber* (La Salle, IL: Open Court, 1967), 256. For more on the distinction between apocalyptic and prophetic hope, see Norman Cohn, *Cosmos, Chaos, and the World to Come* (New Haven, CT: Yale University Press, 1999), 165. See also Bill Arnold, "Old Testament Eschatology and the Rise of Apocalypticism," in Walls, *The Oxford Handbook of Eschatology*.

20. For more on Buber's critique of religion, see Donald J. Moore, *Martin Buber: Prophet of Religious Secularism* (New York: Fordham University Press, 1996).

21. Martin Buber, *Two Types of Faith* (London: Routledge & Paul, 1951), 162.

22. Mendes-Flohr, *Divided Passions*, 230. See also Zachary Braiterman, *(God) after Auschwitz* (Princeton, NJ: Princeton University Press, 1998), 63.

23. Martin Buber, *Pointing the Way: Collected Essays*, ed. and trans. Maurice S. Friedman (Harper and Row, 1963), 203. Buber states: "[The] paradoxical subject of the late apocalyptic is a future that is no longer in time . . . all that may yet come in history no longer has an historical character. Man cannot achieve this future, but he also has nothing more to achieve" (ibid.).

24. It should be noted that Buber closely followed Cohen's argument in the *Religion of Reason* that Messianism and eschatology suggest different relationships to temporality and politics. According to Susannah Heschel, for nineteenth century thinkers such as Cohen, Geiger, and Graetz, apocalypticism was designated an alien import resulting from the political turmoil of the late Second Temple period. The separation of messianism from apocalypticism in Buber's writings also has to be understood as part the polemic to identify Jesus as part of a Jewish messianic tradition which then gets later corrupted by the early Christian appropriation of

messianism into a form of apocalypticism, particularly due to Paul's influence. See Susannah Heschel, *Abraham Geiger and the Jewish Jesus* (Chicago: University of Chicago Press, 1998), 194.

25. Buber, *Israel and the World*, 108.

26. See David Biale, *Gershom Scholem: Kabbalah and Counter-History* (Cambridge, MA: Harvard University Press, 1982), 74.

27. Many of the polarities found in Buber's thought were drawn from Cohen's work. For example, Buber's distinction between the legacy of messianic and apocalyptic faith similarly follows Cohen's distinction in *Religion of Reason* between messianism and eschatology. Cohen's assertion that "Messianism breaks the backbone of nationalism," however, suggested a universalism and idealism that Buber found harder to accept in the post–World War I period. For Buber, the great hope of Jewish nationalism was that it could embody humanistic values while reflecting the unique spirit of Judaism. See Goetschel, *Discipline of Philosophy*. See also Martin Buber and Hermann Cohen, "A Debate on Zionism and Messianism," in Mendes-Flohr and Reinharz, *The Jew in the Modern World*, 571.

28. Michael Walzer, *In God's Shadow: Politics in the Hebrew Bible* (New Haven, CT: Yale University Press, 2012), 184. See also Walzer's discussion on the intention of the rabbis to later "neutralize the disruptive force of prophecy" in Michael Walzer, Menachem Lorberbaum, Noam J. Zohar, and Yair Loberbaum. *The Jewish Political Tradition*, vol. 1, *Authority* (New Haven, CT: Yale University Press, 2003), 205.

29. See Jacob Taubes, "Martin Buber and the Philosophy of History," chap. 2 in *From Cult to Culture: Fragments Toward a Critique of Historical Reason*, ed. Charlotte Fonrobert and Amir Engel (Stanford, CA: Stanford University Press, 2010). See also Edith Wyschogrod, "Hasidism, Hellenism, Holocaust: A Postmodern View," in Kepnes, *Interpreting Judaism in a Postmodern Age*, 310.

30. For further discussion, see Paul Mendes-Flohr, "The Stronger and the Better Jews: Jewish Theological Responses to Political Messianism in the Weimar Republic," in *Jews and Messianism in the Modern Era: Metaphor and Meaning*, ed. Jonathan Frankel (New York: Oxford University Press, 1991), 159–196.

31. Buber, *Prophetic Faith*, 141–142.

32. Buber, *Pointing the Way*, 204. For further discussion, also see Mendes-Flohr, *Divided Passions*, 185.

33. Buber, *Origin and Meaning of Hasidism* 106.

34. See David Hartman, "Learning to Hope," chap. 7 in *From Defender to Critic*, 149. According to Hartman, there are "two different approaches to hope and messianism: one that anticipates final resolution, the emergence of a new type of human and a new type of history, awaiting redemption irrespective of human action; and another that insists upon *teshuvah*, that expects the enrichment of human spiritual possibilities, but that guarantees no final resolution. These divergent approaches to redemption and hope may have their roots in two distinct his-

toric memories. One attitude may emerge from consideration of the redemption of Israel at the Exodus; the other, from remembrance of the revelation of the Torah at Sinai. The former would seem to undergird a radical, 'rupture' concept of history; the latter, a halakhic, covenantal concept of history" (ibid., 147).

35. See Hartman, "Sinai and Exodus," 380.

36. Hartman distinguishes between halakhic and radical hope in the following terms: "Halakhic hope [is] the courage to bear human responsibility, to persevere in partial solutions, and to accept the burden of living and building within contexts of uncertainty. . . . Halakhic hope liberates action, for it provides a means by which to overcome the paralysis of dejection." By contrast, "Radical hope [is] the expectancy of a future resolution to all human problems . . . a mode of anticipation, a faith that ultimately redemption will come, in its appointed time, irrespective of what we do or don't do. It is not expressed through action, but through inaction, a sustained waiting that in mystical thinking is intimately associated with the messianic concept" (*From Defender to Critic*, 129).

37. Martin Buber, *Paths in Utopia* (Syracuse, NY: Syracuse University Press, 1996), 10.

38. Schilpp and Friedman, *Philosophy of Martin Buber*, 455.

39. Buber, *Paths in Utopia*, 8. See also Maurice S. Friedman, *Martin Buber's Life and Work: The Middle Years, 1923–1945* (New York: Dutton, 1983), 118.

40. See Paul Mendes-Flohr, *The Philosophy of Franz Rosenzweig* (Lebanon, NH: Brandeis University Press, 1988); Peter Eli Gordon, *Rosenzweig and Heidegger: Between Judaism and German Philosophy* (Berkeley: University of California Press, 2003); Mara H. Benjamin, *Rosenzweig's Bible: Reinventing Scripture for Jewish Modernity* (Cambridge: Cambridge University Press, 2009); Rosenstock, *Philosophy and the Jewish Question*; and Batnitzky, *Idolatry and Representation*.

41. In his *Mishneh Torah* Maimonides states, "It is beyond the human mind to fathom the designs of the Creator; for our ways are not His ways, neither are our thoughts His thoughts. All these matters relating to Jesus of Nazareth and the Ishmaelite (Mohammed) who came after him, served to clear the way for King Messiah, to prepare the whole world to worship God with one accord, as it is written, *'For then will I turn to the peoples a pure language, that they may all call upon the name of the Lord to serve Him with one consent'* (Zephaniah 3:9). Thus the messianic hope, the Torah, and the commandments have become familiar topics—topics of conversation (among the inhabitants) of the far isles and many peoples." Quoted in Harold Kasimow and Byron L. Sherwin, eds., *No Religion Is an Island: Abraham Joshua Heschel and Interreligious Dialogue* (Maryknoll, NY: Orbis, 1991), 20.

42. Scholem, *Messianic Idea in Judaism*, 3.

43. See Scholem, "Messianism: A Never-Ending Quest," in *On the Possibility of Jewish Mysticism in Our Time: And Other Essays* (Philadelphia: Jewish Publication Society, 1997).

44. Scholem, *Messianic Idea in Judaism*, 10.

45. For further on the conflictual nature of rabbinic attitudes toward the notion of redemption see Ephraim Urbach, "On Redemption," in *The Sages*, 649–690.

46. For further reading on redemptive sin in Scholem and other Jewish thinkers during the Weimar period, see Benjamin Lazier, *God Interrupted: Heresy and the European Imagination Between the World Wars* (Princeton, NJ: Princeton University Press, 2012). See also Steven Wasserstrom, *Religion After Religion: Gershom Scholem, Mircea Eliade, and Henry Corbin at Eranos* (Princeton, NJ: Princeton University Press, 1999).

47. Gershom Scholem, *On Jews and Judaism in Crisis: Selected Essays* (New York: Schocken, 1976), 25.

48. See Martin Buber, *Between Man and Man* (New York: Macmillan, 1975). Buber proposes the distinction between Persian and Israelite messianism in the following terms: "Unlike *Persian Messianism* in which the future is plotted out down to the 'precise hour,' *Israelite Messianism*, which rejects such precisions because it understands man himself, frail, contradictory, questionable man himself as an element that can both contribute to salvation and hinter it; but final and complete salvation is guaranteed to this form of Messianism as well, in faith in the saving power of God.... In the Christian picture of the universe ... the effect of Messianism persists, though weakened" (ibid., 142).

49. See Gershom Scholem, "Martin Buber's Conception of Judaism," in *On Jews and Judaism in Crisis*, 126–171. Scholem charged: "Buber's sharp turn against the revolutionary element in Jewish Messianism is connected with another important point, his striking aversion to the apocalyptic. Buber is among those—no less than Franz Rosenzweig and a long line of liberal Jewish thinkers—who, at least in his later period, represent a tendency to remove the apocalyptic sting from Judaism" (ibid., 162).

50. Jacob Taubes later was to sum up Scholem's cautionary views on messianic redemption in the following terms: "If the messianic idea in Judaism is not interiorized, it can turn the 'landscape of redemption' into a blazing apocalypse.... For every attempt to bring about redemption on the level of history without transfiguration of the messianic idea leads straight into the abyss" (*Occidental Eschatology*, xvii).

51. For further reading on Scholem's positions on messianism and Zionism, see Löwy, *Redemption and Utopia*, 65. See also Eric Jacobson, *Metaphysics of the Profane: The Political Theology of Walter Benjamin and Gershom Scholem* (New York: Columbia University Press, 2003).

52. Scholem, *Messianic Idea in Judaism*, 35–36.

53. In his essay "Three Sins of Brit Shalom," Scholem argued that for Zionism to succeed it must resist the redemptive hopes offered by Judaism's messianic tradition precisely because the redemptive passions ignited by messianism can eradi-

cate the type of pragmatism required for responsibly running a modern state. See Biale, *Gershom Scholem*, 100. See also Nathan Rotensteich, "Gershom Scholem's Conception of Jewish Nationalism," in *Gershom Scholem: The Man and His Work*, ed. Paul Mendes-Flohr (Albany: State University of New York Press, 1994).

54. For more on Scholem's anarchistic theology, see Biale, *Gershom Scholem*, 127, and Löwy, *Redemption and Utopia*, 66. See also Joseph Dan, "Gershom Scholem and Jewish Messianism," in Mendes-Flohr, *Gershom Scholem*, 73–86.

55. According to Scholem the great challenge presented by the Zionist return of the Jewish people into the concrete realm of power politics was the question of managing the redemptive fervor unleashed whenever Messianic hopes are invoked. Scholem's apprehension reveals itself in the concluding sentences to his essay "Toward an Understanding of the Messianic Idea." Scholem states: "The blazing landscape of redemption (as if it were a point of focus) has concentrated in itself the historical outlook of Judaism. Little wonder that overtones of Messianism have accompanied the modern Jewish readiness for irrevocable action in the concrete realm, when it set out on the utopian return to Zion. It is a readiness which no longer allows itself to be fed on hopes. Born out of the horror and destruction that was Jewish history in our generation, it is bound to history itself and not to meta-history; it has not given itself totally to Messianism. Whether or not Jewish history will be able to endure this entry into the concrete realm without perishing in the crisis of the Messianic claim which has virtually been conjured up—that is the question which out of his great and dangerous past the Jew of this age poses to his present and to his future" (*Messianic Idea in Judaism*, 36).

56. Martin Buber, *Knowledge of Man: Selected Essays* (New York: Humanity Books, 1988), 69. See also Friedman, *Martin Buber*, 98–99.

57. Emil Fackenheim, *Jewish Philosophers and Jewish Philosophy* (Bloomington: Indiana University Press, 1996), 86.

58. Paul Mendes-Flohr, "The Kingdom of God: Martin Buber's Critique of Messianic Politics," *Behemoth: A Journal on Civilization* 1, no. 2 (2008): 32.

59. Buber, *Origin and Meaning of Hasidism*, 74.

60. Ibid., 84.

61. Buber states: "It is a mistake to regard Jewish Messianism as a belief in an event happening once at the end of time and in a single human figure created as the center of this event. The assurance of the co-working strength that is accorded to man, to the generation of man, unites the end of time with the life lived in this present" (*Origin and Meaning of Hasidism*, 107). Buber goes on to state: "The Hasidic message of redemption stands in opposition to the Messianic self-differentiation of one man from other men, of one time from other times, of one act from other actions. All mankind is accorded the co-working power, all time is directly redemptive, all action for the sake of God may be Messianic action. . . . Turning the whole of his life in the world to God and then allowing it to open and unfold in all its

moments until the last—that is man's work toward redemption. We live in an unredeemed world. But out of each human life that is unarbitrary and bound to the world, a seed of redemption falls into the world, and the harvest is God's" (ibid., 111–112).

62. See Mendes-Flohr, "'The Stronger and the Better Jews': Jewish Theological Responses to Political Messianism in the Weimar Republic," in *Jews and Messianism in the Modern Era: Metaphor and Meaning*, ed. Jonathan Frankel (New York: Oxford University Press, 1991), 173. Mendes-Flohr points to an early essay by Buber titled "The Messianic Mystery" (1925) in which the dialectics between actuality and spirituality are represented within the history of Jewish messianism as a tension between the *Meshihiim* (messianic enthusiasts) who insist on quickening redemption versus the *Nistarim* (the hidden ones) who embrace an alternative temporality of humble preparation outside the political realm. Mendes-Flohr's scholarship proposes that there was a more cautionary impulse in Buber that led him toward a spiritualization of messianism.

63. Martin Buber, *I and Thou* (New York: Free Press, 1971).

64. Ibid., 54.

65. See Gabriel Marcel, "Sketch of a Phenomenology and a Metaphysic of Hope," chap. 2 in *Homo Viator: Introduction to a Metaphysic of Hope* (London: Gollancz, 1951).

66. See Marcel, "Martin Buber's Philosophical Anthropology," in *Searchings* (New York: Newman Press, 1967), 73–92. See also Marcel, "I and Thou," in Schilpp and Friedman, *Philosophy of Martin Buber*, 41–48. For more on the philosophical connection between Buber and Marcel, see Levinas, "Martin Buber, Gabriel Marcel, and Philosophy," in *Outside the Subject, Meridian: Crossing Aesthetics* (Stanford, CA: Stanford University Press, 1994), 20–39.

67. Marcel, *Homo Viator*, 61.

68. For more on Marcel's philosophy of hope and existential despair, see Martin, *How We Hope*, 109.

69. Aquinas, *Summa Theologiae*, 215.

70. According to Marcel, "Hope consists in asserting that there is at the heart of being, beyond all data, beyond all inventories and all calculations, a mysterious principle which . . . cannot but will that which I will, if what I will deserves to be willed and is, in fact, willed by the whole of my being" (*Philosophy of Existentialism*, 28).

71. Marcel, *Homo Viator*, 61.

72. Marcel states: "[H]ope tends inevitably to *transcend* the particular objects to which it at first seems to be attached." He goes on: "Hope always implies the superlogical connection between a return (*nostos*) and something completely new (*Kaninon ti*)" (*Homo Viator*, 32). See also Jill Hernandez, *Gabriel Marcel's Ethics of Hope: Evil, God, and Virtue* (New York: Bloomsbury Academic, 2011).

73. Martin, *How We Hope*, 126.

74. Buber, *I and Thou*, 94.

75. See Hermann Cohen, *Religion of Reason: Out of the Sources of Judaism* (Atlanta, GA: Scholars Press, 1995). Cohen retained a formal idealized vision of I-Thou relations. Although love of the stranger and "fellowman" was important for Cohen, this love is forever idealized beyond the realm of corporality. In Cohen's words: "How is it possible to love an idea? To which one should retort: How is it possible to love anything but an idea? Does one not love, even in the case of sensual love, only the idealized person, only the idea of the person?" (ibid., 160). By contrast, Buber's redemptive hope emerged from within actual intersubjective relationships of individuals, requiring a mixture of both bodies and ideals. For further discussion of Buber's critique of Cohen's "dissociated spirituality," see Fackenheim, *Jewish Philosophers*, 55.

76. For more on Cohen and messianism, see Alan Mittleman, "Messianic Hope," in *Covenant and Hope: Christian and Jewish Reflections: Essays in Constructive Theology from the Institute for Theological Inquiry*, ed. Robert W. Jenson and Eugene Korn (Grand Rapids, MI: William B. Eerdmans Publishing, 2012), 220–243; Robert Erlewine, *Monotheism and Tolerance: Recovering a Religion of Reason* (Bloomington: Indiana University Press, 2010); and Kavka, *Jewish Messianism*.

77. Martin Buber, *Eclipse of God: Studies in the Relation between Religion and Philosophy* (New York: Harper, 1988), 58.

78. Buber, *I and Thou*, 80.

79. Buber, *Between Man and Man*, 61.

80. Martin Buber, *A Believing Humanism: My Testament, 1902–1965* (Amherst, NY: Prometheus Books), 177.

81. Martin Buber, *Good and Evil* (New York: Prentice Hall, 1980), 92.

82. Buber, *Knowledge of Man*, 50.

83. Buber, *I and Thou*, 69.

84. Buber, *Between Man and Man*, 77.

85. See Silberstein, *Martin Buber's Social and Religious Thought*. Silberstein correlates Buber's critique of idolatry with philosophy in the following terms: "Buber's distinctive interpretation of religion entails a unique conception of idolatry. In their need for stability, permanence, and continuity, people create systems of dogma and moral principles. Thus, as is the case with all social institutions, organized religion is, like ancient idolatry, an expression of the desire to possess and control. . . . The same anxieties that motivate people to formulate ideological and philosophical systems also lead them to transform God into an It, an object that can be analyzed, possessed, and used" (ibid., 219–220).

86. Buber, *I and Thou*, 161.

87. Wolfson, *Giving Beyond the Gift*, 25.

88. Buber, *I and Thou*, 80.

89. It should be noted that part of Buber's critique of metaphysics was also directed at the German idealism of his teacher Hermann Cohen. For more on Buber's critique of Cohen's brand of German Idealism and neo-Kantianism, see Buber, "The Love of God and the Idea of Deity," in *Israel and the World*, 53. For a compelling response to Buber's critique of philosophy, see Iris Murdoch, "Martin Buber and God," chap. 15 in *Metaphysics as a Guide to Morals* (New York: Vintage, 2003).

90. For more on the distinction between Hellenistic occularcentrism versus Judaic "hearing," see Martin Jay, *Downcast Eyes: The Denigration of Vision in Twentieth-Century French Thought* (Berkeley: University of California Press, 1994), 555.

91. Buber, *Between Man and Man*, 127.

92. Silberstein, *Martin Buber's Social and Religious Thought*, 126.

93. Buber, *Between Man and Man*, 142.

94. Buber states: "The philosophical anthropologist must stake nothing less than his real wholeness, his concrete self. And more; it is not enough for him to stake his self as an object of knowledge. He can know the wholeness of the person and through it the wholeness of man only when he does not leave his subjectivity out and does not remain an untouched observer. He must enter, completely and in reality, into the act of self-reflection, in order to become aware of human wholeness ... he must carry out this act of entry into the unique dimension as an act of his life without a prepared philosophical security; that is, he must expose himself to all that can meet you when you are really living. Here you do not attain to knowledge by remaining on the shore and watching the foaming waves, you must make the venture and cast yourself in, you must swim ... in this way, and in no other, do you reach anthropological insight. So long as you 'have' yourself, have yourself as an object, your experience of man is only as of a thing among things" (*Between Man and Man*, 124).

95. Buber defined his alternative epistemological approach for the philosophical anthropologist in the following terms: "He must enter, completely and in reality, into the act of self-reflection, in order to become aware of human wholeness ... he must carry out this act of entry into the unique dimension as an act of his life without a prepared philosophical security; that is, he must expose himself to all that can meet you when you are really living. Here you do not attain to knowledge by remaining on the shore and watching the foaming waves, you must make the venture and cast yourself in, you must swim ... in this way, and in no other, do you reach anthropological insight" (*Between Man and Man*, 124).

96. According to Buber, "only when the individual knows the other in all his otherness as himself ... and from there breaks through to the *other*, has he broken through his solitude in a strict and transforming meeting" (*Between Man and Man*, 202).

97. Buber states: "I have no teaching. I only point to something. I point to reality. I point to something in reality that had not or had too little been seen. I take him who listens to me by the hand and lead him to the window. I open the window and point to what is outside" (Schilpp and Friedman, *Philosophy of Martin Buber*, 693). This ambivalence on Buber's part was perhaps best captured in his Zen master–like response to Charles Hartshorne's essay on Buber's metaphysics when he stated "I am no metaphysician and I am one of the greatest metaphysicians" (ibid., 717).

98. Buber states: "The great deed of Israel is not that it taught the one real God . . . but that it pointed out that this God can be addressed by man in reality, that man can say Thou to Him, that he can stand face to face with Him, that he can have intercourse with Him . . . life as being addressed and answering, addressing and receiving answer" (*Origin and Meaning of Hasidism*, 91).

99. Buber, *I and Thou*, 125.

100. Buber states: "All the enthusiasm of the philosophers for *monologue*, from Plato to Nietzsche, does not touch the simple experience of faith, that speaking with God is something *toto genere*, different from 'speaking with oneself;' whereas, remarkably, it is not something *toto genere* different from speaking with another human being" (*Between Man and Man*, 192).

101. Levinas later summarized Buber's critique of metaphysics and traditional epistemology in the following terms: "Truth, therefore, is not grasped by a dispassionate subject . . . but by a commitment in which the other remains in his otherness. Although the Absolute could not be attained for the philosophers of antiquity except by means of contemplative detachment, and the impossibility of the latter is precisely what led to the separation of being and truth in the Parmenides of Plato, commitment, for Buber, is what gains access to otherness . . . Thus the problem of truth raised by Parmenides is resolved in terms of a social or inter-subjective relation." Levinas continues his assessment, "Buber asserts . . . truth does not consist in a correspondence with being, but is the correlate of a life authentically lived . . . The truth is wholly an attitude towards, an inquiry into, a struggle for, the truth, i.e., the authenticity of a particular existence rather than an agreement between appearance and reality" (Schilpp and Friedman, *Philosophy of Martin Buber*, 141).

102. As Buber states: "Philosophizing and philosophy, in contrast, begin ever anew with one's definitely looking away from his concrete situation, hence with the primary act of abstraction." For Buber, by contrast, this is the opposite of what is achieved through revelation and religious community. Buber states: "Religious expression is bound to the concrete situation" (*Eclipse of God*, 37–38). Thus, in contrast to Hermann Cohen, Kaplan argues that for Buber, "Reverence of the absolute does not mean metaphysical ideation, but religious event" (Schilpp and Friedman, *Philosophy of Martin Buber*, 265).

103. Buber, *Between Man and Man*, 168.

104. Buber, *I and Thou*, 11.

105. Ibid., 12.

106. Buber, *Between Man and Man*, 174.

107. Norman O'Brown, *Life Against Death: The Psychoanalytical Meaning of History* (Middletown, CT: Wesleyan University Press, 1959), 84.

108. Paul Pfuetze states: "Buber, in rejecting metaphysics, has described his standpoint as being on the *narrow ridge* to indicate that there is no sureness of expressible knowledge about the absolute, but only the certainty of meeting what remains undisclosed. The I-Thou relation as such does not procure objective criteria. Uncertainty and insecurity are inherent in human existence. Hence the necessity for faith, venture, risk" (Schilpp and Friedman, *Philosophy of Martin Buber*, 538). For more on Buber's critique of metaphysics in relationship to American Pragmatism, see Paul E. Pfuetze, *Self, Society, Existence: Human Nature and Dialogue in the Thought of George Herbert Mead and Martin Buber* (Westport, CT: Greenwood Press, 1973).

109. Jean-Francois Lyotard, *The Postmodern Condition: A Report on Knowledge* (Minneapolis, MN: University of Minnesota Press, 1984).

110. See Emmanuel Levinas, "Martin Buber and the Theory of Knowledge," in *Philosophy of Martin Buber*, 133–150.

111. Buber, *I and Thou*, 126.

112. Buber, *Between Man and Man*, 168. Starting with Sartre, Buber belongs in the standard tradition of left-wing critiques of Heidegger's existentialism. However, scholars like Thomas Sheehan have pointed out that the complexity and nuance of Heidegger's work also have intersubjective and possibly even democratic strands that would suggest a more hospitable concern for the type of hope generated through intersubjective encounter. See Sheehan, "A Paradigm Shift in Heidegger's Research," *Continental Philosophy Review* 34, no. 2 (June 2001): 183–202. See also Zygmunt Bauman's discussion of Heidegger's *Mitsein* in comparison with Buber's *I and Thou* in which he argues that both carry an assumption of symmetry and solidarity in Bauman, *Postmodern Ethics* (Oxford, UK: Blackwell, 1994), 49; and Haim Gordon, *The Heidegger-Buber Controversy: The Status of the I-Thou* (Westport, CT: Greenwood Press, 2001).

113. Heidegger, *Being and Time*, II.4, sec. 345.

114. Buber, *Paths in Utopia*, 73.

115. Buber, *Between Man and Man*, 87.

116. Ibid., 170.

117. Buber, *I and Thou*, 94.

118. Buber, *Paths in Utopia*, 65.

119. Ibid., 133.

120. Buber, *Between Man and Man*, 119.

121. Ibid., 205.

122. According to Buber: "[Through our connection with finitude,] there is a participation in infinity, which is given by the ability to know at all . . . when we recognize man's finitude we must at the same time recognize his participation in infinity . . . as the twofold nature of the processes in which alone man's existence becomes recognizable. The finite has its effect on him and the infinite has its effect on him; he shares in finitude and shares in infinity" (Ibid., 121).

123. Buber, *Between Man and Man*, 15.

124. Ibid., 61.

125. Buber, *Pointing the Way*, 229.

126. Schilpp and Friedman, *Philosophy of Martin Buber*, 193.

127. Buber, *Between Man and Man*, 174.

128. According to Buber: "something happens to man . . . man receives, and what he receives is not a content (*einen Inhalt*) but a presence,(*eine Gegenwart*) a presence as strength . . . The meaning we receive can be put to the proof in action only by each person in the uniqueness of his being and in the uniqueness of his life. No prescription can lead us to the encounter, and none leads from it . . . the mystery—has remained what it was" (*I and Thou*, 158).

129. In his essay "Fragments on Revelation," Buber states: "Revelation is continual, and everything is fit to become a sign of revelation. What is disclosed to us in the revelation is not God's essence as it is independent of our existence, but His relationship to us and our relation to Him" (*Believing Humanism*, 113).

130. Martin Buber, *For the Sake of Heaven*, 2nd ed. (Philadelphia: Jewish Publication Society of America, 1953), 106. See also Phil Huston, *Martin Buber's Journey to Presence* (New York: Fordham University Press, 2007) and Horwitz, *Buber's Way to "I and Thou."*

131. Hans Ulrich Gumbrecht, *Production of Presence: What Meaning Cannot Convey* (Stanford, CA: Stanford University Press, 2004), 107.

132. As Buber states: "The factual revelation means the breaking of the united light of God into human multiplicity, that is, the breaking of the unity into contradiction. We know no other revelation than that of the meeting of the divine and the human in which the human has a factual share. . . . But it is also not given to us simply and once for all to distinguish between the divine and the human with it. In other words: there is no security against the necessity of living fear and trembling; there is nothing else than the certainty we share in the revelation. Nothing can relieve us of the task of opening ourselves as we are, as a whole and a unity, to the continual revelation that can make all, all things and all events, in history and in our lives, into its signs" (*Believing Humanism*, 113-114).

133. Franz Rosenzweig, *On Jewish Learning*, ed. Nahum Norbert Glatzer (Madison: University of Wisconsin Press, 1955), 111.

134. For more on Buber's exchange with Rosenzweig regarding revelation and commandments, see Eisen, *Rethinking Modern Judaism*, 188.

135. For more on the physiological component of hope, especially in relation to physical and physiological adversity, see Groopman, *The Anatomy of Hope*.

136. Edith Wyschogrod, *An Ethics of Remembering: History, Heterology, and the Nameless Others* (Chicago, IL: University of Chicago Press, 1998), 248. Wyschogrod states: "To be what it is, hope must create the future in the mode of the now. It is the nature of hope to be a desire for presence, a presence that must be deferred."

137. Buber, *Pointing the Way*, 225.

138. See Anson Rabinbach, "Between Apocalypse and Enlightenment: Benjamin, Bloch, and Modern German-Jewish Messianism," chap. 1 in *The Shadow of Catastrophe: German Intellectuals Between Apocalypse and Enlightenment* (Berkeley: University of California Press, 2001), 27.

139. Ernst Bloch, *Atheism in Christianity: The Religion of the Exodus and the Kingdom* (New York: Verso, 2009), 94.

3. THE GOD OF EXODUS AND THE SCHOOL OF HOPE

1. For more on Benjamin, Bloch, and Buber's engagement with eschatological hope, see Mendes-Flohr, "To Brush History Against the Grain: The Eschatology of the Frankfurt School and Ernst Bloch," in *Divided Passions*, 370–371. See also Jürgen Habermas, "The German Idealism of the Jewish Philosophers," in *Religion and Rationality: Essays on Reason, God, and Modernity* (Cambridge, MA: MIT Press, 2002).

2. See Ernst Bloch, *Man on His Own: Essays in the Philosophy of Religion* (New York: Herder and Herder, 1970), 72.

3. See Thomas H. West, *Ultimate Hope without God: The Atheistic Eschatology of Ernst Bloch* (New York: Peter Lang, 1991) and Jamie Owen Daniel and Tom Moylan, *Not Yet: Reconsidering Ernst Bloch* (New York: Verso, 1997). See also Martin Jay, "Ernst Bloch and the Extension of Marxist Holism to Nature," chap. 5 in *Marxism and Totality: The Adventures of a Concept from Lukács to Habermas* (Berkeley: University of California Press, 1984).

4. See Ernst Bloch, "Karl Marx, Death, and the Apocalypse," part 2 in *The Spirit of Utopia* (Stanford, CA: Stanford University Press, 2000).

5. For more on Benjamin and Bloch's joint experimentation with psychedelic drugs, see Gershom Scholem, *Walter Benjamin: The Story of a Friendship* (Philadelphia: Jewish Publication Society of America, 1981), 177. See also Löwy, *Redemption and Utopia*; David Kaufmann, "Thanks for the Memory: Bloch, Benjamin, and the Philosophy of History," chap. 3 in *Not Yet! Reconsidering Ernst Bloch*, ed. Jamie Owen Daniel and Tom Moylan (New York: Verso, 1997); Anson Rabinbach, "Between Enlightenment and Apocalypse: Benjamin, Bloch and Modern German Jewish Messianism," *New German Critique* no. 34 (Winter 1985): 78–124; Margaret Cohen, *Profane Illumination: Walter Benjamin and the Paris of Surrealist Revolution* (Berkeley: University of California Press, 1995); Pierre Bouretz, *Witnesses for*

the Future: Philosophy and Messianism (Baltimore, MD: John Hopkins University Press, 2010).

6. See Hannah Arendt, "Between Pariah and Parvenu," in *The Origins of Totalitarianism* (New York: Harcourt Brace, 1951), 56–67.

7. See Martin Jay, "The Politics of Translation: Siegfried Kracauer and Walter Benjamin on the Buber-Rosenzweig Bible," in *Permanent Exiles: Essays on the Intellectual Migration from Germany to America* (New York: Columbia University Press, 1985).

8. For more on Benjamin's emphasis on experience (*Erfahrung*), see Jay, *Permanent Exiles*, 212, and Biale, *Gershom Scholem*, 115.

9. See Jay, *Marxism and Totality*. See also Habermas, "Themes in Postmetaphysical Thinking," in *Postmetaphysical Thinking* (Cambridge, UK: Polity Press, 1994), 33.

10. See Susan A. Handelman, *Fragments of Redemption: Jewish Thought and Literary Theory in Benjamin, Scholem, and Levinas* (Bloomington: Indiana University Press, 1991); Robert Alter, *Necessary Angels: Tradition and Modernity in Kafka, Benjamin, and Scholem* (Cambridge, MA: Harvard University Press, 1991); and Rose, *Judaism and Modernity*.

11. For more on the relationship between memory and the messianic in Benjamin's thought, see Eric Jacobson, "The Messianic Idea in Walter Benjamin's Early Writings," chap. 1 in *Metaphysics of the Profane*. See also Susan Buck-Morss, *Origin of Negative Dialectics* (New York: Free Press, 1979), *The Dialectics of Seeing: Walter Benjamin and the Arcades Project* (Cambridge, MA: MIT Press, 1991), and, *Dreamworld and Catastrophe*; Peter Osborne, *Walter Benjamin: Critical Evaluations in Cultural Theory* (New York: Routledge, 2004); Gillian Rose, *The Melancholy Science: An Introduction to the Thought of Theodor W. Adorno* (New York: Columbia University Press, 1979); Michael P. Steinberg, *Walter Benjamin and the Demands of History* (Ithaca, NY: Cornell University Press, 1996); Richard Wolin, *Walter Benjamin: An Aesthetic of Redemption* (Berkeley: University of California Press, 1994); and Michael Levine, *A Weak Messianic Power: Figures of a Time to Come in Benjamin, Derrida, and Celan* (New York: Fordham University Press, 2013).

12. Walter Benjamin, *Illuminations: Essays and Reflections* (New York: Schocken Books, 1969), 256.

13. Ibid., 254.

14. Ibid., 264.

15. For more on the influence of Kafka on Benjamin, see Handelman, *Fragments of Redemption*, 40, and Rose, *Judaism and Modernity*. For more on Benjamin's paradoxical mixture of personal despair with messianic hope, see Scholem, *Walter Benjamin*; Rose, *Melancholy Science*; and Jay, *Refractions of Violence*.

16. Benjamin, *Illuminations*, 116. For more on Benjamin's paradoxical mixture of personal despair with messianic hope, see Scholem, *Walter Benjamin*, and Michael Morgan, *Interim Judaism: Jewish Thought in a Century of Crisis* (Bloomington:

Indiana University Press, 2001), 65. See also Rose, *The Melancholy Science*; Jay, *Refractions of Violence*; and Rabinbach, *In the Shadow of Catastrophe*.

17. For more on the influence of Kafka on Benjamin, see Handelman, *Fragments of Redemption*, 40.

18. Benjamin, *Illuminations*, 144.

19. See Wolin, "Reflections on Jewish Secular Messianism," in *Jews and Messianism in the Modern Era*, 193. See also Jacob Taubes, "Nihilism as World Politics and Aestheticized Messianism: Walter Benjamin and Theodor W. Adorno," in *The Political Theology of Paul*, trans. Dana Hollander (Stanford, CA: Stanford University Press, 2003), 71, and Andrew Benjamin, *Present Hope: Philosophy, Architecture, Judaism* (New York: Routledge, 1997).

20. Theodor Adorno, *Minima Moralia* (New York: Verso, 1974), 247.

21. For more on the influence of Aristotle's metaphysics on Bloch, see Peter Thompson and Slavoj Žižek, eds., *The Privatization of Hope: Ernst Bloch and The Future of Utopia* (Durham, NC: Duke University Press, 2013), 92.

22. Bloch, *Man on His Own*, 37.

23. Bloch, *Principle of Hope*, 4.

24. Ibid., 32.

25. John Locke, *An Essay Concerning Human Understanding* (Oxford: Oxford University Press, 1975), 231.

26. E. J. Hobsbawm, *Revolutionaries* (New York: New Press, 2001), 165. For more on Bloch's philosophy as a bridge between Feuerbach and Marx's critique of religion, see Capps, *Future of Hope*, 19.

27. See Emmanuel Levinas, "Another Thinking of Death: Starting from Bloch," and "A Reading of Bloch," in *God, Death, and Time, Meridian, Crossing Aesthetics* (Stanford, CA: Stanford University Press, 2000), 88–106.

28. According to Bloch: "What was intended in the great religions, instead of the many single hopes, was hope itself. . . . The only truth of the divine ideal is the utopia of the kingdom, and the premise is that no God remains on high, where none is or has ever been anyway" (*Man on His Own*, 216).

29. Ibid., 213.

30. See Bloch, "Hunger, Something in a Dream, God of Hope, Thing-for-us," in *The Frankfurt School on Religion: Key Writings by the Major Thinkers*, ed. Eduardo Mendieta (New York: Routledge, 2005), 49.

31. Bloch, *Principle of Hope*, 3:1235.

32. Bloch, *Atheism in Christianity*, 79.

33. West, *Ultimate Hope without God*, 196.

34. Bloch states: "The specific prophetic contribution . . . lay in the idea of . . . free moral choice in one's fate . . . it marks the difference between the prophet Jonah and the destruction of Nineveh which he averted, and the Greek 'prophetess' Cassandra, who could only foresee the curse of the Atrides, without being able to fore-

stall it. . . . The prophets taught a mature freedom of choice extending even to fate; they taught the power of human decision. That is why they all speak of the future not as of an immutable category but hypothetically, as a changeable, chooseable one. . . . Man can at least now choose his destiny" (*Atheism in Christianity*, 89).

35. Ibid., 90.

36. Ibid., 20. Bloch also states, "Again and again in the underground Bible, the serpent stands for an underground movement which has light in its eyes, instead of hollow submissive slave-guilt" (73).

37. Ibid., 94.

38. Ibid., 81.

39. For more on Bloch's notion of the negative, see *Atheism in Christianity*, 232–233.

40. Ibid., xxv.

41. Wolfson, *Giving Beyond the Gift*, xviii.

42. Bloch, *Man on His Own*, 162.

43. Ibid., 72.

44. Ibid., 162.

45. Bloch, *Atheism in Christianity*, xxi.

46. Ibid., 81.

47. Ibid., 123.

48. Ibid., 245.

49. See Buber, "Jewish Religiosity," in *On Judaism*, 79–94.

50. Bloch suggests a metaphysics of becoming (similar to kabbalistic notions of *Ayin*, or Buddhist notions of emptiness) based on the conviction that "nothing is complete; nothing is conclusive; nothing has a solid core" (*Man on His Own*, 72). See also West, *Ultimate Hope without God*, 283. For more on Bloch's metaphysics and Christianity, see Bernard Schumacher, *A Philosophy of Hope: Josef Pieper and the Contemporary Debate on Hope* (New York: Fordham University Press, 2003).

51. See Hartman, "Sinai and Exodus," 381.

52. Ernst Bloch, "Can Hope Be Disappointed," in *Literary Essays*, Meridian (Stanford, CA: Stanford University Press, 1998), 345.

53. Moltmann, *Theology of Hope*, 26.

54. See Konrad Paul Liessmann, "Despair and Responsibility: Affinities and Differences in the Thought of Hans Jonas and Günther Anders," in *The Legacy of Hans Jonas: Judaism and the Phenomenon of Life*, eds. Hava Tirosh-Samuelson and Christian Wiese (Leiden, NL: Brill, 2010). Anders summed up this sentiment in the following terms: "The religious and philosophical ethics that have existed until now have become, without exception, completely obsolete; they were exploded along with Hiroshima and exterminated in Auschwitz" (quoted in ibid., 136).

55. See Daniel Bell, *The End of Ideology: On the Exhaustion of Political Ideas in the Fifties* (Cambridge, MA: Harvard University Press, 2000).

56. See J. Judd Owen, *Religion and the Demise of Liberal Rationalism: The Foundational Crisis of the Separation of Church and State* (Chicago: University of Chicago Press, 2001); Pieper, *Hope and History*; and Roskies, *Against the Apocalypse*.

57. Capps, *Future of Hope*, 93.

58. Ibid., 8.

59. Ibid., 33.

60. Ibid., 28.

61. Ibid., 31.

62. Ibid., 33.

63. For more on the transition away from vertical transcendence and otherworldliness, see ibid., 12 and 39.

64. Moltmann, *Theology of Hope*, 25. John Gray follows Moltmann when he states: "To remain within the boundaries of what is believed to be practicable is to abdicate hope and adopt an attitude of passive acceptance that amounts to complicity with oppression" (*Black Mass*, 18).

65. For Moltmann's commentary on Buber in relation to the prophetic "God of promise" and Buber's *Prophetic Faith*, see *Theology of Hope*, 30, 48, 102, 116, 117, 103, and 128. For more on Moltmann's use of Buber's "God of promise" as an alternative to Greek logos, see Ricoeur, "Freedom in the Light of Hope," in *The Conflict of Interpretations*, 411.

66. Moltmann, *Theology of Hope*, 48.

67. Ibid., 30.

68. See Ricoeur, "Hope and the Structure of Philosophical Systems," in *Figuring the Sacred*. See also "Freedom in the Light of Hope," in *Conflict of Interpretations*, 402–424. For more on Ricoeur's engagement with the phenomena of hope, see G. B. Madison, "Ricoeur and the Hermeneutics of the Subject," in *The Philosophy of Paul Ricoeur*, ed. Lewis Edwin Hahn (Chicago: Open Court, 1994), 89.

69. John Polkinghorne, *The God of Hope and the End of the World* (New Haven, CT: Yale University Press, 2003), 94–95. Polkinghorne states: "[T]here is only one possible source: the eternal faithfulness of the God who is the Creator and Redeemer of history. Here Christianity relies heavily upon its Jewish roots. It is only God who can bring new life and raise the dead, whose spirit breathes life into dry bones and makes them live (Ezekiel 37:9–10). Hope lies in the divine *chesed*, God's steadfast love, and not in some Hellenistic belief in an unchanging realm of ideas or an intrinsic immorality of the human soul."

70. Moltmann, *Theology of Hope*, 34. Moltmann goes on to state: "for the philosophers fix their eyes on the presence of things and reflect only on their qualities and quiddities. But the apostle drags our gaze away from contemplating the present state of things, away from their essence and attributes, and directs it towards the future" (ibid., 35). See also Kelly, *Eschatology and Hope*.

71. Walter Brueggemann, *Hope within History* (Louisville, KY: Westminster John Knox Press, 1986), 84.

72. Ibid., 80.

73. Walter Brueggemann, *Hopeful Imagination: Prophetic Voices in Exile* (Minneapolis, MN: Augsburg Fortress Publishers, 1986), 81.

74. See Charles Vernoff, "Hope," in *Contemporary Jewish Religious Thought*. 417–421.

75. Capps, *Future of Hope*, 68.

76. Ibid., 84.

77. Ibid., 75.

78. Fackenheim states, "On the one hand, the Messiah is represented as coming when man has become good enough to make his coming possible. This is the working aspect. On the other hand, he is represented as coming when man has become wicked enough to make his coming necessary" (ibid., 75).

79. Ibid., 91.

80. For more on Fackenheim's philosophy of hope and messianism, see Braiterman, *(God) after Auschwitz*, and Sharon Portnoff, *Reason and Revelation Before Historicism: Strauss and Fackenheim* (Toronto, ON: University of Toronto Press, 2011).

81. See Ken Koltun-Fromm, *Material Culture and Jewish Thought in America* (Bloomington: Indiana University Press, 2010).

82. See Lawrence Friedman, *The Lives of Erich Fromm: Love's Prophet*, (New York: Columbia University Press, 2013).

83. Erich Fromm, *You Shall Be as Gods: A Radical Interpretation of the Old Testament and Its Tradition* (New York: Holt Rinehart and Winston, 1966), 133.

84. Erich Fromm, *The Revolution of Hope: Toward a Humanized Technology* (New York: Harper and Row, 1968). Fromm states: "Hope is paradoxical. It is neither *passive waiting* nor is it unrealistic forcing of circumstances that cannot occur. It is like the crouched tiger, which will jump only when the moment for jumping has come. Neither tired reformism nor pseudo-radical adventurism is an expression of hope. To hope means to be ready at every moment for that which is not yet born, and yet not become desperate if there is no birth in our lifetime" (ibid., 9).

85. Ibid., 154.

86. Fromm argues that there is an important distinction to be made between "*irrational faith*" which he identifies with a passive "submission to something given" by fixating on an object such as "an idol, a leader, or an ideology," versus "*rational faith*" which leads to an "inner activeness" (ibid., 14).

87. Ibid., 8.

88. Ibid., 1.

89. As Fromm states: "Many people... react to the disappointment of their hopes by adjustment to the average optimism.... They reduce their demands to what they can get and do not even dream of that which seems to be out of their reach. They are well-adjusted members of the herd and they never feel hopeless because nobody else seems to feel hopeless. They present the picture of a peculiar kind of *resigned optimism* which we see in so many members of contemporary Western society—the optimism usually being conscious and the resignation unconscious" (ibid., 21).

90. For more on the relationship between religious thought and postmodernism, see Robert Audi, *Religious Commitment and Secular Reason* (Cambridge, UK: Cambridge University Press, 2000); Robert Audi, *Moral Value and Human Diversity* (New York: Oxford University Press, 2007); Robert Audi and Nicholas Wolterstorff, *Religion in the Public Square: The Place of Religious Convictions in Political Debates, Point/Counterpoint* (Lanham, MD: Rowman and Littlefield Publishers, 1997); and Stanley J. Grenz and John R. Franke, *Beyond Foundationalism: Shaping Theology in a Postmodern Context* (Louisville, KY: Westminster John Knox Press, 2001).

91. Jürgen Habermas, *Postmetaphysical Thinking*, 51.

4. RICHARD RORTY'S SOCIAL HOPE AND POSTMETAPHYSICAL REDEMPTION

1. Rorty, *Contingency, Irony, and Solidarity*, 86.

2. Rorty, *Philosophy and Social Hope*, 20.

3. Ibid., 32.

4. Rorty states: "Greek descriptions of our situation presuppose that humanity itself has an intrinsic nature—that there is something unchangeable called 'the human' which can be contrasted with the rest of the universe. Pragmatism sets that presupposition aside and urges that humanity is an open-ended notion, that the word 'human' names a fuzzy but promising project rather than an essence. So, pragmatists transfer to the human future the sense of awe and mystery which the Greeks attached to the non-human.... It coalesces with the awe we feel before works of imagination, and becomes a sense of awe before humanity's ability to become what it once merely imagined, before its capacity for self-creation" (ibid., 52).

5. Ibid., 166.

6. Richard Rorty, *Objectivity, Relativism, and Truth* (Cambridge: Cambridge University Press, 1991), 213.

7. Rorty, *Consequences of Pragmatism*, xix.

8. Rorty, *Objectivity, Relativism, and Truth*. 13.

9. Anindita Niyogi Balslev, *Cultural Otherness: Correspondence with Richard Rorty* (New York: Oxford University Press, 1999), 42–43.

10. In Keith Baker and Peter Reill, *What's Left of Enlightenment? A Postmodern Question* (Stanford, CA: Stanford University Press, 2002), 19.

11. Rorty, *Consequences of Pragmatism*, 166.

12. See Rorty, "Trotsky and the Wild Orchids," in *Philosophy and Social Hope*, 3–20. For an excellent study of Rorty's intellectual biography, see Gross, *Richard Rorty*.

13. Rorty, *Ethics for Today*, 22.

14. Rorty, "Redemption from Egotism," 395.

15. Rorty, *Philosophy and Social Hope*, 24.

16. I am indebted to Charles Guignon and David Hiley's proposal that Rorty's antifoundationalism is comprised of an "existential and pragmatic strand" stemming from his critique of Cartesian duality. See Charles Guignon and David R. Hiley, *Richard Rorty* (Cambridge: Cambridge University Press, 2003), 22.

17. Rorty et al., *The Revival of Pragmatism: New Essays on Social Thought, Law, and Culture* (Durham, NC: Duke University Press, 1998), 30.

18. Rorty et al., *Revival of Pragmatism*, 28.

19. Rorty, *Philosophy and Social Hope*, 61.

20. Ibid., 201.

21. Ibid., 204–205.

22. Ibid., 153.

23. Rorty, *Consequences of Pragmatism*, 197.

24. For more on Rorty and the problem of power, see Peter McLaren, Ramin Farahmandpur, and Juha Suoranta, "Richard Rorty's Self-Help Liberalism: A Marxist Critique of America's Most Wanted Ironist," in *Richard Rorty: Education, Philosophy, and Politics*, ed. Michael Peters and Paulo Ghiraldelli Jr. (Lanham, MD: Rowman and Littlefield, 2001).

25. Richard Rorty, *Truth and Progress* (Cambridge: Cambridge University Press, 1998), 185.

26. Rorty, *Contingency, Irony, and Solidarity*, 189.

27. Voparil and Bernstein, *Rorty Reader*, 405. For more on the importance of "we-saying," see Robert Brandom, *Making It Explicit: Reasoning, Representing, and Discursive Commitment* (Cambridge, MA: Harvard University Press, 1994), 4.

28. Rorty, *Contingency, Irony, and Solidarity*, 92. Rorty also proposes: "[T]he more books you read, the more ways of being human you have considered, the more human you become—the less tempted by dreams of escape from time and chance, the more convinced that we humans have nothing to rely on save one another . . . it tells young intellectuals that the only source of redemption is the human imagination" (quoted in Richard J. Bernstein, *Pragmatism, Critique, Judgment: Essays for Richard J. Bernstein*, ed. Seyla Benhabib, and Nancy Fraser [Cambridge, MA: MIT Press, 2004], 13).

29. Rorty, *Contingency, Irony, and Solidarity*, 92.

30. Richard Rorty, *Achieving Our Country: Leftist Thought in Twentieth-Century America* (Cambridge, MA: Harvard University Press, 1998), 96–97.

31. See Randall Auxier and Lewis Hahn, eds., *The Philosophy of Richard Rorty* (Chicago: Open Court, 2010). In his response to Harvey Cormier's essay "Richard Rorty and Cornel West On the Point of Pragmatism," Rorty states: "Unlike West (and perhaps Cormier as well), I do not believe that there is an activity called 'critique' at which philosophers are, or should become, expert. The legacy of Marxism (and, more recently, of Foucault) has led many intellectuals to think that the test of a philosophical outlook is its ability to expose the covert operations of 'power.' But the best criticism of a social practice is not to provide a genealogy of it, nor to expose its hypocrisies. It is to propose an alternative practice—to imagine a better future.... The trouble with *Discipline and Punish* is that Foucault made no proposals for an alternative criminal justice system" (ibid., 103).

32. Rorty, *Contingency, Irony, and Solidarity*, 189.

33. See Rorty, "Religion in the Public Square," in Voparil and Bernstein, *Rorty Reader*, 459.

34. Rorty, *Objectivity, Relativism, and Truth*, 221.

35. Rorty, *Contingency, Irony, and Solidarity*, 87.

36. See Richard Rorty, *Essays on Heidegger and Others* (Cambridge: Cambridge University Press, 1991), 174.

37. Rorty, *Objectivity, Relativism, and Truth*, 213.

38. See Richard Rorty, *Philosophy as Cultural Politics* (Cambridge: Cambridge University Press, 2007). According to Rorty, "To agree with Habermas that reason is communicative and dialogical rather than subject-centered and monological is to substitute responsibility to other human beings for responsibility to a nonhuman standard. It is to lower our sights from the unconditional above us to the community around us ... It helps us limit ourselves to hopes for small, finite, fleeting successes, and to give up the hope of participation in enduring grandeur" (ibid., 77).

39. For more on Rorty's distinction between the vertical and the horizontal, see Rorty, *Consequences of Pragmatism*, 92, and *Philosophy as Cultural Politics*, 88.

40. Jürgen Habermas, Richard Rorty, Leszek Kolakowski, Józef Niznik, John T. Sanders, *Debating the State of Philosophy: Habermas, Rorty, and Kolakowski* (Westport, CT: Praeger, 1996), 44.

41. Richard Rorty, *Philosophy and the Mirror of Nature* (Princeton, NJ: Princeton University Press, 1979), 381. Rorty interprets prophetic hope in the following terms: "So I think of the cautionary use of 'true,' ... as the voice of prophecy. This voice says, Some day the world will be changed, and then this proposition may turn out to be true. That romantic hope for another world which is yet to come is at the heart of the anti-Platonist's quest for spiritual perfection. I am tempted to follow Derrida in thinking of such hope as marking a fundamental difference be-

tween the Jews and the Greeks. I take Platonism and Greek thought generally to say, The set of candidates for truth is already here, and all the reasons which might be given for and against their truth are also already here; all that remains is to argue that matter out. I think of romantic (or, for Derrida, Judaic) hope as saying, Some day all of these truth candidates, and all of these notions of what counts as a good reason for believing them, may be obsolete; for a much better world is to come—one in which we shall have wonderful new truth candidates . . . once one starts thinking of languages and truth-candidates as constantly in the process of change" (Habermas et al., *Debating the State of Philosophy*, 50).

42. Rorty, *Objectivity, Relativism, and Truth*, 208.

43. Rorty, "Philosophy and the Future," in *Rorty and Pragmatism: The Philosopher Responds to His Critics*, ed. Herman J. Saatkamp (Nashville, TN: Vanderbilt University Press, 1995), 197.

44. In his reply to Jeffrey Stout, Rorty states, "There is something that the great prophets of secularism have hoped would go away, and that might someday do so . . . belief in post-mortem rewards and punishments meted out by a nonhuman person on the basis of conducts in this mortal life. In my 'perfect secular utopia' neither hopes of such rewards nor fears of such punishments would play any role in moral or political deliberation" (Auxier and Hahn, *Philosophy of Richard Rorty*, 547).

45. Balslev, *Cultural Otherness*, 42.

46. See Rorty, "Redemption from Egotism: James and Proust as Spiritual Exercises," in Voparil and Bernstein, *Rorty Reader*, 405.

47. Rorty states: "The vocabulary of Greek metaphysics and Christian theology . . . was a useful one for our ancestors' purposes, but that we have different purposes, which will be better served by employing a different vocabulary. Our ancestors climbed up a ladder which we are now in a position to throw away. We can throw it away not because we have reached a final resting place, but because we have different problems to solve than those that perplexed our ancestors" (*Philosophy and Social Hope*, xxii).

48. For more on the distinction between *demythologizing* and what Cornel West insightfully identifies as a process of *demystification* perpetuated by critical theorists, see West, "Theory, Pragmatisms, and Politics," in *Pragmatism: From Progressivism to Postmodernism*, ed. Robert Hollinger and David Depew (Westport, CT: Praeger, 1999), 314.

49. Nancy Frankenberry states: "The most common pragmatist critique of all forms of traditional religious thought, therefore, is that they transpose matters of aspiration too solidly into matters of fact, converting ideal aims into actual powers.", See Frankenberry, "Pragmatism, Truth, and the Disenchantment of Subjectivity," in *Pragmatism and Religion: Classical Sources and Original Essays*, ed. Stuart E. Rosenbaum (Urbana: University of Illinois, 2003), 247.

50. Benhabib and Fraser, *Pragmatism, Critique, Judgment*, 24.

51. Rorty et al., *Revival of Pragmatism*, 24.

52. Rorty, *Philosophy and Social Hope*, 7.

53. See Rorty, "Private and Public Religion," in *Radical Interpretation in Religion*, ed. Nancy Frankenberry, (Cambridge: Cambridge University Press, 2002), 155. Rorty states: "Do not worry too much about whether what you have is a belief, a desire, or a mood. Just insofar as such states as hope, love, and faith promote only such private projects, you need not worry about whether you have a right to have them."

54. Rorty et al., *Revival of Pragmatism*, 31.

55. Habermas et al., *Debating the State of Philosophy*, 29.

56. See Rorty, "Cultural Politics and the Question of the Existence of God," in *Philosophy as Cultural Politics*, 3–26.

57. Rorty, *Philosophy and Social Hope*, 173. For more on Rorty as a verificationist, see Frankenberry, *Radical Interpretation in Religion*, 63.

58. Frankenberry, *Radical Interpretation in Religion*, 62.

59. Habermas et al., *Debating the State of Philosophy*, 14.

60. Frankenberry, *Radical Interpretation in Religion*, 72.

61. Rorty states: "We think of rationality not as the application of criteria, as in a tribunal, but as the achievement of consensus, as in a town meeting, or a bazaar" (*Objectivity, Relativism, and Truth*, 217).

62. Rorty writes: "I want to define rationality as the habit of attaining our ends by persuasion rather than force ... opposition between rationality and irrationality is opposition between words and blows" (Habermas et al., *Debating the State of Philosophy*, 28). For more on Rorty's "coherentist" criterion for rationality, see Rorty, *Philosophy and Social Hope*, 119, and *Objectivity, Relativism, and Truth*, 217.

63. Judith Butler et al., *Power of Religion in the Public Sphere*. 25.

64. See Michael Walzer, *Pluralism, Justice, and Equality* (New York: Oxford University Press 1995) and Crockett Clayton, *Radical Political Theology: Religion and Politics After Liberalism* (New York: Columbia University Press, 2011).

65. Rorty, *Contingency, Irony, and Solidarity*, 192. Rorty also states: "To accept the contingency of starting-points is to accept our inheritance from, and our conversation with, our fellow-humans as our only source of guidance" (*Consequences of Pragmatism*, 166).

66. Habermas et al., *Debating the State of Philosophy*, 48.

67. Ibid., 65.

68. Rorty, *Consequences of Pragmatism*, 203.

69. Matthew Festenstein and Simon Thompson, eds., *Richard Rorty: Critical Dialogues* (Cambridge, UK: Polity Press, 2001), 225.

70. Ibid., 227. See also Michael Walzer, *Thick and Thin: Moral Argument at Home and Abroad* (Notre Dame, IN: University of Notre Dame Press, 2006).

71. Rorty, *Ethics for Today*, 13.

72. Festenstein and Thompson, *Richard Rorty: Critical Dialogues*, 225.

73. Richard Rorty, *Objectivity, Relativism, and Truth*, 206.

74. Rorty states: "What Foucault doesn't give us is what Dewey wanted to give us—a kind of hope which doesn't need reinforcement from the idea of a transcendental or enduring subject" (*Consequences of Pragmatism*, 206).

75. See Simon Critchley, *Deconstruction and Pragmatism* (New York: Routledge, 1996). Rorty states: "I don't find Levinas's *Other* any more useful than Heidegger's *Being*—both strike me as gawky, awkward, and unenlightening. I see ethics as what we have to start creating when we face a choice between two irreconcilable actions, each of which would, in other circumstances, have been equally natural and proper. *Neither my child nor my country is very much like a Levinasian Other*, but when I face a choice between incriminating my child or breaking my country's laws by committing perjury, I start looking around for some ethical principles" (ibid., 41).

76. Balslev, *Cultural Otherness*, 100.

77. Rorty, *Philosophy as Cultural Politics*, 163.

78. Ibid.

79. See John Rawls, *A Theory of Justice* (Cambridge, MA: Belknap Press, 2005). Rawls proposed that the risk involved in tolerating the intolerant is not only a civic virtue, but also has the pragmatic payoff of possibly getting the intolerant to change their views. Rawls states: "The liberties of the intolerant may persuade them to a belief in freedom" (ibid., 218).

80. For more on liberalism and the "notion of 'negative' freedom," see Isaiah Berlin, "Two Concepts of Liberty," in *Four Essays on Liberty* (New York: Oxford University Press, 1969), 122.

81. In Rorty, *Philosophy and Social Hope*, 168–174.

82. Audi and Wolterstorff, *Religion in the Public Square*, 37. See also Owen, *Religion and the Demise of Liberal Rationalism*.

83. It is interesting to note that Rorty's position is not so far from the concerns about idolatry and anthropomorphism found with medieval Jewish philosophers, like Maimonides, who similarly argued that it is impossible to make any definitive statements about God's attributes. Rorty's concerns about invoking privileged knowledge of God's designs within the public arena actually has correlations with debates over negative theology and mystical thought.

84. Habermas et al., *Debating the State of Philosophy*, 106–107.

85. For more on Nicholas Wolterstorff's critique of Rorty see Wolterstorff, "Why We Should Reject What Liberalism Tells Us About Speaking and Acting in Public for Religious Reasons," in *Religion and Contemporary Liberalism*, ed. Paul J. Weithman (Notre Dame, IN: University of Notre Dame Press, 1997), 162–181; and Wolterstorff, "An Engagement with Rorty," in *Understanding Liberal Democracy: Essays in Political Philosophy*, ed. Nicholas Wolterstorff and Terence Cuneo (New York: Oxford University Press, 2012), 41–52.

86. Audi and Wolterstorff, *Religion in the Public Square*, 77.

87. According to Stout, "Rorty's generalized anticlericalism seems to be in tension with anti-antiessentialism" (Auxier and Hahn, *Philosophy of Richard Rorty*, 536).

88. Jeffrey Stout, *Democracy and Tradition*, New Forum Books (Princeton, NJ: Princeton University Press, 2004), 89–90.

89. Ibid., 75.

90. Jeffrey Stout, "Rorty on Religion and Politics," in Auxier and Hahn, *Philosophy of Richard Rorty*, 537 and 527.

91. Ibid., 527.

92. See Martin Jay, "Rorty's Linguistic Transcendentalism," in *Songs of Experience: Modern American and European Variations on a Universal Theme* (Berkeley: University of California Press, 2005), 309.

93. For more on Rorty's critique of "inexplicable," see Isaac Nevo, "Richard Rorty's Romantic Pragmatism," in Hollinger and Depew, *Pragmatism*, 294.

94. Rorty, *Contingency, Irony, and Solidarity*, 146.

95. Rawls, *Theory of Justice*, 218.

96. Robert Brandom, *Rorty and His Critics* (Malden, MA: Blackwell, 2000), 14.

97. Matthew Festenstein, *Pragmatism and Political Theory: From Dewey to Rorty* (Chicago: University Of Chicago Press, 1997), 43.

98. Festenstein and Thompson, *Richard Rorty: Critical Dialogues*, 19.

99. Rorty, *Contingency, Irony, and Solidarity*, 46.

100. See Rorty, "Philosophy as Science, as Metaphor, and as Politics" in *The Institution of Philosophy: A Discipline in Crisis?*, ed. Avner Cohen and Marcelo Dascal (Chicago, IL: Open Court, 1989).

101. Frankenberry, *Radical Interpretation in Religion*, 185.

102. Rorty states: "Tossing a metaphor into a conversation is like suddenly breaking off the conversation long enough to make a face, or pulling a photograph out of your pocket and displaying it, or pointing at a feature of the surroundings, or slapping your interlocutor's face, or kissing him. Tossing a metaphor into a text is like using italics, or illustrations, or odd punctuation or formats. All these are ways of *producing effects* on your interlocutor or your reader, but not ways of conveying a message. To none of these is it appropriate to respond with "What exactly are you trying to say?" (*Contingency, Irony, and Solidarity*, 18).

103. Ibid., 19.

104. Rorty, *Objectivity, Relativism, and Truth*, 163.

105. Paul Ricoeur, *The Rule of Metaphor: The Creation of Meaning in Language*, Routledge Classics (New York: Routledge, 2003), 6.

106. Frankenberry, *Radical Interpretation in Religion*, 182.

107. Rorty, *Objectivity, Relativism, and Truth*, 163.

108. Mitchell Aboulafia, *Transcendence: On Self-Determination and Cosmopolitanism* (Stanford, CA: Stanford University Press, 2010), 6.

109. See Richard J. Bernstein, *The New Constellation: The Ethical-Political Horizons of Modernity/Postmodernity* (Cambridge, MA: MIT Press, 1992), 276–279.

110. Derrida states: "I refuse to renounce the great classical discourse of emancipation. . . . There is no language without the performative dimension of the promise . . . a messianic a priori . . . I do not see how one can pose the question of ethics if one renounces the motifs of emancipation and the messianic" (quoted in Critchley, *Deconstruction and Pragmatism*, 82).

111. Derrida writes: "I do not believe that the themes of undecidability or infinite responsibility are romantic, as Rorty claims. . . . I believe that we cannot give up on the concept of *infinite responsibility*, as Rorty seemed to do at the end of his essay. . . . I would say for Levinas, as for myself, if you give up on the infinitude of responsibility, there is no responsibility" (quoted in Critchley, *Deconstruction and Pragmatism*, 86).

112. See Bernstein, *New Constellation*, 276–279.

113. See John Conway, "Irony, State and Utopia: Rorty's 'We' and the Problem of Transitional Praxis," in Festenstein and Thompson, *Richard Rorty: Critical Dialogues*, 56.

114. Conway concludes the utopianism of Rorty's postmetaphysical hope should be subordinated to the praxis imperatives within traditional pragmatism. "The true pragmatist, after all," Conway argues, "strives to devise a productive use for all available historical resources—including resources as apparently inimical to pragmatic adaptation as is metaphysics for Rorty" (ibid., 74).

115. Rorty, *Contingency, Irony, and Solidarity*, 46.

116. Ibid., 189.

117. Martin, *How We Hope*, 114.

118. John Pettegrew, *A Pragmatist's Progress?* (Lanham, MD: Rowman and Littlefield Publishers, Inc., 2000), 108–109.

119. Brandom, *Rorty and His Critics*, 53. See also Habermas, *Postmetaphysical Thinking*, 133.

120. Habermas, "On the Relation Between the Secular Liberal State and Religion," in *The Frankfurt School on Religion: Key Writings by the Major Thinkers*, ed. Eduardo Mendieta (New York: Routledge, 2005), 339–348.

121. Habermas states: "Secularized citizens, insofar as they are acting in their role as citizens of a state, should neither deny a truth potential to religious worldviews as a matter of principle, nor dispute the right of believing fellow citizens to make contributions to public discussions in religious language. A liberal political culture can even expect of its secularized citizens that they participate in efforts to translate contributions from the religious language into the publicly accessible one" (ibid., 348).

122. For Habermas, Genesis 1:27, which states that all humanity is created in the image of God (*B'stzelem Elo'him*), is the prime example for the type of "saving translation" of religious discourse (ibid., 346).

123. The central dilemma for a liberal contractarian society is its dependence on, according to Habermas, the "willingness, in case of need, to stand in for alien co-citizens who remain anonymous, and *to accept sacrifices* in favor of *general interests*" but that such commitment "can only be suggested to citizens of a liberal society. That is why *political virtues* are essential for the existence of a democracy, even if they are 'charged' in small change only. They are a matter of socialization and habituation to the practices and mentalities of a liberal political culture. The status of a citizen is, so to speak, embedded in a civil society which lives on spontaneous, if you will, *pre-political anchorings*" (ibid., 343). For Lasch's proposal for recovering "a more vigorous form of hope," see Christopher Lasch, *The True and Only Heaven: Progress and Its Critics* (New York: Norton, 1991), 529.

124. See Rorty, "Anticlericalism and Atheism," in Richard Rorty and Gianni Vattimo, *The Future of Religion*, ed. Santiago Zabala (New York: Columbia University Press, 2005), 29–42.

125. Rorty and Vattimo, *Future of Religion*, 56.

126. For more on Rorty's pivot from his position on religion in his earlier essay "Religion as a Conversation-Stopper" see Rorty, "Religion in the Public Square: A Reconsideration," in Voparil and Bernstein, *Rorty Reader*, 456–462.

127. See Shade, *Habits of Hope*.

128. Stephen Fishman and Lucille McCarthy, *John Dewey and the Philosophy and Practice of Hope* (Chicago: University of Illinois Press, 2007), 4.

129. Rorty, *Philosophy and Social Hope*, 120.

130. In his concluding reflections on philosophy and religion post Rorty, G. Elijah Dann sums up the distinction between "religious imagining" and "metaphysics" that Rorty inspires in the following terms: "Religious imagining, in contrast to religious metaphysics, imagines whether there is a God; whether there is an afterworld; whether there is something beyond the physical, wondering how we can explain the love we have for a child or the abject grief at the passing of a loved one" (Rorty, *An Ethics for Today*, 58).

131. For Rorty's distinction between the vertical and the horizontal, see Rorty, *Consequences of Pragmatism*, 92. See also Rorty, *Philosophy as Cultural Politics*, 88.

132. My proposal for understanding Rorty's social hope as a form of what I am terming *horizontal transcendence* draws on Patrick Shade's discussion of "conditioned transcendence" (Shade, *Habits of Hope*, 7). According to Shade "conditioned transcendence" reflects the liminal quality of social hope that is both rooted in the realism of actual conditions while providing the audacity to "act as if" we possessed absolute freedom, and thereby pointing us towards something beyond.

CONCLUSION: BETWEEN PRAGMATIC AND MESSIANIC HOPES

1. Rorty, *Consequences of Pragmatism*, 166.
2. Rorty, *Objectivity, Relativism, and Truth*, 33.
3. See Frankenberry, "Pragmatism, Truth, and the Disenchantment of Subjectivity" in Rosenbaum, *Pragmatism and Religion*, 244.
4. Habermas et al., *Debating the State of Philosophy*, 60.
5. John Rawls, *Political Liberalism* (New York: Columbia University Press, 1993), xx.
6. Mittleman, *Hope in a Democratic Age*, 21.
7. Martin Luther King Jr., "The Other America," speech delivered at Stanford University, April 14, 1967, www.chimesfreedom.com/2015/01/19/martin-luther-king-jr-the-other-america/.
8. See for example, *Achieving Our Country* (1998).
9. Rorty himself admits: "I have no clear sense of what mechanisms might realize that hope" (*Truth and Progress*, 234).
10. Buber, *Between Man and Man*, 175–176.
11. Buber states: "What is legitimately done in the sphere of separation receives its legitimacy from the sphere of wholeness" (*Pointing the Way*, 211).
12. Buber, *Between Man and Man*, 62. For more on Buber's critique of liberalism, see Dan Avnon, *Martin Buber: The Hidden Dialogue* (New York: Rowman and Littlefield, 1998), 151.
13. Buber, *Paths in Utopia*, 87.
14. Schilpp and Friedman, *Philosophy of Martin Buber*, 436.
15. Buber, *I and Thou*, 68.
16. Ibid., 69.
17. Buber, *Paths in Utopia*, 104.
18. For more on the mixture of pragmatism with existentialism within Buber's thought, see Stephen Schwarzschild, *The Pursuit of the Ideal: Jewish Writings of Steven Schwarzschild* (Albany: State University of New York Press, 1990), 190; Pfuetze, *Self, Society, Existence*; Silberstein, *Martin Buber's Social and Religious Thought*; and Paul R. Mendes-Flohr, *Martin Buber: A Contemporary Perspective* (Syracuse, NY: Syracuse University Press, 2002). See also Mordecai Kaplan, "Buber's Evaluation of Philosophic Thought and Religious Tradition," in Schilpp and Friedman, *Philosophy of Martin Buber*, 249–272. For more on Buber and pragmatism, see Robert Weltsch, "Buber's Political Philosophy," in Schilpp and Friedman, *Philosophy of Martin Buber*, 442, and Kavka, "Verification (*Bewährung*) in Martin Buber," 71–98.
19. Buber, *Pointing the Way*, 217.
20. For more on Buber and the revitalization of religious thought in relation to postmodernism, see Eugene B. Borowitz, *Renewing the Covenant: A Theology for*

the Postmodern Jew (Philadelphia: Jewish Publication Society of America, 1998). See also Harold Bloom, "Pragmatics of Jewish Culture," in Cornel West and John Rajchman, *Post-Analytic Philosophy* (New York: Columbia University Press, 1985); Peter Ochs and Nancy Levene, *Textual Reasonings: Jewish Philosophy and Text Study at the End of the Twentieth Century* (Grand Rapids, MI: Eerdmans Publishing, 2003); Mendes-Flohr, *Martin Buber*; John D. Caputo and Michael J. Scanlon, *God, the Gift, and Postmodernism* (Bloomington: Indiana University Press, 1999); Bloechl, *Religious Experience*; and Sylvain Boni, *The Self and the Other in the Ontologies of Sartre and Buber* (Lanham, MD: University Press of America, 1982).

21. This ambivalence on Buber's part was perhaps best captured in his statement, "I am no metaphysician and I am one of the greatest metaphysicians" (Schilpp and Friedman, *Philosophy of Martin Buber*, 717).

22. See James W. Walters, *Martin Buber and Feminist Ethics: The Priority of the Personal*, (Syracuse, NY: Syracuse University Press, 2003). Walters proposed that "both feminist ethics and Buberian thought exemplify the hallmarks of postmodernism" through their mutual commitment to "relational ethics" based on lived experience, and "focus on the concrete person in the caring relation" as the basis for critiquing the "system-building" within traditional epistemology (ibid., 85).

23. See Eugene B. Borowitz, *Choices in Modern Jewish Thought: A Partisan Guide* (Springfield, NJ: Behrman House, 1995). Borowitz states, "Making the I-Thou relationship the basis of ethics conveys no useful content to anyone seeking moral guidance. Its subjectivity does nothing to prevent possible horrible abuses" (160). Fackenheim similarly charged that Buber's construction of subjectivity and writings on revelation "fail to confront radical evil" (*Jewish Philosophers and Jewish Philosophy*, 81). See also Emil Fackenheim, "Martin Buber's Concept of Revelation," and Marvin Fox, "Some Problems in Buber's Moral Philosophy," in Schilpp and Friedman, *Philosophy of Martin Buber*, 273–296 and 151–170, respectively.

24. For more on Buber's controversial approach to revelation, see Eisen, *Rethinking Modern Judaism*, 203.

25. In the words of Fackenheim: "Revelation must assume a content for it to count as revelation and not as the mere fantasies of an individual psyche" (Schilpp and Friedman, *Philosophy of Martin Buber*, 290).

26. Buber, *Eclipse of God*, 127.

27. Fackenheim, *Jewish Philosophers and Jewish Philosophy*, 79.

28. Menachem Kellner, ed., *The Pursuit of the Ideal: Jewish Writings of Steven Schwarzschild* (Albany: State University of New York Press, 1990), 190. According to Schwarzschild: "Buber's own response to the question here raised is vacuous, despite its complexity and sophistication. It amounts to saying that there are no answers, and indeed, that there should not be any answers. Each instance of each relationship is expected to produce its own determination of the proper proportion of it-ness and thou-ness, of goodness and evil.... One may sympathize with people

who say that they speak to God every day; it becomes worrisome when they say that God speaks to them everyday... Buber is really incapable of specifying any evil" (ibid., 192).

29. Scholem, *On Jews and Judaism in Crisis*, 159.

30. Buber, *Paths in Utopia*, 134.

31. Buber, *Believing Humanism*, 95. For more on Buber's theory of recognition, see Buber, *Origin and Meaning of Hasidism*, 91, 159.

32. See Paul Pfuetze, "Martin Buber and American Pragmatism," in Schilpp and Friedman, *Philosophy of Martin Buber*, 511–542, and Pfuetze, *Self, Society, Existence*. Following in these debates on Buber and pragmatism, Shmuel Eisenstadt locates Buber in the middle ground between what is now considered to be neopragmatism's postmodernist critique of foundationalism and what Eisenstadt refers to as "a continuing search for ultimate values." See Eisenstadt, "Buber in the Postmodern Age; Utopia, Community, and Education in the Contemporary Era," in Mendes-Flohr, *Martin Buber*, 174–183. For more on Buber in relation to pragmatism and postmodernism see Michael Zank, ed., *New Perspectives on Martin Buber* (Tübingen: JCB Mohr, 2006).

33. Rorty states: "The distinction between causes and reasons ties in with the difference between Bloom's desire for openness and the philosopher's desire for completeness. Bloom quotes Rabbi Tarphon as saying, 'It is not necessary for you to complete the work, but neither are you free to desist from it.' He [Bloom] glosses this as 'If it were necessary for any among us to complete the work, then we might break off in despair, but the work can never be completed.' The work in question is that of enlarging oneself. That requires being ready to be bowled over by tomorrow's experiences—to remain open to the possibility that the next book you read, or the next person you meet, will change your life" (Voparil and Bernstein, *Rorty Reader*, 392).

34. See Buber, "Distance and Relation," in Buber, *Knowledge of Man*, 49–61.

35. Buber, *Between Man and Man*, 4.

36. For more on religion and the liberal public square, see Audi, *Moral Value*; Audi, *Religious Commitment and Secular Reason*; Audi and Wolterstorff, *Religion in the Public Square*; Kent Greenawalt, *Private Consciences and Public Reasons* (New York: Oxford University Press, 1995); Stuart Hampshire, *Public and Private Morality* (Cambridge: Cambridge University Press, 1978); and Brendan Sweetman, *Why Politics Needs Religion: The Place of Religious Arguments in the Public Square* (Downers Grove, IL: InterVarsity Press, 2006).

37. See Stephen Mulhall and Adam Swift, *Liberals and Communitarians* (Malden, MA: Blackwell Publishing, 1996); Andrea Baumeister, *Liberalism and the Politics of Difference* (Edinburgh: Edinburgh University Press, 2000); Michael Walzer, *Politics and Passion: Toward a More Egalitarian Liberalism* (New Haven, CT: Yale University Press, 2006); Crockett, *Radical Political Theology*; Nancy L. Rosenblum,

Obligations of Citizenship and Demands of Faith (Princeton, NJ: Princeton University Press, 2000); and Paul Weithman, *Religion and the Obligations of Citizenship* (Cambridge: Cambridge University Press, 2002).

38. See Michael J. Sandel, *Democracy's Discontent: America in Search of a Public Philosophy* (Cambridge, MA: Belknap Press, 1998); Sandel, *Liberalism and Its Critics* (New York: New York University Press, 1984); and Sandel, *Liberalism and the Limits of Justice* (Cambridge: Cambridge University Press, 1998).

39. See Thomas Nagel, "The Absurd," in *Mortal Questions* (Cambridge: Cambridge University Press, 1979), 11–23. Nagel states: "The collision between the seriousness with which we take our lives and the perpetual possibility of regarding everything about which we are serious as arbitrary, or open to doubt... We cannot live human lives without energy and attention, nor without making choices which show that we take some things more seriously than others. Yet we have always available a point of view outside the particular form of our lives, from which the seriousness appears gratuitous. These two inescapable viewpoints collide in us, and that is what makes life absurd. It is absurd because we ignore the doubts that we know cannot be settled, continuing to live with nearly undiminished seriousness in spite of them" (ibid., 13).

40. Hartman states: "Despite the presence of various themes in the Biblical story itself, the memory of the Exodus from Egypt provides a theological mode where man is basically helpless before God. Men in no way warrant their redemption nor do they cooperate prominently in their deliverance. In this model, God suddenly breaks into history, and from a 'no people,' he creates his elected community" ("Sinai and Exodus," 382).

41. See Hartman, "Sinai and Exodus," 382.

42. Abraham Joshua Heschel, *God in Search of Man: A Philosophy of Judaism* (New York: Farrar, Strauss and Giroux, 1976), 380.

43. For more on pragmatism and education, see Robert B. Westbrook, *Democratic Hope: Pragmatism and the Politics of Truth* (Ithaca, NY: Cornell University Press, 2005); Green, *Pragmatism and Social Hope*; and Kevin McDonough and Walter Feinberg, *Citizenship and Education in Liberal-Democratic Societies: Teaching for Cosmopolitan Values and Collective Identities* (New York: Oxford University Press, 2006).

44. Buber, *Believing Humanism*, 95

45. Buber, *Between Man and Man*, 88. For more on Buber's philosophy of education, see Silberstein, *Martin Buber's Social and Religious Thought*, 188–189. Also see Ernst Simon, "Martin Buber, The Educator," in *The Philosophy of Martin Buber*, 543–576. Adir Cohen, *The Educational Philosophy of Martin Buber* (Plainsboro, NJ: Associated University Presses, 1983); Daniel Murphy, *Martin Buber's Philosophy of Education* (Dublin: Irish Academic Press, 1988); and Joshua Weinstein, *Buber and Humanistic Education* (New York: Philosophical Library, 1975).

46. Martin Buber, *On the Bible: Eighteen Studies* (Syracuse, NY: Syracuse University Press, 2000), 213.

47. See René Vincente Arcilla, *For the Love of Perfection: Richard Rorty and Liberal Education* (New York: Routledge, 1995); Henry A. Giroux, *Pedagogy and the Politics of Hope: Theory, Culture, and Schooling: A Critical Reader* (New York: Westview Press, 1997); and Peters and Ghiraldelli Jr., *Richard Rorty*.

BIBLIOGRAPHY

Aboulafia, Mitchell. *Transcendence: On Self-Determination and Cosmopolitanism*. Redwood, CA: Stanford University Press, 2010.
Adorno, Theodor. *Minima Moralia*. New York: Verso, 1974.
Alter, Robert. *Necessary Angels: Tradition and Modernity in Kafka, Benjamin, and Scholem*. Cambridge, MA: Harvard University Press, 1991.
Altmann, Alexander. "Moses Mendelssohn as Archetypal German Jew." In Reinharz and Schatzberg, *Jewish Response to German Culture*, 17–31.
Aquinas, Thomas. *Summa Theologiae: A Concise Translation*. Allen, TX: Christian Classics, 1991.
Arcilla, René Vincente. *For the Love of Perfection: Richard Rorty and Liberal Education*. New York: Routledge, 1995.
Arendt, Hannah. "Between Pariah and Parvenu." In *The Origins of Totalitarianism*, 56–67. New York: Harcourt Brace, 1951.
Arkush, Allan. *Moses Mendelssohn and the Enlightenment*. Albany: State University of New York Press, 1994.
Arnold, Bill. "Old Testament Eschatology and the Rise of Apocalypticism." In Walls, *Oxford Handbook of Eschatology*, 23–39.
Ascheim, Steven E. *Culture and Catastrophe: German and Jewish Confrontations with National Socialism and Other Crises*. New York: New York University Press, 1996.
Audi, Robert. *Moral Value and Human Diversity*. New York: Oxford University Press, 2007.
———. *Religious Commitment and Secular Reason*. Cambridge, UK: Cambridge University Press, 2000.
Audi, Robert, and Nicholas Wolterstorff. *Religion in the Public Square: The Place of Religious Convictions in Political Debates, Point/Counterpoint*. Lanham, MD: Rowman and Littlefield Publishers, 1997.
Auxier, Randall, and Lewis Hahn, eds. *The Philosophy of Richard Rorty*. Chicago: Open Court, 2010.

Avnon, Dan. *Martin Buber: The Hidden Dialogue*. New York: Rowman and Littlefield, 1998.
Baker, Keith, and Peter Reill. *What's Left of Enlightenment? A Postmodern Question*. Stanford, CA: Stanford University Press, 2002.
Balibar, Étienne, and Warren Montag. *Spinoza and Politics*. Translated by Peter Snowdon. Brooklyn, NY: Verso, 2008.
Balslev, Anindita Niyogi. *Cultural Otherness: Correspondence with Richard Rorty*. New York: Oxford University Press, 1999.
Barth, Karl. *The Epistle to the Romans*. Translated by Edwyn Clement Hoskyns. New York: Oxford University Press, 1950.
Batnitzky, Leora. *How Judaism Became a Religion: An Introduction to Modern Jewish Thought*. Princeton, NJ: Princeton University Press, 2011.
———. *Idolatry and Representation*. Princeton, NJ: Princeton University Press, 2000.
Bauman, Zygmunt. *Modernity and the Holocaust*. Ithaca, NY: Cornell University Press, 2001.
———. *Postmodern Ethics*. Oxford, UK: Blackwell, 1994.
Baumeister, Andrea. *Liberalism and the Politics of Difference*. Edinburgh: Edinburgh University Press, 2000.
Bell, Daniel. *The End of Ideology: On the Exhaustion of Political Ideas in the Fifties*. Cambridge, MA: Harvard University Press, 2000.
Benjamin, Andrew. *Present Hope: Philosophy, Architecture, Judaism*. New York: Routledge, 1997.
Benjamin, Mara H. *Rosenzweig's Bible: Reinventing Scripture for Jewish Modernity*. Cambridge: Cambridge University Press, 2009.
Benjamin, Walter. *Illuminations: Essays and Reflections*. New York: Schocken Books, 1969.
Berger, Peter L. *The Sacred Canopy: Elements of a Sociological Theory of Religion*. New York: Anchor Books, 1990.
Berlin, Isaiah. "The Decline of Utopian Ideals in the West." In *The Crooked Timber of Humanity: Chapters in the History of Ideas*, 20–48. New York: Vintage Books, 1992.
———. "From Hope and Fear Set Free." In *The Proper Study of Mankind: An Anthology of Essays*, edited by Henry Hardy and Roger Hausheer, 91–118. London: Chatto and Windus, 1997.
———. *Political Ideas in the Romantic Age: Their Rise and Influence on Modern Thought*. Princeton, NJ: Princeton University Press, 2006.
———. "Two Concepts of Liberty." In *Four Essays on Liberty*. New York: Oxford University Press, 1969.
Bernstein, Richard J. *The New Constellation: The Ethical-Political Horizons of Modernity/Postmodernity*. Cambridge, MA: MIT Press, 1992.

———. *Pragmatism, Critique, Judgment: Essays for Richard J. Bernstein*. Edited by Seyla Benhabib, and Nancy Fraser. Cambridge, MA: MIT Press, 2004.

Biale, David. *Gershom Scholem: Kabbalah and Counter-History*. Cambridge, MA: Harvard University Press, 1982.

Biemann, Asher D. *Inventing New Beginnings: On the Idea of Renaissance in Modern Judaism*. Stanford, CA: Stanford University Press, 2009.

Birnbaum, Pierre. *Geography of Hope: Exile, the Enlightenment, Disassimilation*. Stanford, CA: Stanford University Press, 2008.

Bloch, Ernst. *Atheism in Christianity: The Religion of the Exodus and the Kingdom*. New York: Verso, 2009.

———. "Hunger, Something in a Dream, God of Hope, Thing-for-us." In *The Frankfurt School on Religion: Key Writings by the Major Thinkers*, edited by Eduardo Mendieta, 49–51. New York: Routledge, 2005.

———. "Karl Marx, Death, and the Apocalypse." Part 2 in *The Spirit of Utopia*. Stanford, CA: Stanford University Press, 2000.

———. *Literary Essays, Meridian*. Stanford, CA: Stanford University Press, 1998.

———. *Man on His Own: Essays in the Philosophy of Religion*. New York: Herder and Herder, 1970.

———. *The Principle of Hope*. Cambridge: MIT Press, 1986.

Bloechl, Jeffrey. *Religious Experience and the End of Metaphysics*. Bloomington: Indiana University Press, 2003.

Bloom, Harold. "The Pragmatics of Contemporary Jewish Culture." In Rajchman and West, *Post-Analytic Philosophy*, 108–128.

Boni, Sylvain. *The Self and the Other in the Ontologies of Sartre and Buber*. Lanham, MD: University Press of America, 1982.

Borowitz, Eugene B. *Choices in Modern Jewish Thought: A Partisan Guide*. Springfield, NJ: Behrman House, 1995.

———. *Our Way to a Postmodern Judaism: Three Lectures*. San Francisco: University of San Francisco, 1993.

———. *Renewing the Covenant: A Theology for the Postmodern Jew*. Philadelphia: Jewish Publication Society of America, 1998.

Bouretz, Pierre. *Witnesses for the Future: Philosophy and Messianism*. Baltimore, MD: John Hopkins University Press, 2010.

Braiterman, Zachary. *(God) after Auschwitz*. Princeton, NJ: Princeton University Press, 1998.

Brandom, Robert. *Making It Explicit: Reasoning, Representing, and Discursive Commitment*. Cambridge, MA: Harvard University Press, 1994.

———. *Rorty and His Critics*. Malden, MA: Blackwell, 2000.

Brenner, Michael. *The Renaissance of Jewish Culture in Weimar Germany*. New Haven, CT: Yale University Press, 1996.

Brueggemann, Walter. *Hope within History*. Louisville, KY: Westminster John Knox Press, 1986.

———. *Hopeful Imagination: Prophetic Voices in Exile*. Minneapolis, MN: Augsburg Fortress Publishers, 1986.

Buber, Martin. *A Believing Humanism: My Testament, 1902–1965*. Amherst, NY: Prometheus Books, 1990.

———. *Between Man and Man*. New York: Macmillan, 1975.

———. *Eclipse of God: Studies in the Relation between Religion and Philosophy*. New York: Harper, 1988.

———. *For the Sake of Heaven*. 2nd ed. Philadelphia: Jewish Publication Society of America, 1953.

———. *Good and Evil*. New York: Prentice Hall, 1980.

———. *Israel and the World: Essays in a Time of Crisis*. Syracuse, NY: Syracuse University Press, 1997.

———. "Jewish Religiosity." Chap. 5 in *On Judaism*. New York: Schocken Books, 1996.

———. *Kingship of God*. Highlands, NJ: Humanities Press, 1990.

———. *The Knowledge of Man: Selected Essays*. Amherst, NY: Humanity Books, 1988.

———. *On the Bible: Eighteen Studies*. Syracuse, NY: Syracuse University Press, 2000.

———. *The Origin and Meaning of Hasidism*. Atlantic Highlands, NJ: Humanities Press International, 1988.

———. *Pointing the Way: Collected Essays*. Edited and translated Maurice S. Friedman. New York: Harper and Row, 1963.

———. *The Prophetic Faith*. New York: Harper and Row, 1960.

———. *Two Types of Faith*. London: Routledge and Paul, 1951.

Buber, Martin, and Hermann Cohen. "A Debate on Zionism and Messianism." In Mendes-Flohr and Reinharz, *The Jew in the Modern World*, 571–576.

Buck-Morss, Susan. *The Dialectics of Seeing: Walter Benjamin and the Arcades Project*. Cambridge, MA: MIT Press, 1991.

———. *Dreamworld and Catastrophe: The Passing of Mass Utopia in East and West*. Cambridge, MA: MIT Press, 2002.

———. *Origin of Negative Dialectics*. New York: Free Press, 1979.

Burrow, J. W. *The Crisis of Reason: European Thought, 1848–1914*. New Haven, CT: Yale University Press, 2002.

Butler, Judith, Jürgen Habermas, Charles Taylor, and Cornel West. *The Power of Religion in the Public Sphere*. Edited by Eduardo Mendieta and Jonathan Van Antwerpen. New York: Columbia University Press, 2011.

Byrne, James M. *Religion and the Enlightenment: From Descartes to Kant*. Louisville, KY: Westminster John Knox Press, 1997.

Capps, Walter H. *The Future of Hope: Essays by Bloch, Fackenheim, Moltmann, Metz, Capps*. Minneapolis, MN: Fortress Press, 1970.

Caputo, John D., and Michael J. Scanlon, *God, the Gift, and Postmodernism*. Bloomington: Indiana University Press, 1999.

Cassirer, Ernst. *The Philosophy of the Enlightenment*. Princeton, NJ: Princeton University Press, 1951.

Clayton, Crockett. *Radical Political Theology: Religion and Politics After Liberalism*. New York: Columbia University Press, 2011.

Cohen, Adir. *The Educational Philosophy of Martin Buber*. Plainsboro, NJ: Associated University Presses, 1983);

Cohen, Arthur. "Redemption." In Cohen and Mendes-Flohr, *Contemporary Jewish Religious Thought*, 417–422.

Cohen, Arthur, and Paul Mendes-Flohr, eds. *Contemporary Jewish Religious Thought*. New York: Free Press, 1988.

Cohen, Hermann. *Religion of Reason: Out of the Sources of Judaism*. Atlanta, GA: Scholars Press, 1995.

———. "The Social Idea as Seen by Plato and by the Prophets." In *Reason and Hope: Sections from the Jewish Writings of Hermann Cohen*, 66–77. Cincinnati, OH: Hebrew Union College, 1993.

Cohen, Margaret. *Profane Illumination: Walter Benjamin and the Paris of Surrealist Revolution*. Berkeley: University of California Press, 1995.

Cohn, Norman. *Cosmos, Chaos, and the World to Come*. New Haven, CT: Yale University Press, 1999.

Critchley, Simon. *Deconstruction and Pragmatism*. New York: Routledge, 1996.

Dan, Joseph. "Gershom Scholem and Jewish Messianism." In Mendes-Flohr, *Gershom Scholem*, 73–86.

Daniel, Jamie Owen, and Tom Moylan. *Not Yet: Reconsidering Ernst Bloch*. New York: Verso, 1997.

Day, J. P. "Hope." *American Philosophical Quarterly* 6, no. 2 (1969): 89–102.

Eagleton, Terry. *Culture and the Death of God*. New Haven, CT: Yale University Press, 2014.

Eisen, Arnold M. *Rethinking Modern Judaism: Ritual, Commandment, Community*. Chicago: University of Chicago Press, 1998.

Eisenstadt, Shmuel. "Buber in the Postmodern Age: Utopia, Community, and Education in the Contemporary Era." In Mendes-Flohr, *Martin Buber*, 174–183.

Erlewine, Robert. *Monotheism and Tolerance: Recovering a Religion of Reason*. Bloomington: Indiana University Press, 2010.

Eshel, Amir. "Cosmopolitanism and Searching for the Sacred Space in Jewish Literature." *Jewish Social Studies* 9, no. 3 (Spring/Summer 2003): 121–138.

Fackenheim, Emil. *Encounters between Judaism and Modern Philosophy: A Preface to Future Jewish Thought*. New York: Basic Books, 1973.

———. *Jewish Philosophers and Jewish Philosophy*. Bloomington: Indiana University Press, 1996.

———. "Martin Buber's Concept of Revelation." In Schilpp and Friedman, *Philosophy of Martin Buber*, 273–296.

Faulconer, James E. *Transcendence in Philosophy and Religion*. Bloomington: Indiana University Press, 2003.

Feiner, Shmuel. *The Jewish Enlightenment*. Philadelphia: University of Pennsylvania Press, 2002.

Festenstein, Matthew. *Pragmatism and Political Theory: From Dewey to Rorty*. Chicago: University Of Chicago Press, 1997.

Festenstein, Matthew, and Simon Thompson, eds. *Richard Rorty: Critical Dialogues*. Cambridge, UK: Polity Press, 2001.

Feuerbach, Ludwig. *The Essence of Christianity*. Amherst, NY: Prometheus Books, 1989.

Fishman, Stephen, and Lucille McCarthy. *John Dewey and the Philosophy and Practice of Hope*. Chicago: University of Illinois Press, 2007.

Fox, Marvin. "Some Problems in Buber's Moral Philosophy." In Schilpp and Friedman, *Philosophy of Martin Buber*, 151–170.

Frankenberry, Nancy. "Pragmatism, Truth, and the Disenchantment of Subjectivity." In *Pragmatism and Religion: Classical Sources and Original Essays*, edited Stuart E. Rosenbaum, 243–264. Urbana: University of Illinois, 2003.

Freudenthal, Gideon. *No Religion without Idolatry: Mendelssohn's Jewish Enlightenment*. Notre Dame, IN: University of Notre Dame, 2012.

Friedman, Lawrence. *The Lives of Erich Fromm: Love's Prophet*. New York: Columbia University Press, 2013.

Friedman, Maurice S. *Encounter on the Narrow Ridge: A Life of Martin Buber*. New York: Paragon House, 1991.

———. *Martin Buber: The Life of Dialogue*, 4th rev. and exp. ed. New York: Routledge, 2002.

———. *Martin Buber's Life and Work: The Early Years, 1878–1923*. New York: Dutton, 1981.

———. *Martin Buber's Life and Work: The Middle Years, 1923–1945*. New York: Dutton, 1983.

Fromm, Erich. *The Revolution of Hope: Toward a Humanized Technology*. New York: Harper and Row, 1968.

———. *You Shall Be as Gods: A Radical Interpretation of the Old Testament and Its Tradition*. New York: Holt, Rinehart and Winston, 1966.

G. B. Madison, "Ricoeur and the Hermeneutics of the Subject." In *The Philosophy of Paul Ricoeur*, ed. Lewis Edwin Hahn, 75–92. Chicago: Open Court, 1994.

Gauchet, Marcel. *The Disenchantment of the World: A Political History of Religion*. Princeton, NJ: Princeton University Press, 1997.

Gay, Peter. *The Enlightenment: An Interpretation.* New York: Norton, 1977.
Giroux, Henry A. *Pedagogy and the Politics of Hope: Theory, Culture, and Schooling: A Critical Reader.* New York: Westview Press, 1997.
———. *Politics After Hope: Obama and the Crisis of Youth, Race and Democracy.* St. Paul, MN: Paradigm Publishers, 2010.
Godfrey, Joseph. *A Philosophy of Human Hope: Studies in Philosophy and Religion.* Boston, MA: Academic Publishers, 1987.
Goetschel, Willi. *The Discipline of Philosophy and the Invention of Modern Jewish Thought.* New York: Fordham University Press, 2013.
Goldstein, Rebecca. *Betraying Spinoza: The Renegade Jew Who Gave Us Modernity.* New York: Schocken, 2006.
Gordon, Haim. *The Heidegger-Buber Controversy: The Status of the I-Thou.* Westport, CT: Greenwood Press, 2001.
Gordon, Peter Eli. *Rosenzweig and Heidegger: Between Judaism and German Philosophy.* Berkeley: University of California Press, 2003.
Gottlieb, Michah. *Faith and Freedom: Moses Mendelssohn's Theological-Political Thought.* New York: Oxford University Press, 2011.
Graetz, Heinrich. "The Stages in the Evolution of Messianic Belief." In *The Structure of Jewish History and Other Essays,* 72–73. Jersey City, NJ: Ktav Publishing House, 1975.
Gray, John. *Black Mass: Apocalyptic Religion and the Death of Utopia.* New York: Macmillan, 2008.
Green, Judith M. *Pragmatism and Social Hope: Deepening Democracy in Global Contexts.* New York: Columbia University Press, 2008.
Greenawalt, Kent. *Private Consciences and Public Reasons.* New York: Oxford University Press, 1995.
Grenz, Stanley J., and John R. Franke. *Beyond Foundationalism: Shaping Theology in a Postmodern Context.* Louisville, KY: Westminster John Knox Press, 2001.
Groopman, Jerome E. *The Anatomy of Hope: How People Prevail in the Face of Illness.* New York: Random House, 2004.
Gross, Neil. *Richard Rorty: The Making of an American Philosophy.* Chicago: University of Chicago Press, 2008.
Guignon, Charles, and David R. Hiley. *Richard Rorty.* Cambridge: Cambridge University Press, 2003.
Gumbrecht, Hans Ulrich. *Production of Presence: What Meaning Cannot Convey.* Stanford, CA: Stanford University Press, 2004.
Habermas, Jürgen. "The German Idealism of the Jewish Philosophers," in *Religion and Rationality: Essays on Reason, God, and Modernity.* Cambridge, MA: MIT Press, 2002.
———. "On the Relation Between the Secular Liberal State and Religion." In *The Frankfurt School on Religion: Key Writings by the Major Thinkers,* ed. Eduardo Mendieta, 339–348. New York: Routledge, 2005.

———. *Postmetaphysical Thinking*. Cambridge, UK: Polity Press, 1994.
Habermas, Jürgen, Richard Rorty, Leszek Kolakowski, József Niznik, John T. Sanders, *Debating the State of Philosophy: Habermas, Rorty, and Kolakowski*. Westport, CT: Praeger, 1996.
Hampshire, Stuart. *Public and Private Morality*. Cambridge: Cambridge University Press, 1978.
———. *Spinoza and Spinozism*. New York: Oxford University Press, 2005.
Handelman, Susan A. *Fragments of Redemption: Jewish Thought and Literary Theory in Benjamin, Scholem, and Levinas*. Bloomington: Indiana University Press, 1991.
———. *The Slayers of Moses*. Albany: State University of New York Press, 1983.
Harding, Vincent. *Hope and History: Why We Must Share the Story of the Movement*. Maryknoll, NY: Orbis Books, 2010.
Hardwick, Charley D., and Donald A. Crosby. *Pragmatism, Neo-Pragmatism, and Religion: Conversations with Richard Rorty*. New York: Peter Lang, 1997.
Hartman, David. "Learning to Hope." Chap. 7 in *From Defender to Critic: The Search for a New Jewish Self*. Woodstock, VT: Jewish Lights Publishing, 2012.
———. "Sinai and Exodus: Two Grounds for Hope in the Jewish Tradition." *Religious Studies* 14, no. 3 (September 1978): 373–387.
Harvey, Van A. *Feuerbach and the Interpretation of Religion*. Cambridge: Cambridge University Press, 1997.
Hernandez, Jill. *Gabriel Marcel's Ethics of Hope: Evil, God, and Virtue*. New York: Bloomsbury Academic, 2011.
Heschel, Abraham Joshua. *God in Search of Man: A Philosophy of Judaism*. New York: Farrar, Strauss and Giroux, 1976.
Heschel, Susannah. *Abraham Geiger and the Jewish Jesus*. Chicago: University of Chicago Press, 1998.
Hess, Jonathan M. *Germans, Jews, and the Claims of Modernity*. New Haven, CT: Yale University Press, 2002.
Hobsbawm, E. J. *Revolutionaries*. New York: New Press, 2001.
Hodge, Roger D. *The Mendacity of Hope: Barack Obama and the Betrayal of American Liberalism*. New York: HarperCollins, 2010.
Horwitz, Rivka. *Buber's Way to "I and Thou": The Development of Martin Buber's Thought and His "Religion as Presence" Lectures*. Philadelphia: Jewish Publication Society of America, 1980.
Huston, Phil. *Martin Buber's Journey to Presence*. New York: Fordham University Press, 2007.
Innerarity, Daniel. *The Future and Its Enemies: In Defense of Political Hope*. Stanford, CA: Stanford University Press, 2012.
Israel, Jonathan I. *Enlightenment Contested: Philosophy, Modernity, and the Emancipation of Man 1670–1752*. New York: Oxford University Press, 2006.

Jacobs, Jonathan A. *Judaic Sources and Western Thought: Jerusalem's Enduring Presence*. New York: Oxford University Press, 2011.

———. *New Directions in Jewish Philosophy*. Bloomington: Indiana University Press, 2010.

Jacobson, Eric. *Metaphysics of the Profane: The Political Theology of Walter Benjamin and Gershom Scholem*. New York: Columbia University Press, 2003.

Jacoby, Russell. *The End of Utopia: Politics and Culture in an Age of Apathy*. New York: Basic Books, 1999.

———. *Picture Imperfect: Utopian Thought for an Anti-Utopian Age*. New York: Columbia University Press, 2005.

James, Susan. *Spinoza on Philosophy, Religion, and Politics: The Theologico-Political Treatise*. New York: Oxford University Press, 2012.

Jay, Martin. *Downcast Eyes: The Denigration of Vision in Twentieth-Century French Thought*. Berkeley: University of California Press, 1994.

———. "Ernst Bloch and the Extension of Marxist Holism to Nature." Chap. 5 in *Marxism and Totality: The Adventures of a Concept from Lukács to Habermas*. Berkeley: University of California Press, 1984.

———. "The Politics of Translation: Siegfried Kracauer and Walter Benjamin on the Buber-Rosenzweig Bible." In *Permanent Exiles: Essays on the Intellectual Migration from Germany to America*, 198–216. New York: Columbia University Press, 1985.

———. *Refractions of Violence*. New York: Routledge, 2003.

———. *Songs of Experience: Modern American and European Variations on a Universal Theme*. Berkeley: University of California Press, 2005.

———. *The Virtues of Mendacity: On Lying in Politics*. Charlottesville: University of Virginia Press, 2012.

Jonas, Hans. "Utopia and the Idea of Progress." In *The Imperative of Responsibility: In Search of an Ethics for the Technological Age*, 160–177. Chicago: University of Chicago Press, 1984.

Kant, Immanuel, *Critique of Pure Reason*. In *The Cambridge Edition of the Works of Immanuel Kant*, edited by Paul Guyer and Allen W. Wood. Cambridge: Cambridge University Press, 1998.

———. *Critique of Practical Reason*. New York: Cambridge University Press, 1997.

———. *Religion within the Boundaries of Mere Reason*. Edited by Allen W. Wood and George di Giovanni. Cambridge: Cambridge University Press, 1998.

Kaplan, Mordecai. "Buber's Evaluation of Philosophic Thought and Religious Tradition." In Schilpp and Friedman, *Philosophy of Martin Buber*, 249–272.

———. "The Belief in God." Chap. 10 in *The Future of the American Jew*. New York: Reconstructionist Press, 1967.

Kasimow, Harold, and Byron L. Sherwin, eds. *No Religion Is an Island: Abraham Joshua Heschel and Interreligious Dialogue*. Maryknoll, NY: Orbis, 1991.

Kaufmann, David. "Thanks for the Memory: Bloch, Benjamin, and the Philosophy of History." Chap. 3 in *Not Yet! Reconsidering Ernst Bloch*, ed. Jamie Owen Daniel and Tom Moylan. New York: Verso, 1997.

Kavka, Martin. *Jewish Messianism and the History of Philosophy*. Cambridge: Cambridge University Press, 2004.

Kavka, Martin. "Verification (*Bewährung*) in Martin Buber." *Journal of Jewish Thought and Philosophy* 20, no. 1 (2012): 71–98.

Kellner, Menachem, ed. *The Pursuit of the Ideal: Jewish Writings of Steven Schwarzschild*. Albany: State University of New York Press, 1990.

Kelly, Anthony. *Eschatology and Hope*. Maryknoll, NY: Orbis Books, 2006.

Kepnes, Steven. *Interpreting Judaism in a Postmodern Age*. New York: New York University Press, 1995.

———. *Reasoning after Revelation: Dialogues in Postmodern Jewish Philosophy*. New York: Westview Press, 2001.

Kesler, Charles R. *I Am the Change: Barack Obama and the Crisis of Liberalism*. New York: HarperCollins, 2012.

King, Martin Luther, Jr. "The Other America." Speech delivered at Stanford University, April 14, 1967. www.chimesfreedom.com/2015/01/19/martin-luther-king-jr-the-other-america/.

———. "Pilgrimage to Nonviolence." Chap. 15 in *Strength to Love*. Minneapolis, MN: Fortress Press, 1981.

Koltun-Fromm, Ken. *Material Culture and Jewish Thought in America*. Bloomington: Indiana University Press, 2010.

———, ed. *Thinking Jewish Culture in America*. Lanham, MD: Lexington Books, 2013.

Koopman, Colin. *Pragmatism as Transition: Historicity and Hope in James, Dewey, and Rorty*. New York: Columbia University Press, 2009.

Landes, Richard. *Heaven On Earth: The Varieties of the Millennial Experience*. New York: Oxford University Press, 2011.

Lasch, Christopher. *The True and Only Heaven: Progress and Its Critics*. New York: Norton, 1991.

Lazier, Benjamin. *God Interrupted: Heresy and the European Imagination Between the World Wars*. Princeton, NJ: Princeton University Press, 2012.

Lear, Jonathan. *Radical Hope: Ethics in the Face of Cultural Devastation*. Cambridge, MA: Harvard University Press, 2009.

Leo Strauss. *Jewish Philosophy and the Crisis of Modernity: Essays and Lectures in Modern Jewish Thought*. Edited by Kenneth Hart Green. Albany: State University of New York Press, 1997.

Lerner, Akiba. "Otherness and Liberal Democratic Solidarity: Buber, Kaplan, Levinas and Rorty's Social Hope." In Koltun-Fromm, *Thinking Jewish Culture in America*, 31–70.

Levinas, Emmanuel. *Existence and Existents*. Pittsburgh: Duquesne University Press, 1978.

———. *God, Death, and Time, Meridian, Crossing Aesthetics*. Stanford, CA: Stanford University Press, 2000.

———. "Martin Buber and the Theory of Knowledge." In Schilpp and Friedman, *Philosophy of Martin Buber*, 133–150.

———. "Martin Buber, Gabriel Marcel, and Philosophy." In *Outside the Subject, Meridian: Crossing Aesthetics*, 20–39. Stanford, CA: Stanford University Press, 1994.

Levine, Michael. *A Weak Messianic Power: Figures of a Time to Come in Benjamin, Derrida, and Celan*. New York: Fordham University Press, 2013.

Librett, Jeffrey S. *The Rhetoric of Cultural Dialogue: Jews and Germans from Moses Mendelssohn to Richard Wagner and Beyond, Cultural Memory in the Present*. Stanford, CA: Stanford University Press, 2000.

Liessmann, Konrad Paul. "Despair and Responsibility: Affinities and Differences in the Thought of Hans Jonas and Günther Anders." Chap. 6 in *The Legacy of Hans Jonas: Judaism and the Phenomenon of Life*, edited by Hava Tirosh-Samuelson and Christian Wiese. Leiden, NL: Brill, 2010.

Lilla, Mark. *The Stillborn God: Religion, Politics, and the Modern West*. New York: Random House, 2008.

Locke, John. *An Essay Concerning Human Understanding*. Oxford: Oxford University Press, 1975.

Lorberbaum, Menachem. *Politics and the Limits of Law: Secularizing the Political in Medieval Jewish Thought*. Stanford, CA: Stanford University Press, 2001.

Löwy, Michael. *Redemption and Utopia: Jewish Libertarian Thought in Central Europe: A Study in Elective Affinity*. London: Athlone Press, 1992.

Lyotard, Jean-Francois. *The Postmodern Condition: A Report on Knowledge*. Minneapolis, MN: University of Minnesota Press, 1984.

Macy, Joanna, and Chris Johnstone. *Active Hope: How to Face the Mess We're in without Going Crazy*. Novato, CA: New World Library, 2012.

Mannheim, Karl. *Ideology and Utopia: An Introduction to the Sociology of Knowledge*. New York: Houghton Mifflin Harcourt, 1985.

Marcel, Gabriel. "Desire and Hope." In *Readings in Existential Phenomenology*, edited by Nathaniel Morris Lawrence and Daniel Denis O'Connor 277–285. Englewood Cliffs, NJ: Prentice-Hall, 1967.

———. "I and Thou." In Schilpp and Friedman, *Philosophy of Martin Buber*, 41–48.

———. "Martin Buber's Philosophical Anthropology." In *Searchings*, 73–92. New York: Newman Press, 1967.

———. *The Philosophy of Existentialism*. New York: Citadel Press, 1962.

———. "Sketch of a Phenomenology and a Metaphysic of Hope." Chap. 2 in *Homo Viator: Introduction to a Metaphysic of Hope*. London: Gollancz, 1951.

Martin, Adrienne. *How We Hope: A Moral Psychology*. Princeton, NJ: Princeton University Press, 2014.

Mason, Richard. *The God of Spinoza: A Philosophical Study*. Cambridge: Cambridge University Press, 1999.

Matustik, Martin Beck. *Radical Evil and the Scarcity of Hope*. Bloomington: Indiana University Press, 2008.

McCammon, Christopher. "Overcoming Deism: Hope incarnate in Kant's Rational Religion." In *Kant and the New Philosophy of Religion*, ed. Chris L. Firestone and Stephen Palmquist, 79–89. Bloomington: Indiana University Press, 2006.

McDonough, Kevin, and Walter Feinberg. *Citizenship and Education in Liberal-Democratic Societies: Teaching for Cosmopolitan Values and Collective Identities*. New York: Oxford University Press, 2006.

McLaren, Peter, Ramin Farahmandpur, and Juha Suoranta. "Richard Rorty's Self-Help Liberalism: A Marxist Critique of America's Most Wanted Ironist." In Peters and Ghiraldelli Jr., *Richard Rorty*, 139–162.

Mendelssohn, Moses. *Jerusalem: Or on Religious Power and Judaism*. Edited by Alexander Altmann. Lebanon, NH: Brandeis University Press, 1983.

———. "The Right to Be Different. 1783." In Mendes-Flohr and Reinharz, *The Jew in the Modern World*, 68–69.

Mendes-Flohr, Paul. *Divided Passions: Jewish Intellectuals and the Experience of Modernity*. Detroit, MI: Wayne State University Press, 1991.

———. *From Mysticism to Dialogue: Martin Buber's Transformation of German Social Thought*. Detroit, MI: Wayne State University Press, 1989)

———. *Gershom Scholem: The Man and His Work*. Albany: State University of New York Press, 1994.

———. "The Kingdom of God: Martin Buber's Critique of Messianic Politics," *Behemoth: A Journal on Civilization* 1, no. 2 (2008): 26–38.

———, ed. *Martin Buber: A Contemporary Perspective*. Syracuse, NY: Syracuse University Press, 2002.

———. *The Philosophy of Franz Rosenzweig*. Lebanon, NH: Brandeis University Press, 1988.

———. "'The Stronger and the Better Jews': Jewish Theological Responses to Political Messianism in the Weimar Republic." In *Jews and Messianism in the Modern Era: Metaphor and Meaning*, edited by Jonathan Frankel, 159–196. New York: Oxford University Press, 1991.

Mendes-Flohr, Paul, and Jehuda Reinharz, eds. *The Jew in the Modern World: A Documentary History*. New York: Oxford University Press, 1995.

Minowitz, Peter. *Straussophobia: Defending Leo Strauss and Straussians against Shadia Drury and Other Accusers*. Lanham, MD: Lexington Books, 2009.

Mittleman, Alan. *Hope in a Democratic Age*. New York: Oxford University Press, 2009.

———. "Messianic Hope." In *Covenant and Hope: Christian and Jewish Reflections: Essays in Constructive Theology from the Institute for Theological Inquiry*, edited by Robert W. Jenson and Eugene Korn, 220–243. Grand Rapids, MI: William B. Eerdmans Publishing, 2012.

Moltmann, Jürgen "Progress and Abyss: Remembrances of the Future of the Modern World." In Volf and Katerberg, *Future of Hope*, 10–11.

———. *Theology of Hope: On the Ground and the Implications of a Christian Eschatology*. London: SCM Press, 2002.

Moore, Donald J. *Martin Buber: Prophet of Religious Secularism*. New York: Fordham University Press, 1996.

Morgan, Michael. *Interim Judaism: Jewish Thought in a Century of Crisis*. Bloomington: Indiana University Press, 2001.

Moses, Stephane. *System and Revelation: The Philosophy of Franz Rosenzweig*. Detroit, MI: Wayne State University Press, 1991.

Mosse, George L. *Confronting the Nation: Jewish and Western Nationalism*. Lebanon, NH: Brandeis University Press, 1993.

———. *German Jews Beyond Judaism*. Bloomington: Indiana University Press, 1985.

———. "Jewish Emancipation: Between Bildung and Respectability." In Reinharz and Schatzberg, *Jewish Response to German Culture*, 1–16.

Mulhall, Stephen, and Adam Swift. *Liberals and Communitarians*. Malden, MA: Blackwell Publishing, 1996.

Murdoch, Iris. "Martin Buber and God." Chap. 15 in *Metaphysics as a Guide to Morals*. New York: Vintage, 2003.

Murphy, Daniel. *Martin Buber's Philosophy of Education*. Dublin: Irish Academic Press, 1988.

Muyskens, James L. *The Sufficiency of Hope: Conceptual Foundations of Religion*. Philadelphia: Temple University Press, 1979.

Nadler, Steven. *A Book Forged in Hell: Spinoza's Scandalous Treatise and the Birth of the Secular Age*. Princeton, NJ: Princeton University Press, 2011.

———. *Spinoza's Heresy: Immortality and the Jewish Mind*. New York: Oxford University Press, 2001.

Nagel, Thomas. "The Absurd." In *Mortal Questions*, 11–23. Cambridge: Cambridge University Press, 1979.

Niebuhr, Reinhold. "Optimism, Pessimism, and Religious Faith." In *The Essential Reinhold Niebuhr: Selected Essays and Addresses*, edited by Robert McAfee Brown, 3–17. New Haven, CT: Yale University Press, 1986.

Nietzsche, Friedrich. "The Antichrist." In *The Portable Nietzsche*, edited and translated by Walter Kaufman, 565–656. New York: Penguin Books, 1976.

Novak, David. "Jewish Eschatology." In Walls, *The Oxford Handbook of Eschatology*, 113–131.

O'Brown, Norman. *Life Against Death: The Psychoanalytical Meaning of History*. Middletown, CT: Wesleyan University Press, 1959.

Obama, Barack. *The Audacity of Hope: Thoughts on Reclaiming the American Dream*. New York: Crown, 2006.

———. "Remarks at a Victory Celebration in Chicago, Illinois." November 7, 2012. www.gpo.gov/fdsys/pkg/DCPD-201200873/pdf/DCPD-201200873.pdf.

Ochs, Peter, and Nancy Levene, *Textual Reasonings: Jewish Philosophy and Text Study at the End of the Twentieth Century*. Grand Rapids, MI: Eerdmans Publishing, 2003.

Olson, Alan M. *Transcendence and the Sacred*. Notre Dame, IN: University of Notre Dame Press, 1994.

Osborne, Peter. *Walter Benjamin: Critical Evaluations in Cultural Theory*. New York: Routledge, 2004.

Owen, Judd. *Religion and the Demise of Liberal Rationalism: The Foundational Crisis of the Separation of Church and State*. Chicago: University of Chicago Press, 2001.

Peters, Curtis H. *Kant's Philosophy of Hope*. New York: Peter Lang, 1993.

Peters, Michael A. and Paulo Ghiraldelli Jr., eds. *Richard Rorty: Education, Philosophy, and Politics*. Lanham, MD: Rowman and Littlefield, 2001.

Pettegrew, John. *A Pragmatist's Progress?*. Lanham, MD: Rowman and Littlefield, 2000.

Pfuetze, Paul. "*Martin Buber and American Pragmatism*," in Schilpp and Friedman, *Philosophy of Martin Buber*, 511–542.

———. *Self, Society, Existence: Human Nature and Dialogue in the Thought of George Herbert Mead and Martin Buber*. Westport, CT: Greenwood Press, 1973.

Pieper, Josef. *Hope and History*. San Francisco: Ignatius Press, 1994.

Plant, Raymond. *Politics, Theology and History*. Cambridge: Cambridge University Press, 2001.

Polkinghorne, John. *The God of Hope and the End of the World*. New Haven, CT: Yale University Press, 2003.

Portnoff, Sharon. *Reason and Revelation Before Historicism: Strauss and Fackenheim*. Toronto, ON: University of Toronto Press, 2011.

Preus, J. Samuel. *Spinoza and the Irrelevance of Biblical Authority*. Cambridge: Cambridge University Press, 2001.

Rabinbach, Anson. "Between Apocalypse and Enlightenment: Benjamin, Bloch, and Modern German-Jewish Messianism." Chap. 1 in *The Shadow of Catastrophe: German Intellectuals Between Apocalypse and Enlightenment*. Berkeley: University of California Press, 2001.

———. "Between Enlightenment and Apocalypse: Benjamin, Bloch and Modern German Jewish Messianism." *New German Critique* no. 34 (Winter 1985): 78–124.

Rajchman, John, and Cornel West, eds. *Post-Analytic Philosophy*. New York: Columbia University Press, 1985.
Rawls, John. *Political Liberalism*. New York: Columbia University Press, 1993.
———. *A Theory of Justice*. Cambridge, MA: Belknap Press, 2005.
Ray, Matthew Alun. *Subjectivity and Irreligion: Atheism and Agnosticism in Kant, Schopenhauer, and Nietzsche*. Surry, UK: Ashgate Publishing, 2004.
Reinharz, Jehuda, and Walter Schatzberg. *The Jewish Response to German Culture: From the Enlightenment to the Second World War*. Lebanon, NH: University Press of New England, 1985.
Ricoeur, Paul. "The Critique of Religion." In *The Philosophy of Paul Ricoeur*, ed. Charles E. Reagan and David Stewart, 213–222. Boston, MA: Beacon Press, 1978.
———. "Freedom in the Light of Hope." In *The Conflict of Interpretations: Essays in Hermeneutics*, edited by Don Ihde, 402–424. Evanston, IL: Northwestern University Press, 1974.
———. "Hope and the Structure of Philosophical Systems." In *Figuring the Sacred: Religion, Narrative, and Imagination*, edited by Mark I. Wallace, 293–302. Minneapolis: Fortress Press, 1995.
———. *The Rule of Metaphor: The Creation of Meaning in Language*. New York: Routledge, 2003.
Rorty, Richard. *Achieving Our Country: Leftist Thought in Twentieth-Century America*. Cambridge, MA: Harvard University Press, 1998.
———. "Anticlericalism and Atheism." In *The Future of Religion*, by Richard Rorty and Gianni Vattimo, edited Santiago Zabala, 29–42. New York: Columbia University Press, 2005.
———. *Consequences of Pragmatism: Essays, 1972–1980*. Minneapolis: University of Minnesota Press, 1982.
———. *Contingency, Irony, and Solidarity*. Cambridge: Cambridge University Press, 1989.
———. "Cultural Politics and the Question of the Existence of God." In *Radical Interpretation in Religion*, edited by Nancy Frankenberry, 53–77. Cambridge: Cambridge University Press, 2002.
———. *Essays on Heidegger and Others*. Cambridge: Cambridge University Press, 1991.
———. *An Ethics for Today: Finding Common Ground between Philosophy and Religion*. New York: Columbia University Press, 2010.
———. *Objectivity, Relativism, and Truth*. Cambridge: Cambridge University Press, 1991.
———. *Philosophy and Social Hope*. New York: Penguin Books, 1999.
———. "Philosophy and the Future," In *Rorty and Pragmatism: The Philosopher Responds to His Critics*, edited by Herman J. Saatkamp, 197–205. Nashville, TN: Vanderbilt University Press, 1995.

———. *Philosophy and the Mirror of Nature*. Princeton, NJ: Princeton University Press, 1979.
———. *Philosophy as Cultural Politics*. Cambridge: Cambridge University Press, 2007.
———. "Philosophy as Science, as Metaphor, and as Politics." In *The Institution of Philosophy: A Discipline in Crisis?*, edited by Avner Cohen and Marcelo Dascal, 13–33. Chicago, IL: Open Court, 1989.
———. "Redemption from Egotism: James and Proust as Spiritual Exercises." In Voparil and Bernstein, *Rorty Reader*, 389–406.
———. "Religion in the Public Square: A Reconsideration." In Voparil and Bernstein, *Rorty Reader*, 456–462.
———. *Truth and Progress*. Cambridge: Cambridge University Press, 1998.
Rorty, Richard, et al., *The Revival of Pragmatism: New Essays on Social Thought, Law, and Culture*. Durham, NC: Duke University Press, 1998.
Rose, Gillian. *Judaism and Modernity: Philosophical Essays*. Hoboken, NJ: Blackwell, 1993.
———. *The Melancholy Science: An Introduction to the Thought of Theodor W. Adorno*. New York: Columbia University Press, 1979.
Rose, Paul Lawrence. *German Question/Jewish Question: Revolutionary Anti-semitism from Kant to Wagner*. Princeton, NJ: Princeton University Press, 1992.
Rosenblum, Nancy L. *Obligations of Citizenship and Demands of Faith*. Princeton, NJ: Princeton University Press, 2000).
Rosenstock, Bruce. *Philosophy and the Jewish Question: Mendelssohn, Rosenzweig, and Beyond*. New York: Fordham University Press, 2009.
Rosenzweig, Franz. *On Jewish Learning*. Edited by Nahum Norbert Glatzer. Madison: University of Wisconsin Press, 1955.
Roshwald, Ariel. *The Endurance of Nationalism: Ancient Roots and Modern Dilemmas*. Cambridge: Cambridge University Press, 2006.
Roskies, David G. *Against the Apocalypse: Responses to Catastrophe in Modern Jewish Culture*. Syracuse, NY: Syracuse University Press, 1999.
Rossi, Philip J., and Michael J. Wreen. *Kant's Philosophy of Religion Reconsidered*. Bloomington: Indiana University Press, 1991.
Rotensteich, Nathan. "Gershom Scholem's Conception of Jewish Nationalism." In Mendes-Flohr, *Gershom Scholem*, 104–119.
———. *Jewish Philosophy in Modern Times: From Mendelssohn to Rosenzweig*. New York: Holt, Rinehart, and Winston, 1968.
Rothstein, Edward, Herbert Muschamp, and Martin Marty. *Visions of Utopia*. New York: Oxford University Press, 2003.
Saint Augustine. *The City of God*. Translated by Marcus Dods. New York: Modern Library, 1993.

Sandel, Michael J. *Democracy's Discontent: America in Search of a Public Philosophy*. Cambridge, MA: Belknap Press, 1998);
——. *Liberalism and Its Critics*. New York: New York University Press, 1984);
——. *Liberalism and the Limits of Justice*. Cambridge: Cambridge University Press, 1998.
Sarachek, Joseph. *The Doctrine of the Messiah in Medieval Jewish Literature*. New York: Hermon Press, 1968.
Schilpp, Paul Arthur, and Maurice S. Friedman, eds. *The Philosophy of Martin Buber*. La Salle, IL: Open Court, 1967.
Scholem, Gershom. *The Messianic Idea in Judaism and Other Essays on Jewish Spirituality*. New York: Schocken Books, 1980.
——. "Messianism: A Never-Ending Quest," in *On the Possibility of Jewish Mysticism in Our Time: And Other Essays*. Philadelphia: Jewish Publication Society, 1997.
——. *On Jews and Judaism in Crisis: Selected Essays*. New York: Schocken, 1976.
——. *Walter Benjamin: The Story of a Friendship*. Philadelphia: Jewish Publication Society of America, 1981.
Schultz, Bart. "Obama's Political Philosophy: Pragmatism, Politics, and the University of Chicago." *Philosophy of the Social Sciences* 39, no. 2 (2009): 127–173.
Schumacher, Bernard. *A Philosophy of Hope: Josef Pieper and the Contemporary Debate on Hope*. New York: Fordham University Press, 2003.
Schwartz, Regina. *Transcendence: Philosophy, Literature, and Theology Approach the Beyond*. New York: Routledge, 2004.
Schwarzschild, Stephen. *The Pursuit of the Ideal: Jewish Writings of Steven Schwarzschild*. Albany: State University of New York Press, 1990);
Scioli, Anthony, and Henry Biller. *Hope in the Age of Anxiety*. New York: Oxford University Press, 2009.
Seeskin, Kenneth. *Jewish Philosophy in a Secular Age*. Albany: State University of New York Press, 1990.
Shade, Patrick. *Habits of Hope: A Pragmatic Theory*. Nashville, TN: Vanderbilt University Press, 2001.
Sheehan, Thomas. "A Paradigm Shift in Heidegger's Research," *Continental Philosophy Review* 34, no. 2 (June 2001): 183–202.
Silberstein, Laurence J. *Martin Buber's Social and Religious Thought: Alienation and the Quest for Meaning*. New York: New York University Press, 1989.
Smith, Steven B. *Spinoza, Liberalism, and the Question of Jewish Identity*. New Haven, CT: Yale University Press, 1998.
Snyder, C. R. *Psychology of Hope: You Can Get Here from There*. New York: Free Press, 2003.
Sorkin, David. *The Religious Enlightenment: Protestants, Jews, and Catholics from London to Vienna*. Princeton, NJ: Princeton University Press, 2008.

———. *The Transformation of German Jewry 1780–1840*. New York: Oxford University Press, 1987.
Spinoza, Benedictus de. *A Theologico-Political Treatise and a Political Treatise*. New York: Dover, 1951.
Steinberg, Michael P. *Walter Benjamin and the Demands of History*. Ithaca, NY: Cornell University Press, 1996.
Stout, Jeffrey. *Democracy and Tradition, New Forum Books*. Princeton, NJ: Princeton University Press, 2004.
———. *Flight from Authority: Religion, Morality, and the Quest for Autonomy*. Notre Dame, IN: University of Notre Dame, 1987.
Strauss, Leo. *Spinoza's Critique of Religion*. New York: Schocken Books, 1965.
Sweetman, Brendan. *Why Politics Needs Religion: The Place of Religious Arguments in the Public Square*. Downers Grove, IL: InterVarsity Press, 2006.
Taubes, Jacob. "Martin Buber and the Philosophy of History." Chap. 2 in *From Cult to Culture: Fragments Toward a Critique of Historical Reason*, edited by Charlotte Fonrobert and Amir Engel. Stanford, CA: Stanford University Press, 2010.
———. "Nihilism as World Politics and Aestheticized Messianism: Walter Benjamin and Theodor W. Adorno." In *The Political Theology of Paul*, translated by Dana Hollander, 70–76. Stanford, CA: Stanford University Press, 2003.
———. *Occidental Eschatology*. Translated by David Ratmoko. Stanford, CA: Stanford University Press, 2009.
Tewes, Henning, and Jonathan Wright. *Liberalism, Anti-Semitism, and Democracy: Essays in Honour of Peter Pulzer*. New York: Oxford University Press, 2001.
Thompson, Peter, and Slavoj Žižek, eds. *The Privatization of Hope: Ernst Bloch and the Future of Utopia*. Durham, NC: Duke University Press, 2013.
Todorov, Tzvetan. *Hope and Memory: Lessons from the Twentieth Century*. Princeton, NJ: Princeton University Press, 2003.
Tomasoni, F. *Modernity and the Final Aim of History: The Debate over Judaism from Kant to the Young Hegelians*. New York: Springer, 2003.
Tucker, Robert C. *The Marx-Engels Reader*. 2nd ed. New York: W. W. Norton.
Urbach, Ephraim. *The Sages: Their Concepts and Beliefs*. Cambridge, MA: Harvard University Press, 1979.
Vernoff, Charles. "Hope." In Cohen and Medes-Flohr, *Contemporary Jewish Religious Thought*, 417–421.
Volf, Miroslav, and William H. Katerberg, eds. *The Future of Hope: Christian Tradition Amid Modernity and Postmodernity*. Grand Rapids, MI: William B. Eerdmans, 2004.
Voparil, Christopher J., and Richard J. Bernstein, eds. *The Rorty Reader*. Hoboken, NJ: Wiley-Blackwell, 2010.
Walls, Jerry L., ed. *The Oxford Handbook of Eschatology*. New York: Oxford University Press, 2008.

Walters, James W. *Martin Buber and Feminist Ethics: The Priority of the Personal,*. Syracuse, NY: Syracuse University Press, 2003.
Walzer, Michael. *In God's Shadow: Politics in the Hebrew Bible*. New Haven, CT: Yale University Press, 2012.
Walzer, Michael. *Pluralism, Justice, and Equality*. New York: Oxford University Press 1995.
———. *Politics and Passion: Toward a More Egalitarian Liberalism*. New Haven, CT: Yale University Press, 2006.
———. *Thick and Thin: Moral Argument at Home and Abroad*. Notre Dame, IN: University of Notre Dame Press, 2006.
Walzer, Michael, Menachem Lorberbaum, Noam J. Zohar, and Yair Loberbaum. *The Jewish Political Tradition*, vol. 1, *Authority*. New Haven, CT: Yale University Press, 2003.
Wasserstrom, Steven. *Religion After Religion: Gershom Scholem, Mircea Eliade, and Henry Corbin at Eranos*. Princeton, NJ: Princeton University Press, 1999.
Weinstein, Joshua. *Buber and Humanistic Education*. New York: Philosophical Library, 1975.
Weithman, Paul. *Religion and the Obligations of Citizenship*. Cambridge: Cambridge University Press, 2002.
Weltsch, Robert. "Buber's Political Philosophy." In Schilpp and Friedman, *Philosophy of Martin Buber*, 435–450.
West, Cornel. *The American Evasion of Philosophy*. Madison: University of Wisconsin Press, 1989.
———. "Last Words on the Black Prophetic Tradition in the Age of Obama". In *Black Prophetic Fire*, 161–165. Boston, MA: Beacon Press, 2014.
———. "The Politics of American Neo-Pragmatism." Afterword in Rajchman and West, *Post-Analytic Philosophy*.
———. *Restoring Hope: Conversations on the Future of Black America*. Boston, MA: Beacon Press, 1999.
———. "Theory, Pragmatisms, and Politics." In *Pragmatism: From Progressivism to Postmodernism*, edited by Robert Hollinger and David Depew, 314–326. Westport, CT: Praeger, 1999.
West, Thomas H. *Ultimate Hope without God: The Atheistic Eschatology of Ernst Bloch*. New York: Peter Lang, 1991.
Westbrook, Robert B. *Democratic Hope: Pragmatism and the Politics of Truth*. Ithaca, NY: Cornell University Press, 2005.
Wolfson, Elliot. *Giving Beyond the Gift: Apophasis and Overcoming Theomania*. New York: Fordham University Press, 2014.
Wolin, Richard. "Reflections on Jewish Secular Messianism." In *Jews and Messianism in the Modern Era: Metaphor and Meaning*, ed. Jonathan Frankel, 186–196. New York: Oxford University Press, 1991.

———. *Walter Benjamin: An Aesthetic of Redemption*. Berkeley: University of California Press, 1994);

Wolterstorff, Nicholas. "An Engagement with Rorty." In *Understanding Liberal Democracy: Essays in Political Philosophy*, edited by Nicholas Wolterstorff and Terence Cuneo, 41–52. New York: Oxford University Press, 2012.

———. "Why We Should Reject What Liberalism Tells Us About Speaking and Acting in Public for Religious Reasons." In *Religion and Contemporary Liberalism*, edited Paul J. Weithman, 162–181. Notre Dame, IN: University of Notre Dame Press, 1997.

Wood, Allen W. *Kant's Ethical Thought*. Cambridge: Cambridge University Press, 1999.

———. *Kant's Moral Religion*. Ithaca, NY: Cornell University Press, 1970.

Wyschogrod, Edith. *An Ethics of Remembering: History, Heterology, and the Nameless Others*. Chicago, IL: University of Chicago Press, 1998.

———. "Hasidism, Hellenism, Holocaust: A Postmodern View," in Kepnes, *Interpreting Judaism in a Postmodern Age*, 301–324.

———. *Saints and Postmodernism: Revisioning Moral Philosophy*. Chicago: University of Chicago Press, 1990.

Wyschogrod, Michael. *The Body of Faith: God and the People Israel*. New York: Rowman and Littlefield Publishers, 1996.

Yovel, Yirmiyahu. *Kant and the Philosophy of History*. Princeton, NJ: Princeton University Press, 1980.

———. *Kant's Practical Philosophy Reconsidered*. New York: Springer, 1989.

———. *Spinoza and Other Heretics*. Vol. 1. Princeton, NJ: Princeton University Press, 1992.

Zank, Michael, ed. *New Perspectives on Martin Buber*. Tübingen: JCB Mohr, 2006.

INDEX

"The Absurd" (Nagel), 122–123
Adam knew his wife, 58–59
Adorno, Theodor, 68
afterlife, Kant, 34
agents of justice, 101
agents of love, 101
Albo, Joseph, 24–25
apocalyptic faith: *versus* messianic, 44–46; psychological needs and, 44; rupture paradigm, 46–47; Scholem on, 49–50
Aquinas, Thomas, 21; eternal life, 24; foundational narratives, 22–24; hope as imperfect virtue, 23; *Summa Theologiae*, 23
atheism, messianism and, 73–74
Atheism in Christianity (Bloch), 72
The Audacity of Hope (Obama), 10
Augustine (Saint), 21; *The City of God*, 22; foundational narratives, 22–23
Auschwitz, poetry after, 83

becoming: *versus* Being, 71; consciousness and, 69–70; force-for-becoming, 73
Being and Time (Heidegger), 61
Being *versus* becoming, 71
Benjamin, Walter: Adorno's negative dialictics, 68; Bloch and, 66–67; on despair, 68; memory, 67; messianic hope, 67
biblically inspired redemptive narratives, 21–22; Aquinas, 22–24; Augustine, 22–23
Bloch, Ernst, 17, 64; *Atheism in Christianity*, 72; Benjamin and, 66–67; de-Hellenization of faith, 79–80; *The Future of Hope*, 79; God of Exodus, 71–73; hope, consciousness and, 70–71; horizontal redemptive hope, 71; "Karl Marx, Death and the Apocalypse," 69; Marxism and, 65–66, 69; metaphysics of becoming, 155n50; not-yet messianism, 65–78; *The Principle of Hope*, 69–70; prophetic contribution, 154n34; school of hope and, 78; *The Spirit of Utopia*, 66
Bloechl, Jeffrey, *Religious Experience and the End of Metaphysics*, 89
Brueggemann, Walter: *Hope Within History*, 81–82; *Hopeful Imagination: Prophetic Voices in Exile*, 81–82
Buber, Martin, 2, 16–17, 19–20; Cohen, Hermann, and, 44–45, 141n24; 142n27; distancing, 121; encounters, 117; eschatological hope, 42–43, 140n14; finitude and the infinite, 62; Hasidism and, 46–47, 52; "Hope for This Hour," 64; *I and Thou*, 53–54; Israelite messianism, 144n48; I-Thou, 53; Jewish messianism, 145n61; Jewish mysticism and, 42; *The Kingship of God*, 42; messianism and, 42, 45–46; *Paths in Utopia*, 47; Pauline transformation of prophetic hope, 44; Persian messianism, 144n48; philosophical anthropologist, 148nn94,95; philosophy *versus* faith experience, 149n100; political theology *versus* political philosophy, 52; pragmatism, 115–117; priestly principle, 43–44; *Prophetic Faith*, 43; prophetic hope, 43–45; religion, 75; religiosity, 75; revelation, 63–64, 151n132; solidarity, 118–123; subjectivity, 58–61; teaching *versus* pointing to something, 149n97; *Two Types of Faith*, 44

Capps, Walter: *The Future of Hope,* 79; "Mapping the Hope Movement," 79; school of hope and, 78
children, I-Thou, 59–60
Christianity: interiorization of redemption and, 141n15; Rosenzweig on, 48
The City of God (Augustine), 22
civic good, 13–14
Cohen, Herman, 22; Buber and, 141n24, 142n27; I-Thou relationships, 55, 147n75; prophetic hope, 44–45
commandment, hope and, 82–86
"The Commandment to Hope" (Fackenheim), 83–86
communion experiences, 54; drive for, 61
consciousness: anticipatory, relationships and, 76; becoming and, 69–70; hope and, 70–71; negation of present and, 76
Contemporary Jewish Religious Thought (Vernoff), 82–83
"The Continuity Between the Enlightenment and Postmodernism" (Rorty), 91
Conway, John, 108
cosmic order, 5
crisis with reason, 89
Critique of Pure Reason (Kant), 30–31

Dann, G. Elijah, 166n130
despair: in Benjamin, 68; Fackenheim and, 83; hope and, 8–9; hope narratives and, 10–11; hope over, 84
determinism *versus* hope for redemption, 21
dialogic encounters, 55
the divine, self-sufficiency, 28
drive for communion, 61

ecumenism, American pragmatism and, 103–104
education, 123–125
egalitarian utopia, 91
empiricists, 29–31
the Enlightenment: hope and, 8; secular utopian hopes, 26
eschatological hope, 42–43, 140n14; prophetic hope and, 45–46
eternal life, 24
ethical relativism, Rorty and, 95
Ethics (Spinoza), 27
existential solidarity, 118–123
experience: of communion, 54; encounter and, 53; Jay, Martin, 5–6; lived, 53; original sin and, 23; secular redemptive narratives, 26–27

Fackenheim, Emil, 17; on Buber, 117; commandment, 84; *The Future of Hope,* 79; school of hope and, 78; "The Commandment to Hope," 83–86
"Failed Prophecies, Glorious Hopes" (Rorty), 94
faith: de-Hellenization, 79–80; Kant, 32; knowledge and, 30–31; necessity, 34; as psychological impediment, 35–39; secularization, 35
fate *versus* hope for redemption, 21
fear, danger of, 27
Feuerbach, Ludwig, 35; religion, 36
force-for-becoming, 73
forward look *versus* upward look, 70–71, 75–76
Frankenberry, Nancy, raft metaphor, 113–114
Frankfurt School, 38–39
Freud, Sigmund, 35
Fromm, Eric: blind optimism, 87–88; resigned optimism, 158n89; *The Revolution of Hope,* 87–88; *The Revolution of Hope: Toward a Humanized Technology,* 18; *You Shall Be as Gods,* 86–87
The Future of Hope symposium, 78–79; de-Hellenization of faith, 79–80
The Future of Religion (Zabala), 89

Genealogy of Morality (Nietzsche), 37
God: hope and, 23–24, 32–33; of Parmenides *versus* God of Exodus, 80–81; promise *versus* presence, 81
God of Exodus, 71–73
Graetz, Heinrich, 22; eschatological hope and, 42–43
Gumbrecht, Hans Ulrich, 63

Habermas, Jürgen, 14; liberal contractarian society, 166n123; postmetaphysical thinking, 89; secularized citizens, 165n121
halakhic hope, 47, 143n36
happiness, moral perfection and, 31–32
Hartman, David, 46–47, 76; approaches to hope and messiansim, 142n34; halakhic hope, 143n36; radical hope, 143n36
Hasidism: Buber and, 46–47, 52; sublimation of redemptive fervor, 52
Hegel, Georg: *The Philosophy of Right,* 69; Young Hegelians, 36
Heidegger, Martin: *Being and Time,* 61; on hope, 60–61

history: historian's as practitioner of memory, 67; purpose and meaning, 22; and redemption, 48–52; as teacher, 33
hope: affective, 5; attainable goals, 24; blind optimism and, 87–88; cognitive, 5; commandment and, 82–86; as coping mechanism, 37; danger of, 27; despair and, 8–9; encounter and, 113–118; *versus* faith, 82; *versus* fantasies, 24; future of, education, 123–125; future possibilities and, 7; God and, 23–24, 32–33; idealism and, 6; intellectual reflection as source, 78–79; justificatory rationale, 6; Kant, 31–32; normative, 54; paradox of, 86–89; phenomenology of, 5; post Shoah, 82–83; postmetaphysical, 103–112; proximate, 6–7; rational agency and, 6; realism and, 6; revelation and, 64; transcendental source and, 2–3; ultimate, 6–7; *versus* wishes, 24
"Hope for This Hour" (Buber), 64
hope narratives: foundational, 22–24
Hope Within History (Brueggemann), 81–82
Hopeful Imagination: Prophetic Voices in Exile (Brueggemann), 81–82
hopeover, 1
horizontal projection, 79
horizontal redemptive hope, 71
horizontal transcendence, 111, 119, 166n132
human agency in redemptive process, 46–47

I and Thou (Buber), 53–54
"Idea for a Universal History from a Cosmopolitan Point of View" (Kant), 33
idealism, hope and, 6
idolatrous impulses, 57
idolatry, religion and, 70, 73
I-It consciousness, 56–57, 60
individual good, 13–14
intellectual reflection as source of hope, 78–79
interiorization of redemption, Christianity and, 141n15
intersubjective recognition, 58–59
Israelite messianism, 144n48
Israelite political theology, 42
I-Thou relationships, 53, 116; children, 59–60; Cohen, Herman, 55, 147n75; intersubjective recognition, 58–59; to know the other, 58–59; phenomenology of hope and, 55; presence, 63–64; responsibility for the other, 56; trust of eternity and, 62–63; vision, disengagement and, 57–58. *See also* relationships

Jay, Martin, 105; *Songs of Experience,* 6
Jeffersonian compromise, 99
Jerusalem (Mendelsohn), 29
Jewish hope, Vernoff on, 82
"Justice as a Larger Loyalty" (Rorty), 100–101

Kant, Immanuel, 21; afterlife, 34; *Critique of Pure Reason,* 30–31; faith, 32; necessity, 34; hope, 31–32; hope, God and, 32–33; "Idea for a Universal History from a Cosmopolitan Point of View," 33; Kingdom of Ends, 62; moral perfection, 33; morality, rationality and, 30; "Perpetual Peace," 33; postulates of pure practical reason, 32–34; *Religion with the Boundaries of Mere Reason,* 32; Supreme Being, 32
"Karl Marx, Death and the Apocalypse" (Bloch), 69
Kingdom of Ends, 62
The Kingship of God (Buber), 42
knowing the other, 58–59
knowledge: faith and, 30–31; synthetic, 30–31

Le Radeau de la Méduse (Gericault), 113–114
liberal boundaries between public and private, 121–122
liberal tolerance, social dynamism and, 102–103
liberalism, 95
literature teaching as spiritual exercise, 111
loyalty, 100–102

Maimonides, Moses, 24–25; redemption, 133n12
"Mapping the Hope Movement" (Capps), 79
Marcel, Gabriel, phenomenology of hope, 53–54
Marx, Karl, 35; *The Philosophy of Right* (Hegel), 69, utopian narratives, 16–17
Marxism: Bloch and, 65–66, 69; religious narratives and, 94
meaning effects, 63
memory, Benjamin and, 67
Mendelsohn, Moses, *Jerusalem,* 29
messianic hope: apocalyptic hope and, 41–47; Benjamin, 67; evolution, 43–44; Graetz, 42–43; post-WWI, 40–41; relationships and, 55

messianism, 20; *versus* apocalyptic faith, 44–46; atheism and, 73–74; the infinite and the particular, 51; Israelite, 144n48; left-wing German politics, 45–46; maximalist political disposition, 49–50; Persian, 144n48; process, 46; Scholem, Gershom, 48–50; soteriological hope and, 44
metaphors, Rorty, 106–107
Metz, Johannes, school of hope and, 78
midrash, 5
Moltmann, Jürgen, 35; God of Parmenides *versus* God of Exodus, 80–81; school of hope and, 78; *Theology of Hope: On the Ground and the Implications of a Christian Eschatology*, 77, 80
moral confidence, secular redemptive narratives, 38–39
moral perfection, happiness and, 31–32
Mosaic man *versus* Socratic man, 58

Nachmanides, 24–25
Nagel, Thomas, "The Absurd," 122–123
neopragmatism, 90–91; Rorty, 16, 20; utopian hopes, 97. See also Rorty, Richard
Nietzsche, Friedrich, 35–37; *Genealogy of Morality*, 37; hope as coping mechanism, 37; metaphysics, 37–38
normative hope, 54
not-yet messianism, Bloch, 65–78

Obama, Barack, 1; *The Audacity of Hope*, 10; redemptive narratives and, 9–15; reelection speech, 10–11

paradox of hope, 86–89
Paths in Utopia (Buber), 47
"Perpetual Peace" (Kant), 33
Persian messianism, 144n48
phenomenology of hope, 5, 53–64; I-Thou encounters, 55
Philosophy and the Mirror of Nature (Rorty), 20
The Philosophy of Right (Hegel), 69
political theology, *versus* political philosophy, 52
possibility, hope and, 7
postfoundational ethics, Rorty, 96
postideological phase, 78
postmetaphysical hope, 103–112
postmetaphysical solidarity, 100–103
postmetaphysical thinking, Habermas and, 89
postmetaphysical utopianism, 97–100
postulates of pure practical reason, 32–34

postutopian phase, 78
pragmatic solidarity, 118–123
presence effects, 63
The Principle of Hope (Bloch), 69–70
private pursuits, 98–99
projection, horizontal *versus* vertical, 79
Prophetic Faith (Buber), 43
prophetic hope, 43–45; eschatology and, 45–46
proximate hopes, 6–7

raft metaphor, 113–114
Rawls, John, 105; ecumenical pragmatism, 110–111
realism, hope and, 6
reason: crisis with, 89; emancipation, 35; postulates of pure practical reason, 32; virtue and, 31
redemption: human involvement, 46–47; Maimonides, 133n12; Rorty, 19
redemptive hope: abuses, 15–20; disenchantment, 34; phenomenology, 53–64; social control and, 27; sources, 4–5; term use, 7; uses, 15–20
redemptive narratives: American founding mythology, 11; biblically inspired, 6–7, 21–22; danger in, 8; disenchantment, 36; need for, 1; religious, premodern, 24–25; secular, 26–27; Western, evolution, 16; Young Hegelians, 36
relationships: anticipatory consciousness, 76; communion experiences and, 54; dialogic encounters, 55; hope and encounter, 113–118; messianic hope and, 55; normative hope and, 54; responsibility for the other, 56; self and, 53, 55, 61. See also I-Thou relationships
religion: Buber on, 75; Feuerbach, 36; idolatry and, 70, 73; negation and, 72–73; premodern redemptive hope narratives, 24–25; redemptive traditions, 5; social hierarchies, 86–87; Spinoza on, 27–29; upward look *versus* forward look, 70–71, 75–76
Religion after Metaphysics (Vattimo), 89
"Religion as a Conversation Stopper" (Rorty), 103
Religion within the Boundaries of Mere Reason (Kant), 32
religiosity, 75
Religious Experience and the End of Metaphysics (Bloechl), 89
resigned optimism, 158n89
responsibility for other, 56
revelation, 63; hope and, 63–64

The Revolution of Hope (Fromm), 87–88
The Revolution of Hope: Toward a Humanized Technology (Fromm), 18
Rorty, Richard, 2–3, 17; contingency, iron, and solidarity, 93; "The Continuity Between the Enlightenment and Postmodernism," 91; demythologizing, 98; ethical relativism and, 95; excess of living in hope, 121; "Failed Prophecies, Glorious Hopes," 94; harmonization of science and religion, 94–95; heavenly voice lack, 108–109; idolatry, 163n83; Jewish thinkers and, 20; "Justice as a Larger Loyalty," 100–101; literature as spiritual exercise, 111; loyalty, 100–102; metaphors, 106–107, 164n102; neopragmatism, 90–93, 120; *Philosophy and the Mirror of Nature,* 20; postfoundational ethics, 96; postmetaphysical hope, 103–112; postmetaphysical solidarity, 100–103; postmetaphysical utopiansim, 97–100; private autonomy, 122; prophetic hope, 160n41; raft metaphor (Frankenberry), 113–114; on recovery, 94; redemption, 19; "Religion as a Conversation Stopper," 103; religious discourses, 93–94; social cooperation, 99–100; solidarity and, 18–19; to Jeffrey Stout, 161n44; transitional praxis, 108; utilitarian tolerance, 93; utopian liberalism, 93; vulnerability and, 95; on Western culture, 92–93
Rosenzweig, Franz, *Star of Redemption,* 47–48
rupture paradigm of apocalyptic faith, 46–47

sacred/profane and public/private, 110
Scholem, Gershom, 25–26; apocalyptic destruction, 49–50; Buber and, 118; history and redemption, 48–50; Zionism, 144n53, 145n55; on Zionism, 50–51
school of hope, 18, 78
Schwarzschild, Steven, 118
science and religion, harmonizing, 94–95
secular messianism, 139n3
secular redemptive narratives, 26–27; moral confidence and, 38–39
self: otherness and, 58–60; relationships and, 53, 55, 61
self creation, 98–99
self-preservation, 105–106
self-sufficiency of the divine, 28

Shoah: hope after, 82–83; hope and poetry after Auschwitz, 83
social control, redemptive hope and, 27
social cooperation, 99–100
social dynamism, liberal tolerance and, 102–103
social goods, 13–14
social hierarchies, religion and, 86–87
social hope, 2
solidarity, 2, 18, 61–62, 90–91; education, 123–125; existential, 118–123; postmetaphysical, 100–103; pragmatic, 118–123; truth and, 3
Songs of Experience (Jay), 6
soteriological hope, messianism and, 44
soteriology, historical transformation and, 45
soulcraft, 14, 101–102
Spinoza: *Ethics,* 27; fear, abuse of, 27–28; fear, danger of, 27; hope, abuse of, 27–28; hope, danger of, 27; rational reflection, 28; redemptive narratives and civil administration, 26–27; *The Theological-Political Treatise,* 27–28
The Spirit of Utopia (Bloch), 66
Star of Redemption (Rosenzweig), 47–48
statecraft, 14, 101–102
Stout, Jeffrey, 104, 161n44
Strauss, Leo, 13
subjectivity, Buber and, 58–61
Summa Theologiae (Aquinas), 23
Supreme Being, Kant, 32
synthetic knowledge, 30–31, 95

technology, post-WWI, 16
The Theological-Political Treatise (Spinoza), 27–28
Theology of Hope: On the Ground and the Implications of a Christian Eschatology (Moltmann), 77, 80
theomania, 57
tolerance, right of, 105–106
transcendence, 12–13
transcendental source of hope, 2–3
transitional praxis, 119
trust of eternity, 62–63
truth, solidarity and, 3
Two Types of Faith (Buber), 44

ultimate hopes, 6–7
unsocial sociability, 33
utopian liberalism, 93

Vattimo, Gianni, *Religion after Metaphysics,* 89

Index   197

Vernoff, Charles: *Contemporary Jewish Religious Thought,* 82–83; hope *versus* faith, 82
vertical projection, 79
virtue, reason and, 31

Walzer, Michael, 45
Wiesel, Eli, commandment to hope, 85

Wolsterstorff, Nicholas, 104
WWI, messianic hope revival, 40–41

You Shall Be as Gods (Fromm), 86–87
Young Hegelians, 36

Zabala, Santiago, *The Future of Religion,* 89
Zionism, 145n55; Fackenheim, 84; Scholem on, 50–51, 144n53

COMMONALITIES
Timothy C. Campbell, series editor

Roberto Esposito, *Terms of the Political: Community, Immunity, Biopolitics*. Translated by Rhiannon Noel Welch. Introduction by Vanessa Lemm.

Maurizio Ferraris, *Documentality: Why It Is Necessary to Leave Traces*. Translated by Richard Davies.

Dimitris Vardoulakis, *Sovereignty and Its Other: Toward the Dejustification of Violence*.

Anne Emmanuelle Berger, *The Queer Turn in Feminism: Identities, Sexualities, and the Theater of Gender*. Translated by Catherine Porter.

James D. Lilley, *Common Things: Romance and the Aesthetics of Belonging in Atlantic Modernity*.

Jean-Luc Nancy, *Identity: Fragments, Frankness*. Translated by François Raffoul.

Miguel Vatter, *The Republic of the Living: Biopolitics and the Critique of Civil Society*.

Miguel Vatter, *Between Form and Event: Machiavelli's Theory of Political Freedom*.

Maurizio Ferraris, *Where Are You? An Ontology of the Cell Phone*. Translated by Sarah De Sanctis.

Irving Goh, *The Reject: Community, Politics, and Religion after the Subject*.

Kevin Attell, *Giorgio Agamben: Beyond the Threshold of Deconstruction*.

J. Hillis Miller, *Communities in Fiction*.

Roberto Esposito, *Categories of the Impolitical*. Translated by Connal Parsley.

Remo Bodei, *The Life of Things, the Love of Things*. Translated by Murtha Baca.

Gabriela Basterra, *The Subject of Freedom: Kant, Levinas*.

Roberto Esposito, *Two: The Machine of Political Theology and the Place of Thought*. Translated by Zakiya Hanafi.

Akiba J. Lerner, *Redemptive Hope: From the Age of Enlightenment to the Age of Obama*.

Emanuele Coccia, *Sensible Life: A Micro-ontology of the Image*. Translated by Scott Stuart. Introduction by Kevin Attell.

Adriana Cavarero and Angelo Scola, *Thou Shalt Not Kill: A Political and Theological Dialogue*. Translated by Margaret Adams Groesbeck and Adam Sitze.

Massimo Cacciari, *Europe and Empire: On the Political Forms of Globalization*. Edited by Alessandro Carrera. Translated by Massimo Verdicchio.

www.ingramcontent.com/pod-product-compliance
Lightning Source LLC
Chambersburg PA
CBHW020109020526
44112CB00033B/1105